The Prentice Hall
Custom Program for CIS

Camden County College
Custom PHIT Exploring Microsoft Office 2007

Access 2007

PEARSON
Custom
Publishing

PEARSON
Prentice
Hall

Director of Database Publishing: Michael Payne
Marketing Manager: Kelly Forsberg
Operations Manager: Eric M. Kenney
Development Editor: Katherine J. Thompson
Production Manager: Jennifer Berry
Cover Designers: Blair Brown and Kisten Kiley

Cover Art: "Cheetah" courtesy of Marvin Mattelson/Getty Images. "Tabs" courtesy of Andrey Prokhorov/iStockphoto. "Open Doors" courtesy of Spectral-Design/iStockphoto. "Compass" courtesy of Laurent Hamels/Getty Images. "Fortune Teller" courtesy of Ingvald Kaldhussaeter/iStockphoto.

This special edition published in cooperation with Pearson Custom Publishing.

Printed in the United States of America.

Please visit our web site at *www.pearsoncustom.com*

Attention bookstores: For permission to return unused stock, fax request to 617-848-6608.

ISBN–13: 9780536222329

ISBN–10: 0536222320

Package ISBN–13: N/A

Package ISBN–10: N/A

PEARSON CUSTOM PUBLISHING
75 Arlington Street, Suite 300, Boston, MA 02116
A Pearson Education Company

Contents

Access

Introduction to Access

Finding Your Way through a Database

Objectives

After reading this chapter you will be able to:

1. Explore, describe, and navigate among the objects in an Access database.
2. Understand the difference between working in storage and memory.
3. Practice good file management.
4. Back up, compact, and repair Access files.
5. Create filters.
6. Sort table data on one or more fields.
7. Know when to use Access or Excel to manage data.
8. Use the Relationship window.
9. Understand relational power.

Hands-On Exercises

Exercises	Skills Covered
1. INTRODUCTION TO DATABASES Open: chap1_ho1-3_traders.accdb Copy, rename, and backup: chap1_ho1-3_traders_solution.accdb chap1_ho1_traders_solution.accdb	• Create a Production Folder and Copy an Access File • Open an Access File • Edit a Record • Navigate an Access Form and Add Records • Recognize the Table and Form Connectivity and Delete a Record • Back up and Compact the Database
2. DATA MANIPULATION: FILTERS AND SORTS Open: chap1_ho1-3_traders_soution.accdb (from Exercise 1) Copy, rename, and backup: chap1_ho1-3_traders_solution.accdb (additional modifications) chap1_ho2_traders_solution.docx chap1_ho2_traders_solution.accdb	• Use Filter by Selection with an Equal Setting • Use Filter by Selection with a Contains Setting • Use Filter by Form with an Inequity Setting • Sort a Table
3. INTRODUCTION TO RELATIONSHIPS Open: chap1_ho1-3_traders_solution.accdb (from Exercise 2) Copy, rename, and backup: chap1_ho1-3_traders_solution.accdb (additional modifications)	• Examine the Relationships Window • Discover that Changes in Table Data Affect Queries • Use Filter by Form with an Inequity Setting and Reapply a Saved Filter • Filter a Report • Remove an Advanced Filter

From *Exploring Office 2007 Volume I*, Robert T. Grauer, Michelle Hulett, Cynthia Krebs, Maurie Wigman Lockley, Keith Mulbery, and Judy Scheeren. Copyright © 2007 by Pearson Education. Published by Prentice Hall.

CASE STUDY

Medical Research—The Lifelong Learning Physicians Association

Today is the first day of your information technology internship appointment with the *Lifelong Learning Physicians Association*. This medical association selected you for the internship because your résumé indicates that you are proficient with Access. Bonnie Clinton, M.D., founded the organization with the purpose of keeping doctors informed about current research and to help physicians identify qualified study participants. Dr. Clinton worries that physicians do not inform their patients about study participation opportunities. She expressed further concerns that the physicians in one field, e.g., cardiology, are unfamiliar with research studies conducted in other fields, such as obstetrics.

Because the association is new, you have very little data to manage. However, the system was designed to accommodate additional data. You will need to talk to Dr. Clinton on a regular basis to determine the association's changing information needs. You may need to guide her in this process. Your responsibilities as the association's IT intern include many items.

Your Assignment

- Read the chapter, paying special attention to learning the vocabulary of database software.
- Copy the *chap1_case_physicians.accdb* file to your production folder, rename it **chap1_case_physicians_solution.accdb**, and enable the content.
- Open the Relationships window and examine the relationships among the tables and the fields contained within each of the tables to become acquainted with this database.
- Open the Volunteers table. Add yourself as a study participant by replacing record **22** with your own information. You should invent data about your height, weight, blood pressure, and your cholesterol. Examine the values in the other records and enter a realistic value. Do not change the stored birthday.
- Identify all of the volunteers who might be college freshmen (18- and 19-year-olds). After you identify them, print the table listing their names and addresses. Use a filter by form with an appropriately set date criterion to identify the correctly aged participants.
- Identify all of the physicians participating in a study involving cholesterol management.
- Open the *Studies and Volunteers Report*. Print it.
- Compact and repair the database file.
- Create a backup of the database. Name the backup **chap1_case_physicians_backup.accdb**.

Data and Files Everywhere!

You probably use databases often. Each time you download an MP3 file, you enter a database via the Internet. There you find searchable data identifying files by artist's name, music style, most frequently requested files, first lines, publication companies, and song titles. If you know the name of the song but not the recording artist or record label, you generally can find it. The software supporting the Web site helps you locate the information you need. The server for the Web site provides access to a major database that contains a lot of data about available MP3 files.

> Each time you download an MP3 file, you enter a database via the internet.

You are exposed to other databases on a regular basis. For example, your university uses a database to support the registration process. When you registered for this course, you entered a database. It probably told you how many seats remained but not the names of the other students. In addition, Web-based job and dating boards are based on database software. Organizations rely on data to conduct daily operations, regardless of whether the organization exists as a profit or not-for-profit environment. The organization maintains data about employees, volunteers, customers, activities, and facilities. Every keystroke and mouse click creates data about the organization that needs to be stored, organized, and analyzed. Microsoft Access provides the organizational decision-maker a valuable tool facilitating data retrieval and use.

In this section, you explore Access database objects and work with table views. You also learn the difference between working in storage and memory to understand how changes to database objects are saved. Finally, you practice good file management techniques by backing up, compacting, and repairing databases.

Exploring, Describing, and Navigating Among the Objects in an Access Database

A **field** is a basic entity or data element, such as the name of a book or the telephone number of a publisher.

A **record** is a complete set of all of the data (fields) about one person, place, event, or idea.

A **table** is a collection of records. Every record in a table contains the same fields in the same order.

A **database** consists of one or more tables and the supporting objects used to get data into and out of the tables.

To understand database management effectively and to use Access productively, you should first learn the vocabulary. A *field* is a basic entity, data element, or category, such as book titles or telephone numbers. The field does not necessarily need to contain a value. For example, a field might store fax numbers for a firm's customers. However, some of the customers may not have a fax machine so the Fax field is blank for that record. A *record* is a complete set of all of the data (fields) about one person, place, event, or idea. For example, your name, homework, and test scores constitute your record in your instructor's grade book. A *table*, the foundation of every database, is a collection of related records that contain fields to organize data. If you have used Excel, you will see the similarities between a spreadsheet and an Access table. Each column represents a field, and each row represents a record. Every record in a table contains the same fields in the same order. An instructor's grade book for one class is a table containing records of all students in one structure. A *database* consists of one or more tables and the supporting objects used to get data into and out of the tables.

Prior to the advent of database management software, organizations managed their data manually. They placed papers in file folders and organized the folders in multiple drawer filing cabinets. You can think of the filing cabinet in the manual system as a database. Each drawer full of folders in the filing cabinet corresponds to a table within the database. Figure 1 shows a college's database system from before the information age. File drawers (tables) contain student data. Each folder (record) contains facts (fields) about that student. The cabinet also contains drawers (tables) full of data about the faculty and the courses offered. Together, the tables combine to form a database system.

TIP Data Versus Information

Data and Information are not synonymous although the terms often are used interchangeably. Data is the raw material and consists of the table (or tables) that comprise a database. Information is the finished product. Data is converted to information by selecting (filtering) records, by sequencing (sorting) the selected records, or by summarizing data from multiple records. Decisions in an organization are based on information compiled from multiple records, as opposed to raw data.

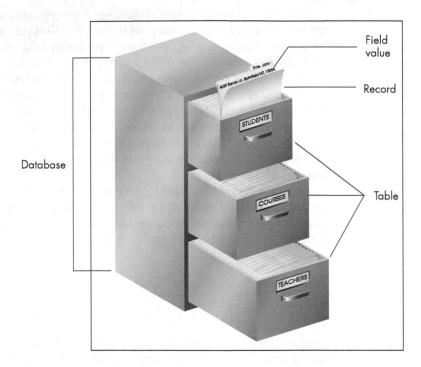

Figure 1 Primitive Database

Identify Access Interface Elements

Figure 2 shows how Microsoft Access appears onscreen. It contains two open windows—an application window for Microsoft Access and a document (database) window for the open database. Each window has its own title bar and icons. The title bar in the application window contains the name of the application (Microsoft Access) and the Minimize, Maximize (or Restore) icons. The title bar in the document (database) window contains the name of the object that is currently open (Employees table). Should more than one object be open at a time, the top of the document window will display tabs for each open object. The Access application window is maximized; therefore, Restore is visible.

Figure 2 An Access Database

Let's look at an example of a database for an international food distribution company—The Northwind Traders. This firm sells specialty food items to restaurants and food shops around the world. It also purchases the products it sells from diversely located firms. The Northwind Traders Company database contains eight tables: Categories, Customers, Employees, Order Details, Orders, Products, Shippers, and Suppliers. Each table, in turn, consists of multiple records, corresponding to the folders in the file cabinet. The Employees table, for example, contains a record for every employee. Each record in the Employees table contains 17 fields—where data about the employee's education, address, photograph, position, and so on are stored. Occasionally a field does not contain a value for a particular record. One of the employees, Margaret Peacock did not provide a picture. The value of that field is missing. Access provides a placeholder to store the data when it is available. The Suppliers table has a record for each vendor from whom the firm purchases products, just as the Orders table has a record for each order. The real power of Access is derived from a database with multiple tables and the relationships that connect the tables.

The database window displays the various objects in an Access database. An Access *object* stores the basic elements of the database. Access uses six types of objects—tables, queries, forms, reports, macros, and modules. Every database must contain at least one table, and it may contain any, all, or none of the other objects. Each object type is accessed through the appropriate tab within the database window. Because of the interrelationships among objects, you may either view all of the objects of a type in a single place or view all of the related objects in a way that demonstrates their inner-connectivity. You select an object for viewing using the Navigation pane. The Navigation pane on the left side groups related objects.

An Access *object* contains the basic elements of the database.

The Reference page describes the tabs and groups on the Ribbon in Access 2007. You do not need to memorize most of these tabs and groups now. You will learn where things are located as you explore using the features.

Reference Page | Access Ribbon

Tab and Group	Description
Home Views Clipboard Font Rich Text Records Sort & Filter Find	The basic Access tab. Contains basic editing functions such as cut and paste along with most formatting actions. As with all groups, Dialog Box Launchers are available and do increase functionality.
Create Tables Forms Reports Other	Brings together all create operations in one area. Includes ability to create queries through the wizard or in Design view.
External Data Import Export Collect Data SharePoint Lists	Contains all of the operations to facilitate collaboration and data exchange.
Database Tools Macro Show/Hide Analyze Move Data Database Tools	The area that contains the operational backbone of Access. Here you create and maintain the relationships of the database. You also analyze the file performance and perform routine maintenance.

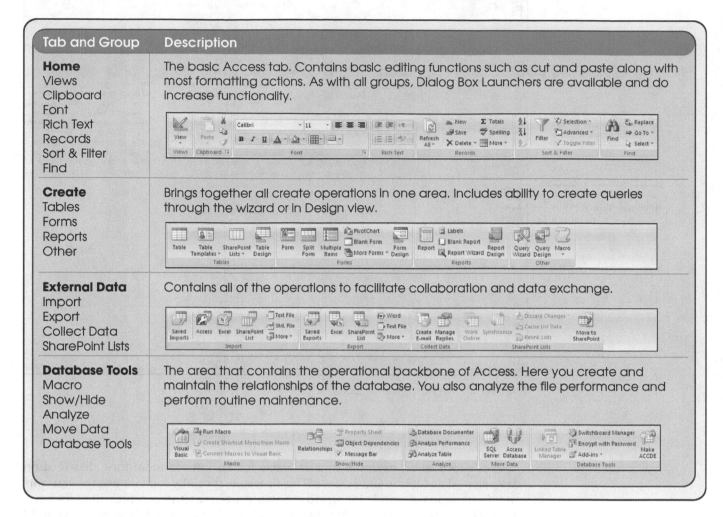

Work with Table Views

The **Datasheet view** is a grid where you add, edit, and delete the records of a table.

The **Design view** is a different grid where you create and modify the properties of the table.

Access provides different ways in which to view a table and most other objects. The **Datasheet view** is a grid containing columns (fields) and rows (records). You can view, add, edit, and delete records of a table in the Datasheet view. You can use the **Design view** to create and modify the table by specifying the fields it will contain and their associated properties. The field type (for example, text or numeric data) and the field length are examples of field properties. If you need the values stored in a particular field to display as currency, you would modify the property of that field to ensure all values display appropriately.

Figure 3 shows the Datasheet view for the Customers table. The first row in the table displays the field names. Each additional row contains a record (the data for a specific customer). Each column represents a field (one fact about a customer). Every record in the table contains the same fields in the same order.

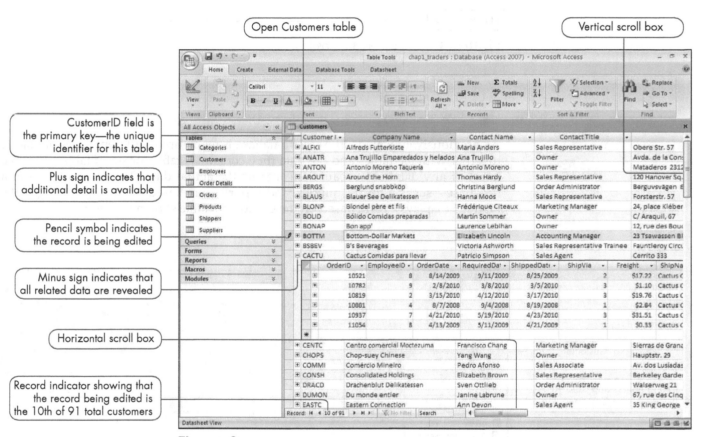

Figure 3   The Customers Table and Related Order Information

The **primary key** is the field that makes each record in a table unique.

The **primary key** is the field (or combination of fields) that makes each record in a table unique. The CustomerID is the primary key in the Customers table; it ensures that every record in a table is different from every other record, and it prevents the occurrence of duplicate records. Primary key fields may be numbers, letters, or a combination of both. In this case the primary key is text (letters).

The Navigation bar at the bottom of Figure 3 shows a table with 91 records and record number 10 as the current record. You can work on only one record at a time. The vertical scroll bar at the right of the window shows that more records exist in the table than you can see at one time. The horizontal scroll bar at the bottom of the window indicates that you cannot see an entire record.

The pencil icon at the left of the record indicates that the data in the current record are being edited and that the changes have not yet been saved. The pencil icon disappears after you complete the data entry and move to another record, because Access saves data automatically as soon as you move from one record to the next.

Figure 4 displays the navigation buttons that you use to move within most Access objects. You may navigate using commands to go to the last and first records, advance and go back one record, and add a new record.

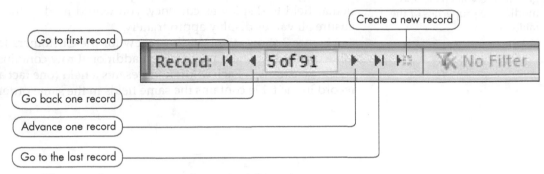

Figure 4 Navigation Buttons

Use Forms, Queries, and Reports

As previously indicated, an Access database is made up of different types of objects together with the tables and the data they contain. A table (or set of tables) is at the heart of any database because it contains the actual data. The other objects in a database—such as forms, queries, and reports—are based on an underlying table. Figure 5 displays a form based on the Customers table shown earlier.

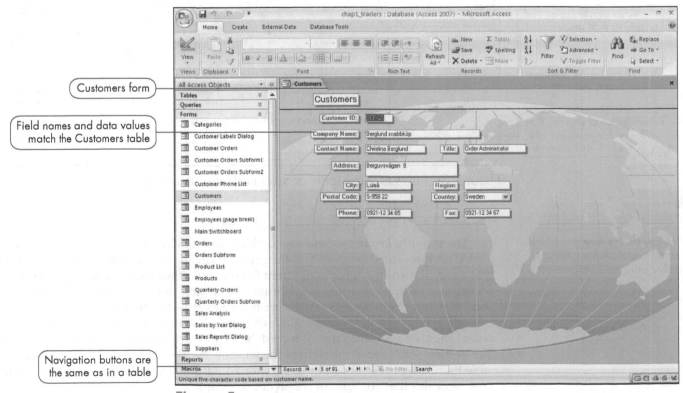

Figure 5 Customers Form

A **form** is an interface that enables you to enter or modify record data.

A **query** provides information that answers a question.

A **criterion** (**criteria**, pl) is a rule or norm that is the basis for making judgments.

A **form** is an interface that enables you to enter or modify record data. Commands may appear in the form to add a new record, print a record, or close the form. The form provides access to all of the data maintenance operations that are available through a table. The status bar and navigation buttons at the bottom of the form are similar to those that appear at the bottom of a table. You use the form in Datasheet view, but create and edit the form structure in Design view.

Figure 6 displays a query that lists the products that the firm purchases from a particular supplier. A **query** provides information that answers a question based on the data within an underlying table or tables. The Suppliers table, for example, contains records for many vendors, but the query in Figure 6 shows only the products that were supplied by a specific supplier. If you want to know the details about a specific supplier, you establish a criterion to specify which supplier you need to know about. A **criterion** (**criteria**, pl) is a rule or norm that is the basis for making judgments. If you need the names of all the suppliers in New York, you set a criterion to identify the New York suppliers. The results would yield only those suppliers from New York. Query results are similar in appearance to the underlying table, except that the query contains selected records and/or selected fields for those records. The query also may list the records in a different sequence from that of the table. (You also can use a query to add new records and modify existing records.) If you have a query open and notice an error in an address field, you can edit the record, and the edited value would immediately and permanently transfer to the table storing that record. Queries may be opened in Datasheet view or Design view. You use the Datasheet view to examine the query output and use the Design view to specify which fields and records to include in the query.

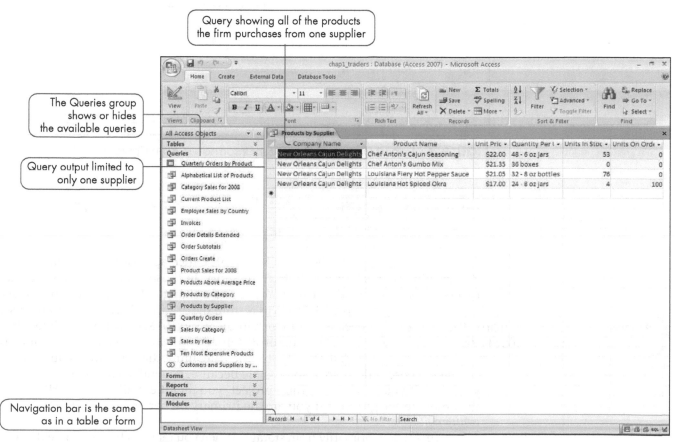

Figure 6   Results of a Query Shown in Datasheet View

A *report* presents database information professionally.

Figure 7 displays a report that contains the same information as the query in Figure 6. A *report* contains professionally formatted information from underlying tables or queries. Because the report information contains a more enhanced format than a query or table, you place database output in a report to print. Access provides different views for designing, modifying, and running reports. Most Access users use only the Print Preview, Print Layout, and Report views of a report.

The report shows the same data as in the query in a user-friendly format

Reports object opened to display a list of available reports

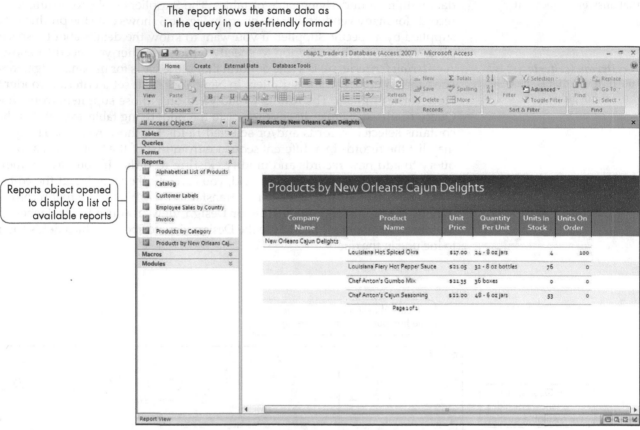

Figure 7 Report Displaying the Query Information from Figure 6

Understanding the Difference Between Working in Storage and Memory

Access is different from the other Microsoft Office applications. Word, Excel, and PowerPoint all work primarily from memory. In those applications you can easily reverse mistakes by using Undo. You make a change, discover that you dislike it, and click Undo to restore the original. These actions are possible because you work in memory (RAM) most of the time while in the other Microsoft Office applications; changes are not saved automatically to the file immediately after you make the changes. These actions are also possible because, generally, you are the only user of your file. If you work on a group project, you might e-mail the PowerPoint file to the others in the group, but you are the primary owner and user of that file. Access is *different*.

Access is different from the other Microsoft Office applications.

Access works primarily from storage. When you make a change to a field's content in an Access table (for example, changing a customer's area code), Access saves your changes as soon as you move the insertion point to a different record; you do not need to click Save. You can click Undo to reverse several editing changes (such as changing an area code and a contact name) for a single record **immediately** after making the changes to that record. However, unlike other Office programs that let you continue

Undoing actions, you cannot use Undo to reverse edits to more than the last record you edited or to restore a field if you delete it.

Multiple users can work on the database simultaneously. As long as no two users attempt to interact with the same record at the same time, the system updates as it goes. This also means that any reports extracting the information from the database contain the most up-to-date data. The only time you need to click Save is when you are creating or changing a structural element, such as a table, query, form, or report.

TIP   Save Edits While Keeping a Record Active

When you want to save changes to a record you are editing while staying on the same record, press Shift+Enter. The pencil icon, indicating an editing mode, disappears, indicating that the change is saved.

Be careful to avoid accidentally typing something in a record and pressing Enter. Doing so saves the change, and you can retrieve the original data if you are lucky enough to remember to click Undo immediately before making or editing other records. Because Access is a relational database, several other related objects (queries, reports, or forms) could also be permanently changed. In Access, one file holds everything. All of the objects—tables, forms, queries, and reports—are saved both individually and as part of the Access collection.

TIP   Data Validation

No system, no matter how sophisticated, can produce valid output from invalid input. Thus, good systems are built to anticipate errors in data entry and to reject those errors prior to saving a record. Access will automatically prevent you from adding records with a duplicate primary key or entering invalid data into a numeric or date field. The database developer has the choice whether to require other types of validation, such as requiring the author's name.

Practicing Good File Management

You must exercise methodical and deliberate file management techniques to avoid damaging data. Every time you need to open a file, this book will direct you to copy the file to your production folder and rename the copied file. Name the production folder with *Your Name Access Production*. You would not copy a real database and work in the copy often. However, as you learn, you will probably make mistakes. Following the practice of working in a copied file will facilitate mistake recovery during the learning process.

Further, it matters to which type of media you save your files. Access does not work from some media. Access runs best from a hard or network drive because those drives have sufficient access speed to support the software. Access speed measures the time it takes for the storage device to make the file content available for use. If you work from your own computer, create the production folder in the My Documents folder on the hard drive. Most schools lock their hard drives so that students cannot permanently save files there. If your school provides you with storage space on the school's network, store your production folder there. The advantage to using the network is that the network administration staff backs up files regularly. If you have no storage on the school network, your next best storage option is a thumb drive, also known as USB jump drive, flash drive, Pen drive, or stick drive.

Access speed measures the time it takes for the storage device to make the file content available for use.

All of the objects in an Access database are stored in a single file. You can open a database from within Windows Explorer by double-clicking the filename. You also can open the database from within Access through the Recent Documents list or by clicking the Microsoft Office Button (noted as Office Button only in this textbook) and selecting Open from the Office menu. The individual objects within a database are opened from the database window.

Backing Up, Compacting, and Repairing Access Files

Data is the lifeblood of any organization. Imagine what would happen to a firm that loses the records of the orders placed but not shipped or the charity that loses the list of donor contribution records or the hospital that loses the digital records of patient X-rays. What would happen to the employee who "accidentally" deleted mission-critical data? What would happen to the other employees who did not lose the mission-critical data? Fortunately, Access recognizes how critical backup procedures are to organizations and makes backing up the database files easy.

Back Up a Database

You back up an Access file (and all of the objects it contains) with just a few mouse clicks. To back up files, click the Office Button and select Manage from the Office menu. When you select Backup, a dialog box, much like a Save As dialog box in the other applications, opens. You may use controls in the Backup dialog box to specify storage location and filename. Access provides a default filename that is the original filename followed by the date. In most organizations, this step is useful because the Information Technology department backs up every database each day.

Compact and Repair a Database

All databases have a tendency to expand with use. This expansion will occur without new information being added. Simply using the database, creating queries and running them, or applying and removing filters may cause the file to store inefficiently. Because the files tend to be rather large to start with, any growth creates problems. Access provides another utility, Compact and Repair, under the Manage submenu in the Office menu that addresses this issue. The Compact and Repair utility acts much like a disk defragmenter utility. It finds related file sectors and reassembles them in one location if they become scattered from database use. You should compact and repair your database each day when you close the file. This step often will decrease file size by 50% or more. Access closes any open objects during the compact and repair procedure, so it is a good idea to close any objects in the database prior to compacting so that you will control if any design changes will be saved or not.

In the next hands-on exercise, you will work with a database from an international gourmet food distributor, the Northwind Traders. This firm purchases food items from suppliers and sells them to restaurants and specialty food shops. It depends on the data stored in the Access database to make daily decisions.

Hands-On Exercises

1 | Introduction to Databases

Skills covered: **1.** Create a Production Folder and Copy an Access File **2.** Open an Access File **3.** Edit a Record **4.** Navigate an Access Form and Add Records **5.** Recognize the Table and Form Connectivity and Delete a Record **6.** Back up and Compact the Database

Step 1 Create a Production Folder and Copy an Access File	Refer to Figure 8 as you complete Step 1.

a. Right-click **My Computer** on the desktop and select **Explore** from the shortcut menu.

This step opens the Explore utility in a two-pane view that facilitates transferring materials between folders.

b. Determine where your production folder will reside and double-click that location. For example, double-click the **My Documents** folder if that is where your files will reside.

For the remainder of this book, it is assumed that your production folder resides in the My Document folder on the hard drive. Your folder may actually exist on another drive. What is important is that you (1) create and use the folder and (2) remember where it is.

c. Right-click anywhere on a blank spot in the right pane of the Exploring window. Select **New** and then select **Folder** from the shortcut menu.

A new folder is created with the default name, New Folder, selected and ready to be renamed.

d. Type **Your Name Access Production** and press **Enter**.

e. Open the folder that contains the student data files that accompany this textbook.

f. Find the file named *chap1_ho1-3_traders.accdb*, right-click the file, and select **Copy** from the shortcut menu.

g. Go to the newly created production folder named with your name. Right-click a blank area in the right side of the Exploring window and select **Paste**.

You have created a copy of the original *chap1_ho1-3_traders.accdb* file. You will work with the copy. In the event that you make mistakes, the original remains intact in the student data folder. You can recopy it and rework the exercise if necessary.

h. Rename the newly copied file **your_name_chap1_ho1-3_traders_solution.accdb**.

You need to remember to rename all of the solution files with your name. If your instructor requests that you submit your work for evaluation using a shared folder on the campus network, each file must have a unique name. You risk overwriting another student's work (or having someone overwrite your work) if you do not name your files with your name and the file designation.

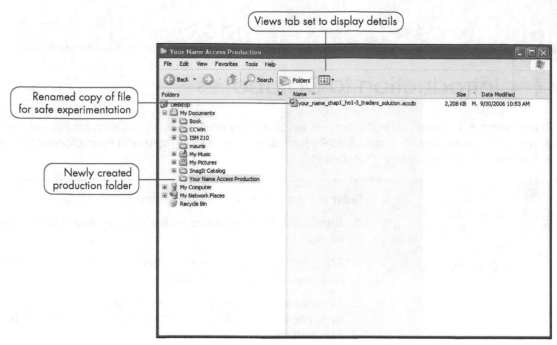

Figure 8 Production Folder Created Showing Copied and Renamed File

Step 2
Open an Access File

Refer to Figure 9 as you complete Step 2.

a. Double-click the *your_name_chap1_ho1-3_traders_solution* file to open it.

This step launches Access and opens the Explore file. From now on, this book will refer to the files without the *your_name* prefix.

b. Click **Options** on the Security Warning toolbar. See Figure 9.

Each time you open an Access file for the remainder of the class, you will need to enable the content. Several viruses and worms may be transmitted via Access files. You may be reasonably confident of the trustworthiness of the files in this book. However, if an Access file arrives as an attachment from an unsolicited e-mail message, you should not open it. Microsoft warns all users of Access files that a potential threat exists every time the file is opened.

c. Click **Enable this content** and then click **OK**.

The Microsoft Office Security Options dialog box closes, and the Security Warning toolbar disappears.

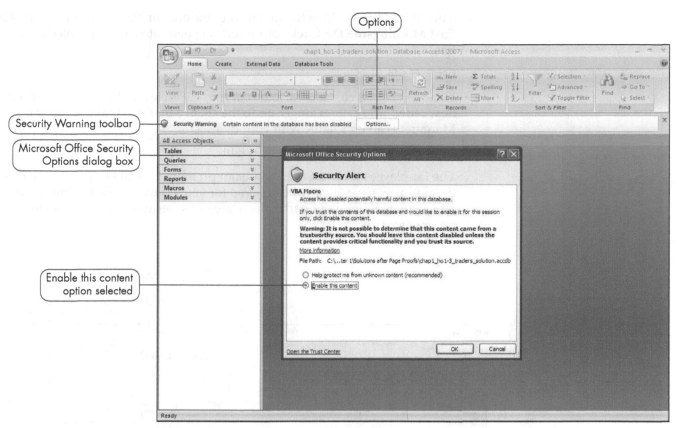

Figure 9 Microsoft Office Security Options Dialog Box

Step 3
Edit a Record

Refer to Figure 10 as you complete Step 3.

a. Click **Tables** in the Navigation pane to expand the list of available tables.

The list of tables contained in the database file opens.

b. Double-click the **Employees table** to open it. See Figure 10.

c. Click the insertion point in the fourth row. Double-click *Peacock* in the LastName field. The entire name highlights. Type **your last name** to replace *Peacock*.

d. Press **Tab** to move to the next field in the fourth row. Replace *Margaret* with **your first name**.

You have made changes to two fields in the same record (row); the pencil displays in the row selector box.

e. Click **Undo** on the Quick Access Toolbar.

Your first name reverts back to Margaret because you have not yet left the record.

f. Type your name again to replace *Margaret* with **your first name**. Press **Enter**.

You should now be in the Title field and your title, *Sales Representative*, is selected. The pencil icon still displays in the row selector.

g. Click anywhere in the third row where Janet Leverling's data are stored.

The pencil icon disappears; your changes to the table have been saved.

h. Click the address field in the first record, the one for Nancy Davolio. Type **4004 East Morningside Dr**. Click your insertion point into Andrew Fuller's name field.

i. Click **Undo**.

Nancy's address changes back to *20th Ave. E*. However, the Undo command is now faded. You can no longer undo the change that you made replacing Margaret Peacock's name with your own.

j. Click **Close** to close the Employees table.

The Employees table closes. You are not prompted about saving your changes, because they have already been saved for you. If you reopen the Employees table, you will find your name, not Margaret's, because Access works in storage, not memory.

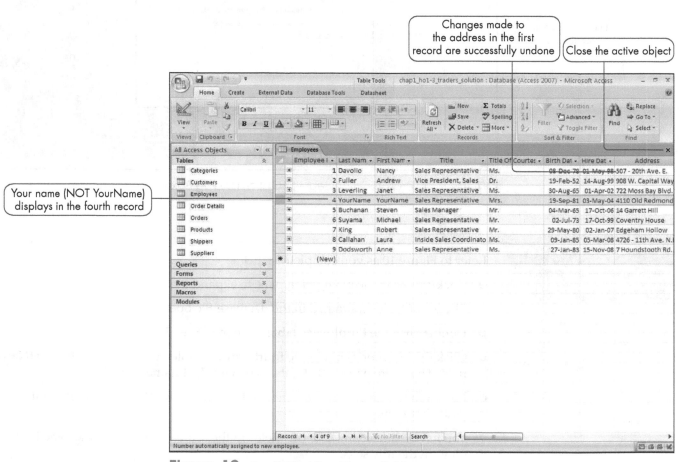

Figure 10 The Edited Employees Table

Refer to Figure 11 as you complete Step 4.

Step 4
Navigate an Access Form and Add Records

a. Click **Tables** in the Navigation pane to close it.

The list of available tables collapses.

b. Click **Forms** in the Navigation pane to expand it.

c. Double-click the **Products form** to open it.

d. Practice with the navigation buttons above the status bar to move from one record to the next. Click **Next record** and then click **Last record**.

e. Click **Find** in the Find group on the Home tab.

The Find command is an ideal way to search for specific records within a table, form, or query. You can search a single field or the entire record, match all or part of the selected field(s), move forward or back in a table, or specify a case-sensitive search. The Replace command can be used to substitute one value for another. Be careful, however, about using the Replace All option for global replacement because unintended replacements are far too common.

f. Type **ikura** in the *Find What* section of the Find and Replace dialog box. Check to make sure that the *Look In* option is set to **Product Name** and the *Match* option is set to **Whole Field**. The *Search* option should be set to **All**. Click **Find Next**.

You should see the information about *ikura*, a seafood supplied by Tokyo Traders.

g. Type **Grandma** in the *Find What* box, click the **Match drop-down arrow**, and select **Any Part of Field**. Click **Find Next**.

You should see information about Grandma's Boysenberry Spread. Setting the match option to any part of the field will return a match even if it is contained in the middle of a word.

h. Close the Find and Replace dialog box.

i. Click **New (blank) record** located on the Navigation bar.

j. Enter the following information for a new product. Press **Tab** to navigate the form.

Field Name	Value to Type
Product Name	Your Name Pecan Pie
Supplier	Grandma Kelly's Homestead (Note, display the drop-down list to enter this information quickly)
Category	Confections (Use the drop-down box here, too)
Quantity Per Unit	1
Unit Price	25.00
Units In Stock	18
Units on Order	50
Reorder Level	20

As soon as you begin typing in the product name box, Access assigns a Product ID, in this case 78, to the record. The Product ID is used as the primary key in the Products table.

k. Close the Products form.

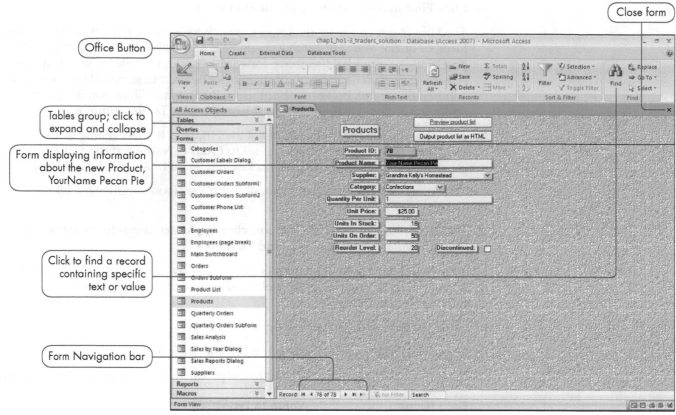

Figure 11 The Newly Created Record In the Products Form

Refer to Figure 12 as you complete Step 5.

a. Click **Forms** in the Navigation pane to close it.

The list of available forms collapses.

b. Click **Tables** in the Navigation pane to expand it.

The list of available tables expands. You need to assure yourself that the change you made to the Products form will transfer to the Products table.

c. Double-click the **Products table** to open it.

d. Click **Last record** on the Navigation bar.

The Products form was designed to make data entry easier. It is linked to the Products table. Your newly created record about the Pecan Pie product name is stored in the Products table even though you created it in the form.

e. Navigate to the fifth record in the table, *Chef Anton's Gumbo Mix*.

f. Use the horizontal scroll bar to scroll right until you see the *Discontinued* field.

The check mark in the Discontinued check box tells you that this product has been discontinued.

g. Click the row selector box at the left of the window (see Figure 12).

The row highlights with a gold-colored border.

h. Press **Delete**.

An error message appears. It tells you that you cannot delete this record because the table, Order Details, has related records. Even though the product is now discontinued and none of it is in stock, it cannot be deleted from the table because related records are connected to it. A customer in the past ordered this product. If you first deleted all of the orders in the Order Details table that referenced this product, you would be permitted to delete the product from the Products table.

i. Read the error message. Click **OK**.

j. Navigate to the last record. Click the *row selector* to highlight the entire row.

k. Press **Delete**. STOP. Read the error message.

A warning box appears. It tells you that this action cannot be undone. This product can be deleted because it was just created. No customers have ever ordered it so no related records are in the system.

l. Click **No**. You do not want to delete this record.

TROUBLESHOOTING: If you clicked Yes and deleted the record, return to Step 4j. Reenter the information for this record. You will need it later in the lesson.

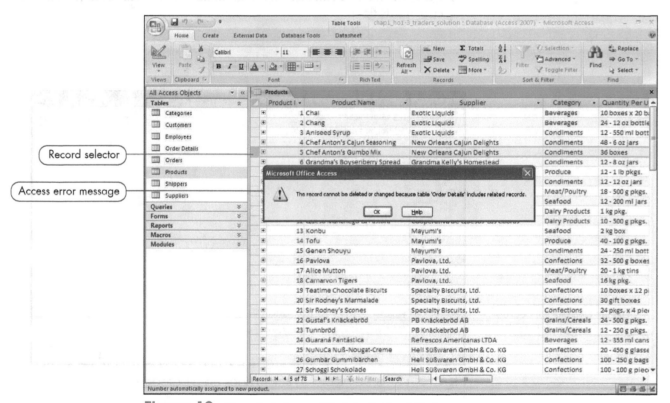

Figure 12 How Databases Work to Protect Data

Step 6

Back up and Compact the Database

Refer to Figure 13 as you complete Step 6.

a. Click the **Office Button** and select **Manage**.

The Manage menu gives you access to three critically important tools.

b. Select **Compact and Repair Database**.

Databases tend to get larger and larger as you use them. This feature acts as a defragmenter and eliminates wasted space. As it runs, it closes any open objects in the database.

c. Click the **Office Button**, select **Manage**, and then select **Back Up Database**.

The Save As dialog box opens. The backup utility assigns a default name by adding a date to your filename.

d. Type **chap1_ho1_traders_solution** and click **Save**.

You just created a backup of the database after completing the first hands-on exercise. The original database *chap1_ho1-3_traders_solution* remains onscreen. If you ruin the original database as you complete the second hands-on exercise, you can use the backup file you just created.

e. Close the file and exit Access if you do not want to continue with the next exercise at this time.

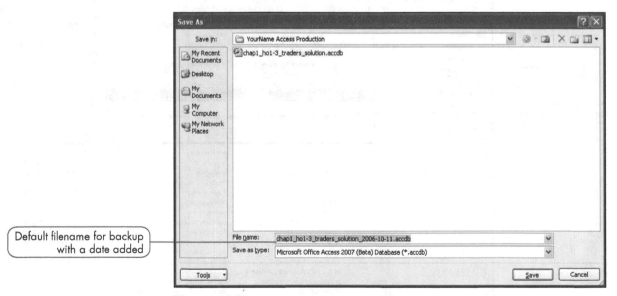

Default filename for backup with a date added

Figure 13 Save As Dialog Box to Back Up a Database

Filters, Sorts, and Access Versus Excel

Microsoft Office provides you with many tools that you may use to identify and extract only the records needed at the moment. For example, you might need to know which suppliers are located in New Orleans or which customers have not ordered any products in the last 60 days. You might use that information to identify possible disruptions to product deliveries or customers who may need a telephone call to see if all is well. Both Access and Excel contain powerful tools that enable you to sift through data and extract the information you need and arrange it in a way that makes sense to you. An important part of becoming a proficient computer user is recognizing when to use which tool to accomplish a task.

In this section you learn how to create filters to examine records and organize these records by sorting table data. You also will examine the logic of Access and Excel in more detail. You will investigate when to use which application to complete a given task.

Creating Filters

A *filter* lets you find a subset of data meeting your specifications.

In the first hands-on exercise, you used data from an existing table to obtain information from the database. You created new records and saw that the changes made in a form update data in the associated table data. You found the pecan pie, but you also saw lots of other products. When all of the information needed is contained in a single table, form, report, or query, you can open the object in the Datasheet view, and then apply a filter to display only the records of interest to you. A *filter* displays a subset of records; from the object according to specified criteria. You use filters to examine data. Applying a filter does not delete any records; it simply hides extraneous records from your view.

Figure 14 displays a Customers table with 91 records. The records in the table are displayed in sequence according to the CustomerID, which is also the primary key (the field or combination of fields that uniquely identifies a record). The status bar indicates that the active record is the sixth in the table. Let's explore how you would retrieve a partial list of those records, such as records of customers in Germany only.

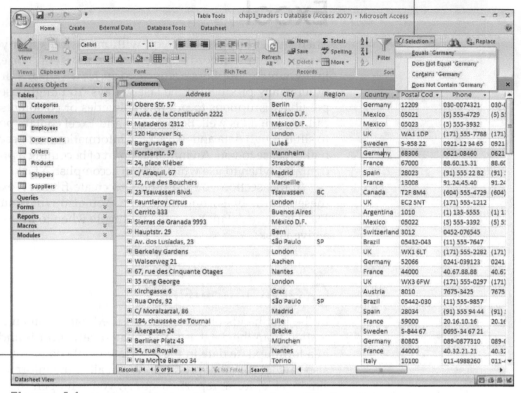

Figure 14 Unfiltered Table with Appropriate Sort Options Selected

Figure 15 displays a filtered view of the same table in which we see only the customers in Germany. The Navigation bar shows that this is a filtered list and that the filter found 11 records satisfying the criteria. (The Customers table still contains the original 91 records, but only 11 records are visible with the filter applied.)

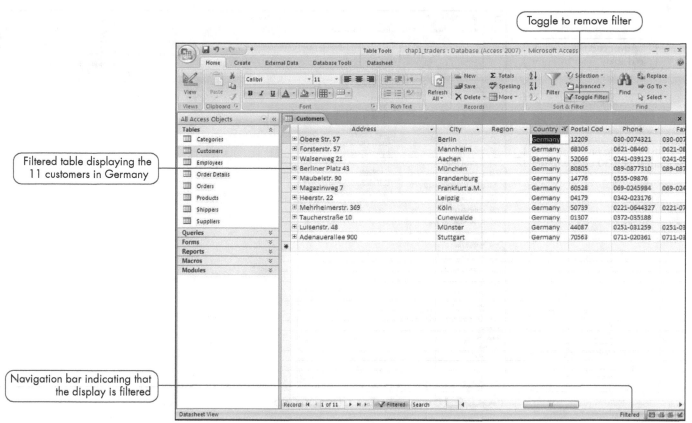

Toggle to remove filter

Filtered table displaying the 11 customers in Germany

Navigation bar indicating that the display is filtered

Figure 15 Filtered Table with Appropriate Sort Options Selected

TIP Use Quick Keyboard Shortcuts

Look for underlined letters in Access menus. They indicate the letters to use for the keyboard shortcuts. For example, when you click in a field and click the Selection down arrow in the Sort & Filter group, you can click the Equals "London" menu selection or simply type the letter e because the letter E in Equals is underlined, indicating a shortcut key.

Filter by Selection selects only the records that match the pre-selected criteria.

Filter by Form permits selecting criteria from a drop-down list, or applying multiple criteria.

An *inequity* examines a mathematical relationship such as equals, not equals, greater than, less than, greater than or equal to, or less than or equal to.

The easiest way to implement a filter is to click in any cell that contains the value of the desired criterion (such as any cell that contains *Account Rep* in the Title field), then click Filter by Selection in the Sort & Filter group. *Filter by Selection* selects only the records that match the pre-selected criteria.

Figure 16 illustrates an alternate and more powerful way to apply a filter. *Filter by Form* permits selecting the criteria from a drop-down list and/or applying multiple criteria simultaneously. However, the real advantage of the Filter by Form command extends beyond these conveniences to two additional capabilities. First, you can specify relationships within a criterion; for example, you can use an inequity setting to select products with an inventory level greater than (or less than) 30. An *inequity* examines a mathematical relationship such as equals, not equals, greater than, less than, greater than or equal to, or less than or equal to. Filter by Selection, on the other hand, requires you to specify criteria equal to an existing value. Figure 16 shows the filtered query setup to select Beverages with more than 30 units in stock.

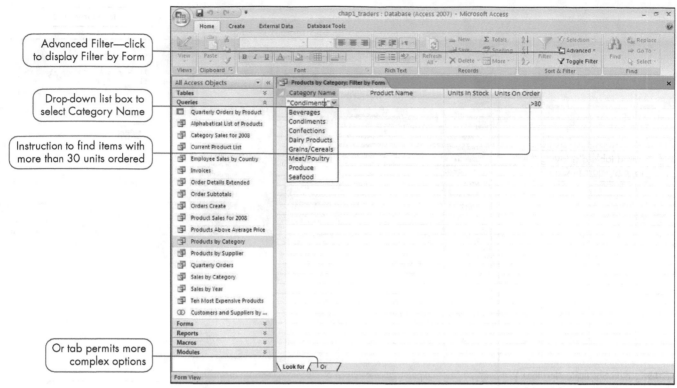

Advanced Filter—click to display Filter by Form

Drop-down list box to select Category Name

Instruction to find items with more than 30 units ordered

Or tab permits more complex options

Figure 16 Filter by Form Design Grid

A second advantage of the Filter by Form command is that you can specify alternative criteria (such as customers in Germany or orders for over 30 units) by clicking the Or tab. (The latter capability is not implemented in Figure 16.) However, the availability of the various filter and sort commands enables you to obtain information from a database quickly and easily without creating a query or report.

Sorting Table Data on One or More Fields

A *sort* lists those records in a specific sequence, such as alphabetically by last name.

Sort Ascending provides an alphabetical list of text data or a small to large list of numeric data.

Sort Descending displays records with the highest value listed first.

You also can change the order of the information by sorting by one or more fields. A *sort* lists those records in a specific sequence, such as alphabetically by last name or by EmployeeID. To sort the table, click in the field on which you want to sequence the records (the LastName field in this example), then click Sort Ascending in the Sort & Filter group on the Home tab. *Sort Ascending* provides an alphabetical list of text data or a small to large list of numeric data. *Sort Descending* is appropriate for numeric fields such as salary, if you want to display the records with the highest value listed first. Figure 17 shows the Customers table sorted in alphabetical order by country. You may apply both filters and sorts to table or query information to select and order the data in the way that you need to make decisions.

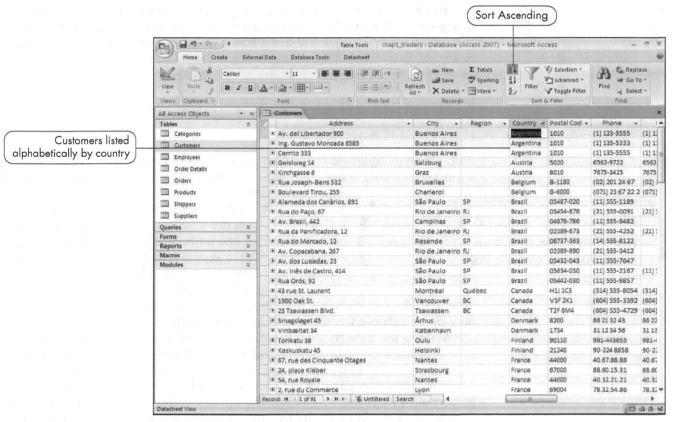

Figure 17 Customers Table Sorted by Country

The operations can be done in any order; that is, you can filter a table to show only selected records, then you can sort the filtered table to display the records in a different order. Conversely, you can sort a table and then apply a filter. It does not matter which operation is performed first, and indeed, you can go back and forth between the two. You can also filter the table further, by applying a second (or third) criterion; for example, click in a cell containing *USA* and apply a Filter by Selection. Then click in a record for Oregon (OR) and apply a Filter by Selection a second time to display the customers from Oregon. You also can click Toggle Filter at any time to display all of the records in the table. Filters are a temporary method for examining subsets of data. If you close the filtered table or query and reopen it, all of the records display.

> ### TIP The Sort or Filter—Which is First?
>
> It doesn't matter whether you sort a table and then apply a filter, or filter first and then sort. The operations are cumulative. Thus, after you sort a table, any subsequent display of filtered records for that table will be in the specified sequence. Alternatively, you can apply a filter and then sort the filtered table by clicking in the desired field and clicking the appropriate sort command. Remember, too, that all filter commands are cumulative, and hence you must remove the filter to see the original table.

You may be familiar with applying a filter, sorting data, or designing a form using Excel. The fact is, Excel can accomplish all of these activities. You need to examine your data needs and think about what your future data requirements may be to decide whether to use Access or Excel.

Knowing When to Use Access or Excel to Manage Data

If you have the ability to control data and turn it into useful information, you possess a marketable skill. It does not matter whether you are planning to become a social worker, a teacher, an engineer, an entrepreneur, a radiologist, a marketer, a day care worker, a musician, or an accountant. You will need to collect, store, maintain, manage, and protect data as well as convert it into information used to make strategic decisions. A widely used program that you probably already know is Excel. This course will help you become familiar with Access. You can accomplish many of the same things in either software. Although the two packages have much in common, they each have advantages. So, how do you choose whether to use Access or Excel?

> If you have the ability to control data and turn it into useful information, you possess a marketable skill.

Making the right choice is critical if you want to find and update your information with maximum performance and accuracy. Ideally, your data needs and the type and amount of data used will determine how to pick the program that will work best. Sometimes organizations use Access when they probably would be better served with Excel and vice-versa. The answer to the question of which to use may depend on who you ask. An accountant probably will use Excel. The information technology professional probably will use a more sophisticated database software like Oracle, but not Access. The middle manager in the marketing or manufacturing department will probably use Access. The question remains.

Select the Software to Use

A contacts list is an example of flat data. Each column of data (names, addresses, and phone numbers) is logically related to the others. If you can store your data logically in a single table or worksheet, then do. Update your data in the same type of file. Data contained in a single page or sheet (not multiple) are called *flat* or *non-relational data*. You would never store your friend's last name on a different sheet from the sheet containing the friend's cell phone number.

> Data contained in a single page or sheet (not multiple) are called *flat or non-relational data*.

Suppose you had a spreadsheet of club members' names and contact information. Your club decides to sell cookies as a fundraiser. You might create a new worksheet listing how many boxes of which type of cookie each member picked up to sell. Your third worksheet might show how much money each member has turned in from the cookie sales. These data are different. They are not flat. Can you imagine needing to know someone's phone number or how many cookie boxes he or she promised to sell while looking at the worksheet of data about how much money has been turned in? These data are multi-dimensional and need to be stored in more than one worksheet or table. This describes relational data. Each table holds a particular type of data (number of boxes collected, contact information, funds turned in). Relational data are best stored in Access. In this example, you would create a database with three tables. You need to adhere to the following rules about assigning data to the appropriate table.

Assign table data so that each table:

- Represents only a single subject
- Has a field(s) that uniquely identifies each record
- Does not contain duplicate fields
- Has no repetition of the same type of value
- Has no fields belonging in other tables

As the quantity and complexity of data increase, the need to organize it efficiently also increases. Access affords better data organization than Excel. Access accomplishes the organization through a system of linkages among the tables. Each record (row) should be designated with a primary key—a unique identifier that sets it apart from all of the other records in the table. The primary key might be an account number, a student identification number, or an employee access code. All data in Excel have a unique identifier—the cell address. In life, you have a Social Security Number. It's the best unique identifier you have. Ever notice how, when at the doctor's office or applying for college admission, you are asked for your Social Security Number as well as your name? Your record in its database system probably uses your Social Security Number as a unique identifier.

You still need to answer the question of when to use Access and when to use Excel.

Use Access

You should use Access to manage data when you:

- Require a relational database (multiple tables or multi-dimensional tables) to store your data or anticipate adding more tables in the future.

  For example, you may set your club membership contact list in either software, but if you believe that you also will need to keep track of the cookie sales and fund collection, use Access.

- Have a large amount of data.

- Rely on external databases to derive and analyze the data you need.

  If frequently you need to have Excel exchange data to or from Access, use Access. Even though the programs are compatible, it makes sense to work in Access to minimize compatibility issues.

- Need to maintain constant connectivity to a large external database, such as one built with Microsoft SQL Server or your organization's Enterprise Resource Planning system.

- Need to regroup data from different tables in a single place through complex queries.

  You might need to create output showing how many boxes of cookies each club member picked up and how much money they turned in along with the club member's name and phone number.

- Have many people working in the database and need strong options to update the data.

  For example, five different clerks at an auto parts store might wait on five different customers. Each clerk connects to the inventory table to find out if the needed part is in stock and where in the warehouse it is located. When the customer says, "Yes, I want that" the inventory list is instantly updated and that product is no longer available to be purchased by the other four customers.

Use Excel

You should use Excel to manage data when you:

- Require a flat or non-relational view of your data (you do not need a relational database with multiple tables).

  This idea is especially true if that data is mostly numeric—for example, if you need to maintain an expense statement.

- Want to run primarily calculations and statistical comparisons on your data.

- Know your dataset is manageable in size (no more than 15,000 rows).

  In the next exercise you will create and apply filters, perform sorts, and develop skills to customize the data presentation to answer your questions.

Hands-On Exercises

2 | Data Manipulation: Filters and Sorts

Skills covered: 1. Use Filter by Selection with an Equal Setting **2.** Use Filter by Selection with a Contains Setting **3.** Use Filter by Form with an Inequity Setting **4.** Sort a Table

Step 1
Use Filter by Selection with an Equal Setting

Refer to Figure 18 as you complete Step 1.

a. Open the *chap1_ho1-3_traders_solution* file if necessary, and click **Options** on the Security Warning toolbar, click the **Enable this content option** in the Microsoft Office Security Options dialog box, and click **OK**.

TROUBLESHOOTING: If you create unrecoverable errors while completing this hands-on exercise, you can delete the *chap1_ho1-3_traders_solution* file, copy the *chap1_ho1_traders_solution* backup database you created at the end of the first hands-on exercise, and open the copy of the backup database to start the second hands-on exercise again.

b. Open the **Customers table**; navigate to record 4 and replace *Thomas Hardy's* name with **your name** in the **Contact Name field**.

c. Scroll right until the **City field** is visible. Look through the record values of the field form until you locate a customer in **London**, for example, the fourth record. Click in the field box to select it.

The word *"London"* will have a gold colored border around it to let you know that it is active.

d. Click **Selection** in the Sort & Filter group on the Home tab.

e. Choose **Equals "London"** from the menu.

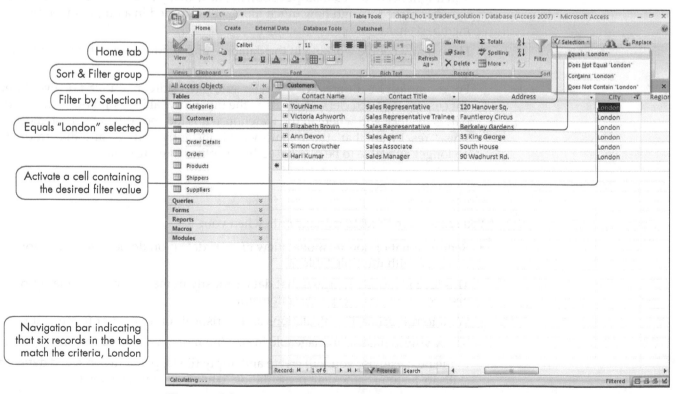

Figure 18 Customers Table Filtered to Display London Records Only

Refer to Figure 19 as you complete Step 2.

a. Find a record with the value **Sales Representative** in the **Contact Title field**. Click your insertion point to activate that field. The first record has a value of *Sales Representative* for the Contact Title field.

Sales Representative will have a gold colored border around it to let you know that it is activated.

b. Click **Selection** on the Sort & Filter group located on the Home tab.

c. Click on **Contains "Sales Representative"** (or type t).

You have applied a second layer of filtering to the customers in London. The second layer further restricts the display to only those customers who have the words Sales Representative contained in their title.

d. Scroll left until you see your name. Compare your results to those shown in Figure 19.

e. Click the **Office Button**, select **Print**, and then select **Quick Print**.

f. Click **Toggle Filter** in the Sort & Filter group to remove the filters.

g. Close the Customers table. Click **No** if a dialog box asks if you want to save the design changes to the Customers table.

TIP   Removing Versus Deleting a Filter

Removing a filter displays all of the records that are in a table, but it does not delete the filter because the filter is stored permanently with the table. To delete the filter entirely is more complicated than simply removing it. Click Advanced on the Sort & Filter group and select the Clear All Filters option from the drop-down list box. Deleting unnecessary filters may reduce the load on the CPU and will allow the database manager to optimize the database performance.

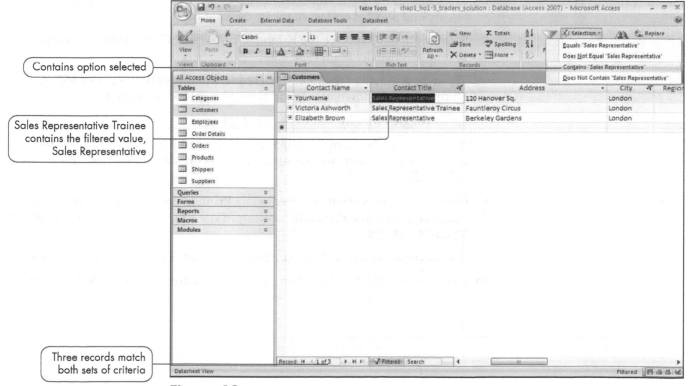

Figure 19 Customers Table Filtered to Display London and Sales Representative Job Titles

Step 3

Use Filter by Form with an Inequity Setting

Refer to Figure 20 as you complete Step 3.

a. Click **Tables** in the Navigation pane to collapse the listed tables.

b. Click **Queries** in the Navigation pane to expand the lists of available queries.

c. Locate and double-click the **Order Details Extended** query to open it.

This query contains information about orders. It has fields containing information about the salesperson, the Order ID, the product name, the unit price, quantity ordered, the discount given, and an extended price. The extended price is a term used to total order information.

d. Click **Advanced** in the Sort & Filter group on the Home tab.

The process to apply a filter by form is identical in a table or a query.

e. Select **Filter By Form** from the list.

All of the records seem to vanish and you see only a list of field names.

f. Click in the **first row** under the **First Name** field.

A down arrow appears at the right of the box.

g. Click the **First Name down arrow**. A list of all available first names appears.

Your name should be on the list. It may be in a different location than that shown in Figure 20 because the list is in alphabetical order.

TROUBLESHOOTING: If you do not see your name and you do see Margaret on the list, you probably skipped Steps 3c and 3d in Hands-On Exercise 1. Close the query without saving changes, turn back to the first hands-on exercise, and rework it, making sure not to omit any steps. Then you can return to this spot and work the remainder of this hands-on exercise.

h. Select **your first name** from the list.

i. Click in the *first row* under the *Last Name field* to turn on the drop-down arrow. Locate and select **your last name** by clicking it.

j. Scroll right until you see the Extended Price field. Click in the *first row* under the Extended Price field and type **<50**.

This will select all of the items ordered where the total was under $50. You ignore the drop-down arrow and type the expression needed.

k. Click **Toggle Filter** in the Sort & Filter group.

You have specified which records to include and have executed the filtering by clicking Toggle Filter. You should have 31 records that match the criteria you specified.

l. Click the **Office Button** and then select **Print**. In the Print dialog box locate the **Pages** control in the *Print Range* section. Type **1** in the *From* box and again in the *To* box. Click **OK**.

You have instructed Access to print the first page of the filtered query results.

m. Close the query. Click **No** when asked if you want to save the design changes.

TIP Deleting Filter by Form Criterion

The Filter by Form command has all of the capabilities of the Filter by Selection command and provides two additional capabilities. First, you can use relational operators such as >, >=, <, or <= as opposed to searching for an exact value. Second, you can search for records that meet one of several conditions (the equivalent of an "Or" operation). Enter the first criterion as you normally would, then click the Or tab at the bottom of the window to display a second form in which you enter the alternate criteria. (To delete an alternate criterion, click the associated tab, and then click Delete on the toolbar.)

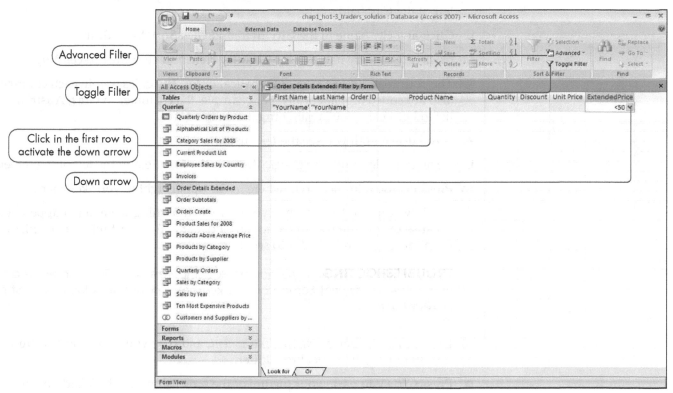

Figure 20   Filter by Selection Criteria Settings

Step 4
Sort a Table

Refer to Figure 21 as you complete Step 4.

a. Click **Queries** in the Navigation pane to collapse the listed queries.

b. Click **Tables** in the Navigation pane to expand the lists of available tables.

c. Locate and double-click the **Customers table** to open it.

This table contains information about customers. It is sorted in ascending order by the Customer ID field. Because this field contains text, the table is sorted in alphabetical order.

d. Click any value in the **Customer ID field**. Click **Sort Descending** in the Sort & Filter group on the Home tab.

Sorting in descending order on a character field produces a reverse alphabetical order.

e. Scroll right until you can see both the **Country** and the **City fields**.

You will sort the customers by country and then by city within the countries. You can sort on more than one field as long as you sort on the primary field (in this case the country) last.

f. Click the field name for **Country**.

The entire column selects.

g. Click the **Country field name box** and hold the left mouse down.

A thick dark blue line displays on the left edge of the Country field column.

h. Check to make sure that you see the thick blue line. When you do, drag the country field to the **left**. When the thick black line moves to between the *Address and City* fields, release the mouse, and the Country field position moves to the left of the City field.

i. Click any city name in the **City field** and click **Sort Ascending**.

j. Click any country name in the **Country field** and click **Sort Ascending**.

The countries are sorted in alphabetical order. The cities within each country also are sorted alphabetically. For example, the customer in Graz, Austria, is listed before the one in Saltzburg.

k. Scroll down until you see the *UK* customers listed.

l. Scroll to the left until the *Contact Name* is the first field in the left of the screen.

m. Press **PrntScrn** located somewhere in the upper right of your keyboard.

You have captured a picture of your screen. If nothing seemed to happen, it is because the picture was saved to the Clipboard. You must retrieve the picture from the Clipboard in order to see it.

TROUBLESHOOTING: Some notebook computers have Print Screen as a function. If the words Print Screen on the key are a different color, you must press **Fn+Print Screen**.

n. Launch Word, open a *new blank document*, and type **your name and section number** on the first line. Press **Enter**.

o. Press **Ctrl+V** to paste your picture of the screenshot into the Word document. Save the document as **chap1_ho2_traders_solution.docx**. Print the Word document.

p. Close the **Customers table**. Do not save the changes.

q. Click the **Office Button**, select **Manage**, and then select **Compact and Repair Database**.

r. Click the **Office Button** again, select **Manage**, and then select **Back Up Database**. Type **chap1_ho2_traders_solution** as the filename and click **Save**.

You just created a backup of the database after completing the second hands-on exercise. The original database *chap1_ho1-3_traders_solution* remains onscreen. If you ruin the original database as you complete the third hands-on exercise, you can use the backup file you just created.

s. Close the file and exit Access if you do not want to continue with the next exercise at this time.

The Cowes customer lists before the London customers

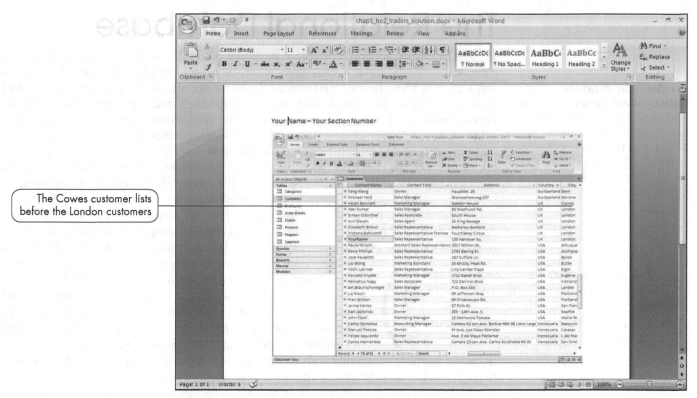

Figure 21 The Customers Table Sorted by Country and then City in Word

The Relational Database

A *relational database management system* is one in which data are grouped into similar collections, called tables, and the relationships between tables are formed by using a common field.

In the previous section you read that you should use Access when you have multi-dimensional data. Access derives power from multiple tables and the relationships among those tables. A *relational database management system* is one in which data are grouped into similar collections called tables, and the relationships between tables are formed by using a common field. The design of a relational database system is illustrated in Figure 22. The power of a relational database lies in the software's ability to organize data and combine items in different ways to obtain a complete picture of the events the data describe. Good database design connects the data in different tables through a system of linkages. These links are the relationships that give relational databases the name. Look at Figure 1. The student record (folder) contains information about the student, but also contains cross-references to data stored in other cabinet drawers, such as the advisor's name or a list of courses completed. If you need to know the advisor's phone number, you can open the faculty drawer, find the advisor's record, and then locate the field containing the phone number. The cross-reference from the student file to the faculty file illustrates how a relationship works in a database. Figure 22 displays the cross-references between the tables as a series of lines connecting the common fields. When the database is set up properly, the users of the data can be confident that if they search a specific customer identification number, they will be given accurate information about that customer's order history and payment balances, and his/her product or shipping preferences.

(The power of a relational database lies in the software's ability to organize data and combine items in different ways to obtain a complete picture of the events the data describe.)

In this section, you will explore the relationships among tables, learn about the power of relational integrity, and discover how the software protects the organization's data.

Using the Relationship Window

The relationship (the lines between the tables in Figure 22) is like a piece of electronic string that travels throughout the database, searching every record of every table until it finds the data satisfying the user's request. Once identified, the fields and records of interest will be tied to the end of the string, pulled through the computer and reassembled in a way that makes the data easy to understand. The first end of the string was created when the primary key was established in the Customers table. The primary key is a unique identifier for each table record. The other end of the string will be tied to a field in a different table. If you examine Figure 22, you will see that the CustomerID is a foreign field in the Orders table. A *foreign key* is a field in one table that also is stored in a different table as a primary key. Each value of the CustomerID can occur only once in the Customers table because it is a primary key. However, the CustomerID may appear multiple times in the Orders table because one customer may make many different purchases. The CustomerID field is a foreign key in the Orders table but the primary key in the Customers table.

A *foreign key* is a field in one table that also is stored in a different table as a primary key.

Examine Referential Integrity

The relationships connecting the tables will be created using an Access feature that uses referential integrity. Integrity means truthful or reliable. When *referential integrity* is enforced, the user can trust the "threads" running through the database and "tying" related items together. The sales manager can use the database to find the names and phone numbers of all the customers who have ordered Teatime Chocolate Biscuits (a specific product). Because referential integrity has been enforced, it will not matter that the order information is in a different table from the customer data. The invisible threads will keep the information accurately connected. The threads also provide a method of ensuring data accuracy. You cannot enter a record in the Orders table that references a ProductID or a CustomerID that does not exist elsewhere in the system. Nor can you easily delete a record in one table if it has related records in related tables.

Referential integrity is the set of rules that ensure that data stored in related tables remain consistent as the data are updated.

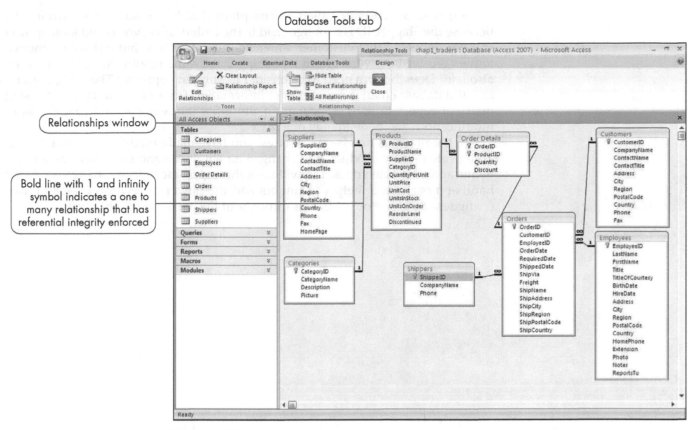

Database Tools tab

Relationships window

Bold line with 1 and infinity symbol indicates a one to many relationship that has referential integrity enforced

Figure 22 The Relationships Window Displaying Table Connections

If this were a real organization's data system, the files would be much, much larger and the data more sophisticated. When learning database skills, you should start with smaller, more manageable files. The same design principles apply regardless of the database size. A small file gives you the ability to check the tables and see if your results are correct. Even though the data amounts are small, you need to develop the work practices needed to manage large amounts of data. With only a handful of records, you can easily count the number of employees at the Washington state office. In addition to learning how to accomplish a task, you also should begin to learn to anticipate the computer's response to an instruction. As you work, ask yourself what the anticipated results should be and then verify. When you become skilled at anticipating output correctly, you are surprised less often.

> As you work, ask yourself what the anticipated results should be and then verify. When you become skilled at anticipating output correctly, you are surprised less often.

Understanding Relational Power

In the previous section you read that you should use Access when you have multidimensional data. Access derives power from multiple tables and the relationships between those tables. This type of database is known as a relational database and is illustrated in Figure 22. This figure describes the database structure. Examine some of the connections. The Employee ID is a foreign field in the Orders table. For example, you can produce a document displaying the history of each order a customer had placed and the employee's name (from the Employees table) that entered the order. The Orders table references the Order Details table where the OrderID is a foreign field. The ProductID relates to the Products table (where it is the primary key). The Category ID is the primary key in the Categories table, but shows up as a foreign field in the Products table. The table connections, even when more than one table is involved, provide the decision-maker power. This feature gives the manager the ability to find out sales by category. How many different beverages were shipped last week? What was the total revenue generated from seafood orders last year?

Suppose a customer called to complain that his orders were arriving late. Because the Shipper ID is a foreign field in the Orders table, you could look up which shipper delivered that customer's merchandise and then find out what other customers received deliveries from that shipper the same month. Are the other orders also late? Does the firm need to reconsider its shipping options? The design of a relational database enables us to extract information from multiple tables in a single query or report. Equally important, it simplifies the way data are changed in that modifications are made in only one place.

In the previous hands-on exercises, you have made modifications to table data. You created a new product, you changed an employee and customer name to your name, and you sorted data. You will trace through some of those changes in the next hands-on exercise to help you understand the power of relationships and how a change made to one object travels throughout the database file structure.

Hands-On Exercises

3 | Introduction to Relationships

Skills covered: 1. Examine the Relationships Window **2.** Discover that Changes in Table Data Affect Queries **3.** Use Filter by Form with an Inequity Setting and Reapply a Saved Filter **4.** Filter a Report **5.** Remove an Advanced Filter

Step 1 **Examine the** **Relationships Window**	Refer to Figure 23 as you complete Step 1. **a.** Open the *chap1_ho1-3_traders_solution* file if necessary, click **Options** on the *security warning* toolbar, click the **Enable this content option** in the Microsoft Office Security Options dialog box, and click **OK**.

TROUBLESHOOTING: If you create unrecoverable errors while completing this hands-on exercise, you can delete the *chap1_ho1-3_traders_solution* file, copy the *chap1_ho2_traders_solution* database you created at the end of the second hands-on exercise, and open the copy of the backup database to start the third hands-on exercise again.

b. Click the **Database Tools tab** and click **Relationships** in the Show/Hide group.

Examine the relationships that connect the various tables. For example, the Products table is connected to the Suppliers, Categories, and Order Details tables.

c. Click **Show Table**.

The Show Table dialog box opens. It tells you that there are eight available tables in the database. If you look in the Relationship window, you will see that all eight tables are in the relationship diagram.

d. Click the **Queries tab** in the Show Table dialog box.

You could add all of the queries to the Relationships window. Things might become cluttered, but you could tell at a glance where the queries get their information.

e. Close the Show Table dialog box.

f. Click the **down arrow** in the All Access Objects bar of the Navigation pane.

g. Click **Tables and Related Views**.

You can now see not only the tables, but also the queries, forms, and reports that connect to the table data. If a query is sourced on more than one table, it will appear multiple times in the Navigation pane. This view provides an alternate method of viewing the relationships connecting the tables.

h. Close the Relationships window. Save the changes.

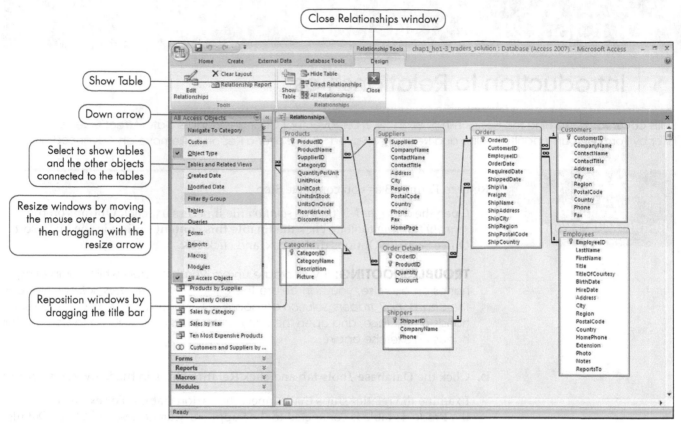

Close Relationships window

Show Table

Down arrow

Select to show tables
and the other objects
connected to the tables

Resize windows by moving
the mouse over a border,
then dragging with the
resize arrow

Reposition windows by
dragging the title bar

Figure 23 The Relationships Window Displaying the Northwind Table Relationships

Step 2

**Discover that Changes
in Table Data Affect
Queries**

Refer to Figure 24 as you complete Step 2.

a. Scroll in the Navigation pane until you see the *Products table and Related Objects*. Locate and double-click the **Order Details Extended query**.

b. Examine the icons on the left edge of the Navigation pane. Figure 24 identifies the object type for each of the objects.

c. Find an occurrence of *your last name* anywhere in the query (record 7 should show your name) and click it to make it active.

The query contains your name because in Hands-On Exercise 1 you replaced Margaret Peacock's name in the Employees table with your name. The Employees table is related to the Orders table, the Orders table to the Order Details table, and the Order Details table to the Products table. Therefore, any change you make to the Employees table is carried throughout the database via the relationships.

d. Click **Filter by Selection** in the Sort & Filter group. Select **Equals "YourName"** from the selection menu.

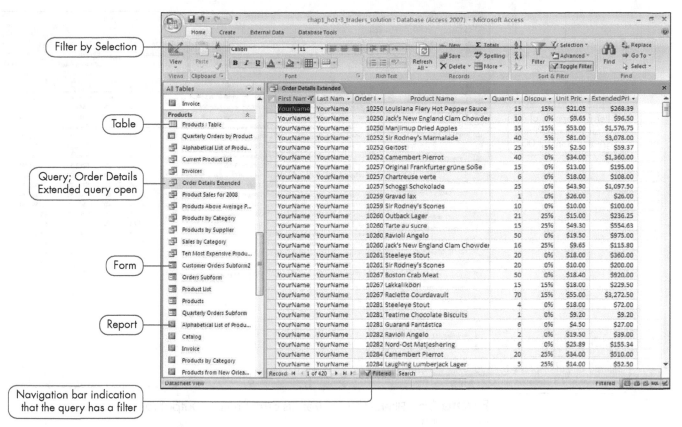

Filter by Selection

Table

Query; Order Details
Extended query open

Form

Report

Navigation bar indication
that the query has a filter

Figure 24 Filtered Query Results

Refer to Figure 25 as you complete Step 3.

Step 3

Use Filter by Form with an Inequity Setting and Reapply a Saved Filter

a. Click **Advanced Filter options**.

b. Select **Filter By Form** from the drop-down list.

Because you already applied a filter to these data, the Filter By Form design sheet opens with one criterion already filled in. Your name displays in the selection box under the Last Name field.

c. Scroll right (or press **Tab**) until the Extended Price field is visible. Click the insertion point in the **first row** under the Extended Price field.

d. Type **>2000**.

The Extended Price field shows the purchased amount for each item ordered. If an item sold for $15 and a customer ordered 10, the Extended Price would display $150.

e. Click **Toggle Filter** in the Sort & Filter group. Examine the filtered results.

Your inequity instruction, >2000, identified the items ordered where the extended price exceeded $2,000.

f. Press **Ctrl+S** to save the query. Close the query by clicking the X in the object window.

g. Open the **Order Details Extended query**.

The filter disengages when you close and reopen the object. However, your filtering directions have been stored with the query design. You may reapply the filter at any time by clicking the Toggle Filter command.

h. Click **Toggle Filter** in the Sort & Filter group.

i. Compare your work to Figure 25. If it is correct, close the query.

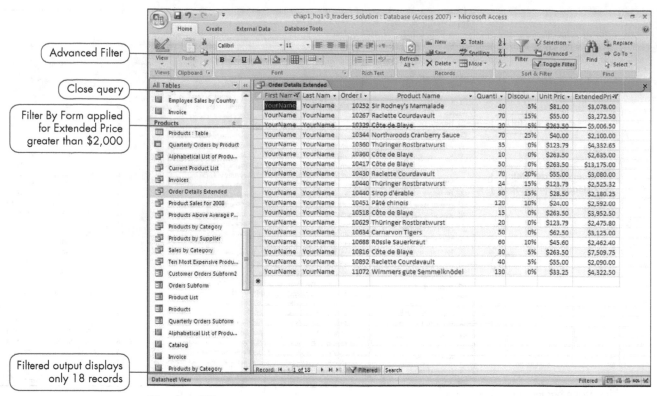

Labels pointing to the figure:
- Advanced Filter
- Close query
- Filter By Form applied for Extended Price greater than $2,000
- Filtered output displays only 18 records

Figure 25 Filtered Query Results after Limiting Output to Extended Prices over $2,000

Step 4
Filter a Report

Refer to Figure 26 as you complete Step 4.

a. Open the **Products by Category report** located in the Navigation pane under the Products group. You may need to scroll down to locate it.

The report should open in Print Preview with a gray stripe highlighting the report title. The Print Preview displays the report exactly as it will print. This report was formatted to display in three columns.

TROUBLESHOOTING: If you do not see the gray stripe and three columns, you probably opened the wrong object. The database also contains a Product by Category query. It is the source for the Products by Category report. Make sure you open the report (shown with the green report icon) and not the query. Close the query and open the report.

b. Examine the Confections category products. You should see **Your Name Pecan Pie**.

You created this product by entering data in a form in Hands-On Exercise 1. You later discovered that changes made to a form affect the related table. Now you see that other related objects also change when the source data changes.

c. Right-click the **gold report tab**. Select **Report View** from the shortcut menu.

The Report view displays the information a little differently. It no longer shows three columns. If you clicked the Print command while in Report view, the columns would print even though you do not see them. The Report view permits limited data interaction (for example, filtering).

d. Scroll down in the report until you see the title *Category: Confections*. **Right-click** the word **Confections** in the title. Select **Equals "Confections"** from the shortcut menu.

Right-clicking a selected data value in an Access table, query, form, or report activates a shortcut to a Filter by Selection menu. Alternatively you can click the selected value, in this case, Confections, and then click the Filter by Selection command in the Sort & Filter group.

e. Right-click the **gold report tab**. Select **Print Preview** from the shortcut menu.

You need to print this report. Always view your reports in Print Preview prior to printing.

f. Click the **Office Button**, select **Print**, and then select **Quick Print** to produce a printed copy of the filtered report. Click **OK**.

The Quick Print command sends your work to the default printer as soon as you click it. You can use this safely when you have already viewed your work in Print Preview.

g. Save and close the report.

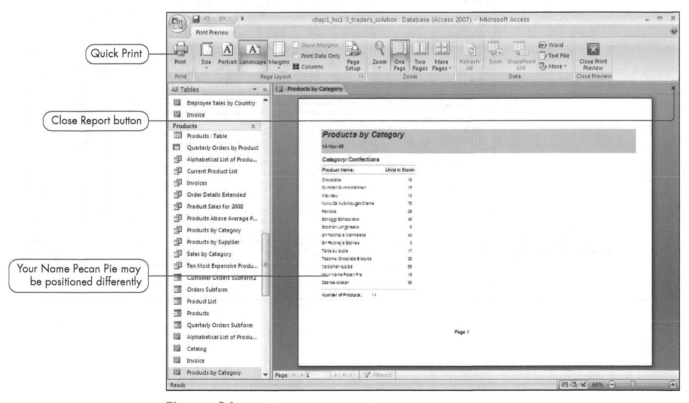

Quick Print

Close Report button

Your Name Pecan Pie may be positioned differently

Figure 26 Filtered Report Results

Refer to Figure 27 as you complete Step 5.

Step 5
Remove an Advanced Filter

Refer to Figure 27 as you complete Step 5.

a. Open the **Order Details Extended query**.

All 2,155 records should display in the query. You have unfiltered the data. However the filter still exists.

b. Click **Toggle Filter** in the Sort & Filter group.

You will see the same 18 filtered records that you printed in Step 3.

c. Click **Advanced** in the Sort & Filter group and click **Clear All Filters**.

d. Close the query. A dialog box opens asking if you want to save changes. Click **Yes**.

e. Open the **Order Details Extended query**.

f. Click **Advanced Filter Options** in the Sort & Filter group.

g. Check to ensure the *Clear All Filters* option is dim. Save and close the query.

h. Click the **Office Button**, select **Manage**, and select **Compact and Repair Database**. Close the file and exit Access.

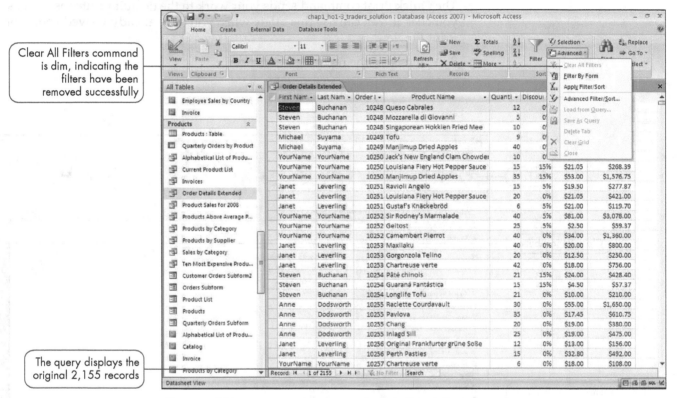

Clear All Filters command is dim, indicating the filters have been removed successfully

The query displays the original 2,155 records

Figure 27 Query Results with Filters Removed

Introduction to Access

Summary

1. **Explore, describe, and navigate among objects in an Access database.** An Access database has six types of objects: tables, forms, queries, reports, macros, and modules. The database window displays these objects and enables you to open an existing object or create new objects. You may arrange these objects by type or by relationship views. The relationship view provides a listing of each table and all other objects in the database that use that table as a source. Thus, one query or report may appear several times, listed once under each table from which it derives information. Each table in the database is composed of records, and each record is in turn composed of fields. Every record in a given table has the same fields in the same order. The primary key is the field (or combination of fields) that makes every record in a table unique.

2. **Understand the difference between working in storage and memory.** Access automatically saves any changes in the current record as soon as you move to the next record or when you close the table. The Undo Current Record command cancels (undoes) the changes to the previously saved record.

3. **Practice good file management.** Because organizations depend on the data stored in databases, database users need to be intentional about exercising good file management practices. You need to be intentional about where you save your files. As you learn new Access skills, you need to make a copy of the database file and practice on the copy. This practice provides a recovery point should you make data-damaging errors.

4. **Create backups, compact, and repair your database.** Because using a database tends to increase the size of the file, you should always close any database objects and compact the database prior to closing the file. This step may reduce the storage requirement by half. Adequate backup is essential when working with an Access database (or any other Office application). A duplicate copy of the database should be created at the end of every session and stored off-site (away from the computer).

5. **Create filters.** A filter is a set of criteria that is applied to a table to display a subset of the records in that table. Microsoft Access lets you Filter by Selection or Filter by Form. The application of a filter does not remove the records from the table, but simply suppresses them from view.

6. **Sort table or query data on one or more fields.** The records in a table can be displayed in ascending or descending order by clicking the appropriate command on the Home tab.

7. **Know when to use Access or Excel to manage data.** Excel data typically is flat. All of the needed information easily presents in a one-dimensional spreadsheet. Use Excel when the data are primarily numeric. Access handles multi-dimensional data more effectively. Use Access when you need to exchange data with other databases, for large amounts of data, or if your data needs are likely to expand.

8. **Use the Relationships window.** The Relationships window provides a summarizing overview of the database design. Use it to discover which fields are stored in what table. It displays the system of linkages among the table data. The Relationships window provides an excellent tool for you to become acquainted with a new database quickly.

9. **Understand relational power.** A relational database contains multiple tables and enables you to extract information from those tables in a single query. The related tables must be consistent with one another, a concept known as referential integrity. Thus, Access automatically implements additional data validation to ensure the integrity of a database. No system, no matter how sophisticated, can produce valid output from invalid input. Changes made in one object travel through the database and affect other, related objects. The relationships are based on linking primary and foreign key fields between tables.

Key Terms

Access speed	Flat or non-relational data	Relational database
Criterion	Foreign key	management system
Database	Form	Report
Datasheet view	Inequity	Sort
Design view	Object	Sort Ascending
Field	Primary key	Sort Descending
Filter	Query	Table
Filter by Form	Record	
Filter by Selection	Referential integrity	

Introduction to Access

Multiple Choice

1. Which sequence represents the hierarchy of terms, from smallest to largest?

   (a) Database, table, record, field
   (b) Field, record, table, database
   (c) Record, field, table, database
   (d) Field, record, database, table

2. Which of the following is not true regarding movement within a record (assuming you are not in the first or last field of that record)?

   (a) Press Tab or the right arrow key to move to the next field.
   (b) Press Spacebar to move to the next field to the right.
   (c) Press Shift+Tab or the left arrow key to return to the previous field.
   (d) Press the Enter key and move to the next record.

3. You're performing routine maintenance on a table within an Access database. When should you execute the Save command?

   (a) Immediately after you add, edit, or delete a record
   (b) Periodically during a session—for example, after every fifth change
   (c) Once at the end of a session
   (d) None of the above since Access automatically saves the changes as they are made

4. Which of the following objects are not contained within an Access database?

   (a) Tables and forms
   (b) Queries and reports
   (c) Macros and modules
   (d) Web sites and worksheets

5. You have opened an Access file. The left pane displays a table with forms, queries, and reports listed under the table. Then another table and its objects display. You notice some of the object names are repeated under different tables. Why?

   (a) The database has been set to Object Type View. The object names repeat because a query or report is frequently based on multiple tables.
   (b) The database has been set to Tables and Related View. The object names repeat because a query or report is frequently based on multiple tables.
   (c) The database has been set to Most Recently Used View. The object names repeat because an object has been used frequently.
   (d) The database objects have been alphabetized.

6. Which of the following is not true of an Access database?

   (a) Every record in a table has the same fields as every other record. The fields are in the same order in each record.
   (b) Every table contains the same number of records as every other table.
   (c) Every record in a table has the same fields as every other record. The fields may be ordered differently depending on the record.
   (d) All records contain the same data as all other records.

7. Which of the following is true regarding the record selector symbol?

   (a) A pencil indicates that the current record already has been saved.
   (b) An empty square indicates that the current record has not changed.
   (c) An asterisk indicates the first record in the table.
   (d) A gold border surrounds the active record.

8. You have finished an Access assignment and wish to turn it in to your instructor for evaluation. As you prepare to transfer the file, you discover that it has grown in size. It is now more than double the original size. You should:

   (a) Zip the database file prior to transmitting it to the instructor.
   (b) Turn it in; the size does not matter.
   (c) Compact and repair the database file prior to transmitting it to the instructor.
   (d) Delete extra tables or reports or fields to make the file smaller.

9. Which of the following will be accepted as valid during data entry?

   (a) Adding a record with a duplicate primary key
   (b) Entering text into a numeric field
   (c) Entering numbers into a text field
   (d) Omitting an entry in a required field

10. In a Replace command, the values for the Find and Replace commands must be:

    (a) The same length
    (b) The same case
    (c) Any part of a word
    (d) Either the same or a different length and case

...continued on Next Page

11. Which of the following capabilities is available through Filter by Selection?

    (a) The imposition of a relational condition

    (b) The imposition of an alternate (OR) condition

    (c) The imposition of an Equal condition

    (d) The imposition of a delete condition

12. You open an Access form and use it to update an address for customer Lee Fong. You exited the record and closed the form. Later you open a report that generates mailing labels. What will the address label for Lee Fong show?

    (a) The new address

    (b) The old address

    (c) The new address if you remembered to save the changes made to the form

    (d) The old address until you remember to update it in the report

13. You have created a Filter by Form in an Order Total field. You set the criterion to >25. Which of the following accurately reflects the instruction given to Access?

    (a) All orders with an Order Total of at least 25

    (b) All orders with an Order Total of less than 25

    (c) All orders with an Order Total over 25

    (d) All orders with an Order Total of 25 or less

14. You have used Find and Replace to find all occurrences of the word "his" with "his/her." You typed only his in the Find box and only his/her in the Replace box. What will the result be?

    (a) History will become His/Herstory

    (b) This will become This/Her

    (c) His will become His/Her

    (d) All of the above

    (e) None of the above

15. You are looking at an Employees table in Datasheet view. You want the names sorted alphabetically by last name and then by first name, e.g., Smith, Andrea is listed before Smith, William. To accomplish this, you must:

    (a) First sort ascending on first name and then on last name

    (b) First sort descending on first name and then on last name

    (c) First sort ascending on last name and then on first name

    (d) First sort ascending on last name and then on first name

Practice Exercises

1 Comfort Insurance

The Comfort Insurance Agency is a midsized company with offices located across the country. You are the human resource director for the company. Your office is located in the home office in Miami. Each employee receives an annual performance review. The review determines employee eligibility for salary increases and the performance bonus. The employee data are stored in an Access database. This database is used by the Human Resource department to monitor and maintain employee records. Your task is to identify the employees who have a performance rating of excellent and a salary under $40,000 per year (if any). Once you identify the appropriate records, you need to sort them alphabetically by the employee's last name. Verify your work by examining Figure 28.

a. Copy the partially completed file in *chap1_pe1_insurance.accdb* from the Exploring Access folder to your production folder. Rename it **chap1_pe1_insurance_solution**. Double-click the filename to open it. Enable the security content by clicking the **Options** command in the Security Warning bar. Select **Enable this content** and then click **OK**.

b. Click the **Database Tools tab** and click **Relationships** in the Show/Hide group. Examine the table structure, relationships, and fields. Once you are familiar with the database, close the Relationships window.

c. Double-click the **Raises and Bonuses query** in the Navigation pane to open it. Find *Debbie Johnson*'s name in the seventh record. Double-click *Debbie* and type your **first name**. Double-click *Johnson* and type your **last name**. Click on a different record to save your change.

d. Examine the number of records in the query and remember it for future reference.

e. Find a record that has a value of *Excellent* in the *Performance field*. The record for Johnny Park (sixth record) is one. Click your insertion point in that field on the word **Excellent**.

f. Activate the **Filter by Selection** in the Sort & Filter group. Select **Equals "Excellent"** from the menu. Examine the number of records in the query and remember it for future reference.

g. Click **Advanced Filter** in the Sort & Filter group and select **Filter By Form**.

h. Position the insertion point in the first row in the *Salary field*. Type **<40000**. (Make sure you apply this number to the Salary field and not the NewSalary field.)

i. Click **Toggle Filter** in the Sort & Filter group. Examine the number of records in the query and remember it for future reference. As you add additional criteria, the number of filtered results should decrease.

j. Click the **first record** in the *LastName* field. Click **Sort Ascending** in the Sort & Filter group on the Home tab to sort the filtered output by the employee's last name alphabetically.

k. Compare your results with Figure 28. Your name will be sorted into the list so your results may not match exactly. The number of records should exactly match.

l. Click the **Office Button** and select **Print**. Select **Quick Print** and click OK. Save the query.

m. Click the **Office Button**, select **Manage**, and select **Compact and Repair Database**. Close the file.

...continued on Next Page

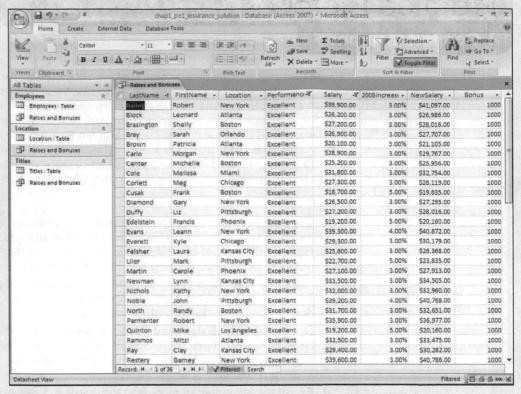

Figure 28 Sorted and Filtered Query Results

2 Member Rewards

The Prestige Hotel chain caters to upscale business travelers and provides state of the art conference, meeting, and reception facilities. It prides itself on its international, four-star cuisines. Last year, it began a member rewards club to help the marketing department track the purchasing patterns of its most loyal customers. All of the hotel transactions are stored in the database. Your task is to update a customer record and identify the customers who had weddings in St. Paul. Verify your work by examining Figure 29.

   a. Copy the partially completed file in *chap1_pe2_memrewards.accdb* from the Exploring Access folder to your production folder. Rename it **chap1_pe2_memrewards_solution**. Double-click the filename to open it. Enable the security content by clicking the **Options** command in the Security Warning bar. Select **Enable this content** and then click **OK**.
   b. Open the **Members Form form** and click **New (blank) record** in the Navigation bar. (It has a yellow asterisk.)
   c. Enter the information below in the form. Press **Tab** to move from field to field.

Field Name	Value
MemNumber	1718
LastName	Your Last Name
FirstName	Your First Name
JoinDate	7/30/2008
Address	124 West Elm Apt 12
City	Your hometown
State	Your state (2 character code)
Zip	00001

...continued on Next Page

Phone	9995551234
Email	Your e-mail
OrderID	9325
ServiceDate	8/1/2008
ServiceID	3
NoInParty	2
Location	20

d. Click **Close form** in the database window (X) to close the form.

e. Double-click the **Members table** in the Navigation pane. Find Boyd Pegel in the first and last name field and replace his name with **your name**.

f. Double-click the **Member Service by City query** in the Navigation pane. Find a record that displays **St Paul** as the value in the *City field*. Click **St Paul** to select that data entry.

g. Select **Filter by Selection** in the Sort & Filter group on the Home tab. Click **Equals "St Paul"**.

h. Find a record that displays **Wedding** as the value in the *ServiceName* field. Click **Wedding** to select that data entry.

i. Select **Filter by Selection** in the Sort & Filter group on the Home tab. Click **Equals "Wedding"**.

j. Click any value in the **FirstName** field. Click **Sort Ascending** in the Sort & Filter group on the Home tab. Click any value in the **LastName** field. Click **Sort Ascending** in the Sort & Filter group on the Home tab.

k. Click the **Office Button**, select **Print**, and click **OK** to print the sorted and filtered query.

l. Save and close the query.

m. Click the **Office Button**, select **Manage**, and then select **Compact and Repair Database**. Close the file.

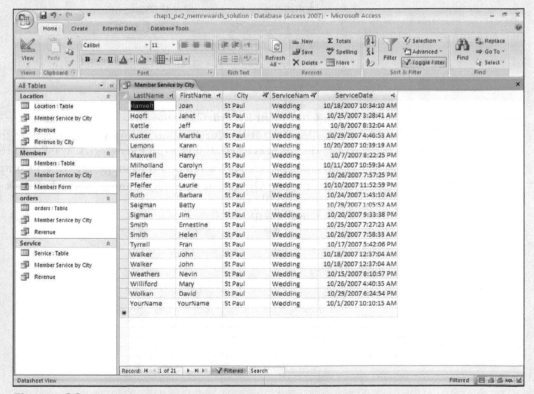

Figure 29 Sorted and Filtered Query Results

The Vancouver Preschool is a dynamic and exciting educational environment for young children. It launches each school year with a fundraiser that helps provide classroom supplies. Patrons are asked to donate goods and services, which are auctioned at a welcome-back-to-school dinner for students, parents, grandparents, and friends. All of the data about the donations are contained in an Access file. Your task is to make some modifications to the data and print a form and a report. Verify your work by comparing it to Figure 30. The report in the figure is displayed at a higher zoom percentage so that you can read the report easily. Your report may appear as a full page.

a. Copy the partially completed file *chap1_pe3_preschool.accdb* from the Exploring Access folder to your production folder. Rename it **chap1_pe3_preschool_solution.accdb**. Double-click the filename to open it. Click **Options** on the Security Warning bar, click **Enable this content,** and then click **OK**.

b. Open the **Donors form**. Navigate to a **new blank record** by clicking the navigation button with the yellow asterisk on it.

c. Enter the information below in the form.

Field Name	Value
DonorID	(New)
FirstName	Your First Name
LastName	Your Last Name
Address	124 West Elm Apt 12
City	Your hometown
State	Your state
Zip	00001
Phone	9995551234
Notes	Your e-mail
Item Donated	Car wash and hand wax
Number Attending	2
Item Value	100
Category	Service

d. Click **Print Record**. Close the form.

e. Open the **Items for Auction** report. Check to ensure that the *car wash and hand wax* donation is listed. If it is, print the report. Close Print preview.

f. Click the **Office Button**, select **Manage**, and select **Compact and Repair Database**.

g. Click the **Office Button**, select **Manage**, and select **Back Up Database**. Use the default backup filename.

h. Close the file.

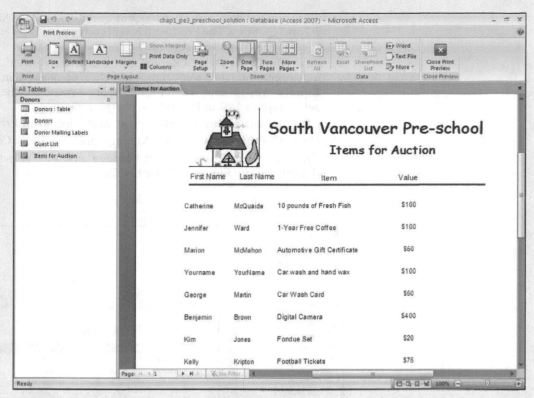

Figure 30 Report

---

4 Custom Coffee

The Custom Coffee Company is a small service organization that provides coffee, tea, and snacks to offices. Custom Coffee also provides and maintains the equipment for brewing the beverages. Although the firm is small, its excellent reputation for providing outstanding customer service has helped it grow. Part of the customer service is determined through a database the firm owner set up to organize and keep track of customer purchases. Verify your work by comparing it to Figure 31. The report in the figure is displayed at a higher zoom percentage so that you can read the report easily. Your report may appear as a full page.

a. Copy the partially completed file *chap1_pe4_coffee.accdb* from the Exploring Access folder to your production folder. Rename it **chap1_pe4_coffee_solution.accdb**. Double-click the filename to open the file. Click **Options** in the Security Warning bar, click **Enable this content**, and then click **OK**.

b. Click the **Navigation pane down arrow** to change the object view from Tables and Related Views to **Object Type**.

c. Examine the other objects, reports, forms, and queries in the database. Click the **Navigation pane down arrow** and restore the **Tables and Related Views** method of looking at the objects.

d. Double-click the **Sales Reps table** to open it. Replace *YourName* with **your name**. Close the table by clicking Close in the database window.

e. Double-click the **Customers Form** to open it. Navigate to a **new blank record** by clicking the navigation button with the yellow asterisk on it. Use **your name** for the *Customer* and *Contact* fields. Invent an address, phone, and email. Type **Miami** for the city and **FL** for the state fields. The *Service Start Date* is **01/17/2005**. The *Credit Rating* is **A**. Type a **2** for the *Sales Rep ID*. It will convert to *S002* automatically.

f. Close the Customers Form.

g. Double-click the **Orders form** to open it. Navigate to a new blank record by clicking the navigation button with the yellow asterisk on it.

h. Type **16** as the *Customer ID*. The database will convert it to *C0016*. In the *Payment Type*, type **Cash**.

...continued on Next Page

i. Type **4** in the *Product ID box* and **2** in *Quantity*. In the next row, type **6** and **1** for *Product ID* and *Quantity*. The Product IDs will convert to P0004 and P0006. Close the form, saving changes if requested.

j. Open the **Order Details Report**. Scroll down to verify that your name appears both as a customer and as a sales rep. Right-click **your name** in the SalesRep field and select **Equals "Your Name"** from the shortcut menu. Right click **Miami** in the City field and select **Equals "Miami"** from the shortcut menu.

k. Click the **Office Button**, select **Print**, and select **Print Preview**. Click **Print**.

l. Click the **Office Button**, select **Manage**, and then select **Compact and Repair Database**.

m. Click the **Office Button**, select **Manage**, and then select **Back Up Database**. Use the default backup filename. Close the file.

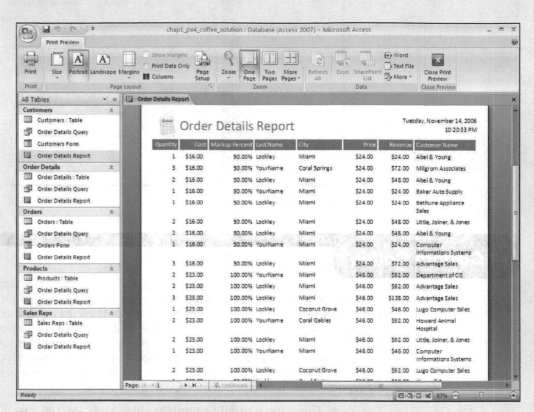

Figure 31 Report Showing Changes Made to Forms

Mid-Level Exercises

1 Object Navigation, Data Entry, and Printing Database Objects

Your little sister lives to play soccer. She told her coach that you have become a computer expert. Coach (who is also the league director) called you to ask for help with the Access database file containing all of the league information. You agreed, and he promptly delivered a disc containing a copy of the league's database. The file contains information on the players, the coaches, and the teams. Players are classified by skill and experience level, with the best players described as "A." The Coaches table classifies coaching status as level 1 (head coaches) or 2 (assistant coaches). Coach asks that you add new players to the database and then identify all of the players not yet assigned to teams. He also needs you to identify the teams without coaches, the unassigned coaches, and asks that you assign each team a head and an assistant coach. Finally, Coach convinces you to volunteer as a coach in the league. Verify your work by looking at Figure 32.

a. Locate the file named *chap1_mid1_soccer.accdb*, copy it to your working folder, and rename it **chap1_mid1_soccer_solution.accdb**. Open the file and enable the content.

b. Open the Relationships window and examine the tables, the relationships, and the fields located in each table. Close the Relationships window.

c. Examine all of the objects in the database and think about the work Coach asked you to do. Identify which objects will assist you in accomplishing the assigned tasks.

d. Open the **Players form** and create a new record. Use your name, but you may invent the data about your address and phone. You are classified as an "A" player. Print the form containing your record. Close the form.

e. Open the **Coaches table**. Replace record 13 with **your instructor's name**. Add **yourself** as a new record. You are a *coach status* **1**.

f. Identify the players not assigned to teams. Assign each player to a team while balancing skill levels. (You would not want one team in the league to have all of the "A" skill level players because they would always win.)

g. Identify the teams without coaches and the coaches not assigned to teams. Assign a head coach and an assistant coach to each team. You may need to assign a person with head coaching qualifications to an assistant position. If you do, change his or her *status* to **2**.

h. After you assign all of the players and coaches to teams, open and print the **Master Coaching List report**.

i. After you assign all of the players and coaches to teams, open and print the **Team Rosters report**. Close the database.

...continued on Next Page

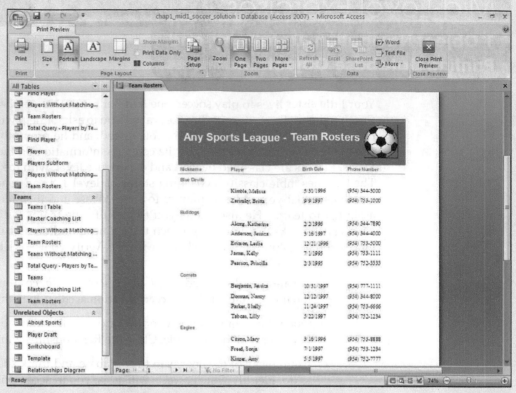

Figure 32 Team Roster Report

2 Sorting and Filtering Table Data Using Advanced Filters

You are the senior partner in a large, independent real estate firm that specializes in home sales. Although you still represent buyers and sellers in real estate transactions, you find that most of your time is spent supervising the agents who work for your firm. This fact distresses you because you like helping people buy and sell homes. There is a database containing all of the information on the properties your firm has listed. You believe that by using the data in the database more effectively, you can spend less time supervising the other agents and spend more time doing the part of your job that you like doing the best. Your task is to determine how many three-bedroom, two-bathroom, and garage properties your firm has listed for sale with a listing price under $400,000. Finally, you need to sort the data by list price in descending order. Refer to Figure 33 to verify that your results match the results shown.

    a. Locate the file named *chap1_mid2_realestate.accdb*; copy it to your working folder and rename it **chap1_mid2_realestate_solution.accdb**. Open the file and enable the content. Open the *Agents* table. Find and replace *YourName* with **your name** in the first and last name fields.

    b. Create a filter by form on the data stored in the *Under 400K query*. Set the criteria to identify **three or more bedrooms, two or more bathrooms,** and **garage** properties you have listed for sale with a listing price **under $400,000.**

    c. Sort the filtered results in **descending** order by the **ListPrice** field.

    d. After you are sure that your results are correct, save the query.

    e. Capture a screenshot of the sorted and filtered Under 400K query. With the sorted and filtered table open on your computer, press **PrintScrn**. Open Word; launch a new blank document, type **your name and section number**, and press **Enter**. Press **Ctrl+V** or

...continued on Next Page

click Paste. Print the word document. Save it as **chap1_mid2_realestate_solution. docx**. Close the Word document.

f. Compact, repair, and back up the database. Name the backup **chap1_mid2_ realestate_backup.accdb**. Close the database.

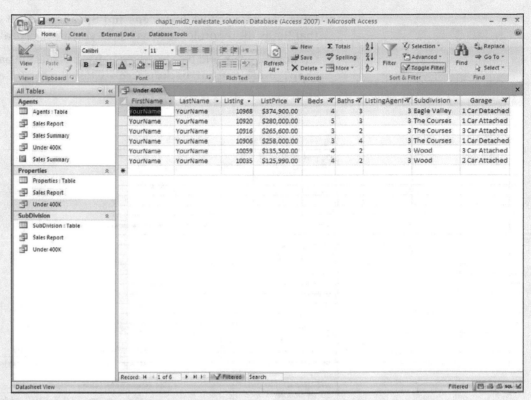

Figure 33 Sorted, Filtered Table

3 Sorting and Filtering Table Data Using Advanced Filters, Printing a Report

You work for the Office of Residence Life at your university as a work/study employee. The dean of student affairs, Martha Sink, PhD, placed you in this position because your transcript noted that you were enrolled in a computing class covering Microsoft Access. Dr. Sink has a special project for you. Each year the Association of Higher Education hosts a national conference to share new ideas and best practices. Next year the conference will be held on your campus, and the Office of Residence life has the responsibility of planning and organizing the events, speakers, and physical meeting spaces. To facilitate the work, the IT department has created a database containing information on the rooms, speakers, and sessions. Dr. Sink needs your assistance with extracting information from the database. Examine Figure 34 to verify your work.

a. Locate the file named *chap1_mid3_natconf.accdb*; copy it to your working folder and rename it **chap1_mid3_natconf_solution.accdb**. Open the file and enable the content. Open the **Speakers table**. Find and replace *YourName* with **your name**. Close the Speakers table.

...continued on Next Page

b. Open the **Speaker - Session Query** and apply a filter to identify the sessions where you or Holly Davis are the speakers. Use Filter by Form and engage the Or tab.

c. Sort the filtered results in descending order by the RoomID field.

d. Capture a screenshot of the sorted and filtered Speaker Session query. With the sorted and filtered query open on your computer press **PrintScrn**. Open Word; launch a new blank document, type **your name and section number**, and press **Enter**. Press **Ctrl+V** or click **Paste**. Print the Word document. Save it as **chap1_mid3_natconf_ solution.docx**. Close the Word document.

e. Open the **Master List – Sessions and Speakers report** in Report View. Apply a filter that limits the report to sessions where you are the speaker. Print the report.

f. Compact, repair, and back up the database. Name the backup **chap1_mid3_natconf_backup.accdb**. Close the database.

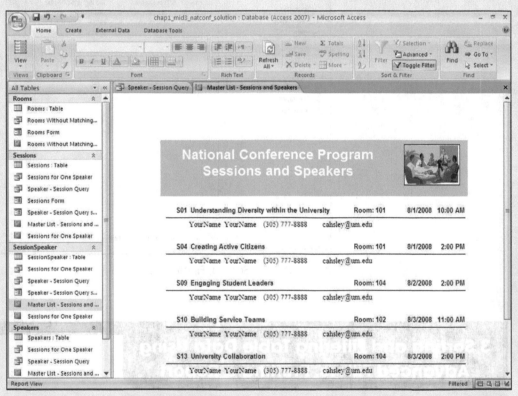

Figure 34 Master Sessions and Speakers Report

Introduction to Access

Capstone Exercise

Your boss expressed a concern about the accuracy of the inventory reports in the bookstore. He needs you to open the inventory database, make modifications to some records, and determine if the changes you make carry through to the other objects in the database. You will make changes to a form and then visit those changes in a table, a query, and a report. When you have verified that the changes update automatically, you will compact and repair the database and make a backup of it.

Database File Setup

You need to copy an original database file, rename the copied file, and then open the copied database to complete this capstone exercise. After you open the copied database, you will replace an existing employee's name with your name.

a. Locate the file named *chap1_cap_bookstore.accdb* and copy it to your working folder.

b. Rename the copied file as **chap1_cap_bookstore_solution.accdb**.

c. Open the *chap1_cap_bookstore_solution.accdb* file and enable the content.

d. Open the **Author Form** form.

e. Navigate to record 7 and replace *YourName* with **your name**.

f. Add a new *Title*, **Computer Wisdom II**. The *ISBN* is **0-684-80416-5**, the *PubID* is **SS**, the *PublDate* is **2007**, the *Price* is **$28.00** (just type 28, no $, period, or zeros), and *StockAmt* is **27** *units*.

g. Navigate to record 6 (or any other record). Close the form.

h. Open the **Author Form** again and navigate to record 7. The changes are there because Access works from storage, not memory. Close the form.

Sort a Query and Apply a Filter by Selection

You need to reorder a detail query so that the results are sorted alphabetically by the publisher name.

a. Open the **Publishers, Books, and Authors Query**.

b. Click in any record in the PubName field and sort the field in alphabetical order.

c. Check to make sure that two books list you as the author.

d. Click *your name* in the Author field and filter the records to show your books.

e. Close the query without saving the changes.

View a Report

You need to examine the Publishers, Books, and Authors report to determine if the changes you made to the Author form carried through to the report.

a. Open the **Publishers, Books, and Authors Report**.

b. Check to make sure that the report shows two books listing you as the author.

c. Print the report.

d. Close the report.

Filter a Table

You need to examine the Books table to determine if the changes you made to the Author form carried through to the related table. You also will filter the table to display books published after 2004 with fewer than 30 copies in inventory.

a. Open the **Books** table.

b. Click **Advanced** in the Sort & Filter group and then select **Filter by Form** from the drop-down list.

c. Create the criteria that will identify all records with fewer than 30 items in stock.

d. Apply the filter.

e. Print the filtered table.

f. Close the table. Do not save the design changes.

Compact and Repair a Database, Backup a Database

Now that you are satisfied that any changes made to a form, table, or query carry through the database, you are ready to compact, repair, and back up your file.

a. Select the option to compact and repair your database.

b. Select the option to create a backup copy of your database, accept the default filename, and save it.

c. Close the file.

Mini Cases

Use the rubric following the case as a guide to evaluate your work, but keep in mind that your instructor may impose additional grading criteria or use a different standard to judge your work.

Applying Filters, Printing, and File Management

GENERAL CASE

The *chap1_mc1_safebank.accdb* file contains data from a small bank. Copy the *chap1_mc1_safebank.accdb* file to your working storage folder, name it **chap1_mc1_safebank_solution.accdb**, and open the copied file. Use the skills from this chapter to perform several tasks. Open the Customer table, replace YourName with your name, and sort the data in alphabetical order by LastName. Print the Customer table. Open the Branch table and make yourself the manager of the Campus branch. Close both tables. Open the Branch Customers query and filter it to show only the accounts at the Campus branch with balances over $1,500.00. Print the filtered query results. Compact, repair, and backup your work.

Performance Elements	Exceeds Expectations	Meets Expectations	Below Expectations
Sort and print table data	Printout displays data sorted in requested order.	The table was successfully printed, but the order is incorrect.	Output missing or corrupted.
Apply filters and print query data	Appropriate filters successfully created and printed.	One of the requested filters but not both work correctly. Output created.	Output missing or corrupted.
Data entry	Data were entered correctly.	Some but not all of the requested data were entered correctly, or other data were overwritten.	Output missing or corrupted.
File management	Database was correctly compacted, repaired, and backed up.	The database was successfully compacted but not backed up or vice-versa.	Files not submitted.

Combining Name Fields

RESEARCH CASE

This chapter introduced you to the power of using Access filters and setting criteria, but you have much more to explore. Copy the file named *chap1_mc2_traders.accdb* to your production folder and rename it **chap1_mc2_traders_solution.accdb**. Open the file and enable the content. Open the Employees table and replace YourName with your first and last names. Open the Revenue report and switch to the appropriate view. Use the tools that you have learned in this chapter to filter the report. You wish to limit the output to only your sales of Seafood. You may need to use Access Help to get the filters to work. Once the report is filtered, print it. Write your instructor a letter explaining how you accomplished this step. Use a letter template in Word, your most professional writing style, and clear directions that someone could follow in order to accomplish this task. Attach the printout of the name list to the letter. Turn the printouts in to the instructor if instructed to do so. Back up, compact, and repair your database.

Performance Elements	Exceeds Expectations	Meets Expectations	Below Expectations
Use online help	Appropriate articles located, and letter indicates comprehension.	Appropriate articles located, but letter did not demonstrate comprehension.	Articles not found.
Report filtered to display only your sales of seafood	Printed list attached to letter in requested format.	Printed list is attached, but the filter failed to screen one or more salespeople or categories.	List missing or incomprehensible.
Summarize and communicate	Letter clearly written and could be used as directions.	Letter text indicates some understanding but also weaknesses.	Letter missing or incomprehensible.
File management	Database was correctly compacted, repaired, and backed up.	Database was successfully compacted but not backed up or vice-versa.	Files not submitted.
Esthetics	Letter template correctly employed.	Template employed but signed in the wrong place or improperly used.	Letter missing or incomprehensible.

Coffee Revenue Queries

DISASTER RECOVERY

A co-worker called you into his office and explained that he was having difficulty with Access 2007 and asked you to look at his work. Copy the *chap1_mc3_coffee.accdb* file to your working storage folder, name it **chap1_mc3_coffee_solution.accdb**, and open the file. Your co-worker explains that the report is incorrect. It shows that Lockley is the sales representative for "Coulter Office Supplies" and the "Little, Joiner, and Jones" customers, when in fact you are those customers' sales representative. Make sure your name replaces YourName in the Sales Reps table. Find the source of the error and correct it. Run and print the report and turn the printout and file in to your instructor if instructed to do so. Compact, repair, and backup your database.

Performance Elements	Exceeds Expectations	Meets Expectations	Below Expectations
Error identification	Correct identification and correction of all errors.	Correct identification of all errors and correction of some errors.	Errors neither located nor corrected.
Reporting	Report opened, run, and printed successfully.	Printout submitted, but with errors.	No printout submitted for evaluation.
File management	Database was correctly compacted, repaired, and backed up.	Database was successfully compacted but not backed up or vice-versa.	Files not submitted.

Access

Relational Databases and Multi-Table Queries

Designing Databases and Using Related Data

Objectives

After you read this chapter you will be able to:

1. Design data.
2. Create tables.
3. Understand table relationships.
4. Share data with Excel.
5. Establish table relationships.
6. Create a query.
7. Specify criteria for different data types.
8. Copy and run a query.
9. Use the Query Wizard.
10. Understand large database differences.

Hands-On Exercises

Exercises	Skills Covered
1. TABLE DESIGN, PROPERTIES, VIEWS, AND WIZARDS Open: a new blank database Save as: chap2_ho1-3_safebank_solution.accdb Back up as: chap2_ho1_safebank_solution.accdb	• Create a New Database • Create a Table by Entering Data • Change the Primary Key, Modify Field Properties, and Delete a Field • Modify Table Fields in Design View • Create a New Field in Design View • Switch Between the Table Design and the Table Datasheet Views
2. IMPORTS AND RELATIONSHIPS Open: chap2_ho1-3_safebank_solution.accdb (from Exercise 1) and chap2_ho2_safebank.xlsx Save as: chap2_ho1-3_safebank_solution.accdb (additional modifications) Back up as: chap2_ho2_safebank_solution. accdb	• Import Excel Data into an Access Table • Import Additional Excel Data • Modify an Imported Table's Design • Add Data to an Imported Table • Establish Table Relationships • Understand How Referential Integrity Protects Data
3. MULTIPLE-TABLE QUERY Open: chap2_ho1-3_safebank_solution.accdb (from Exercise 2) Save as: chap2_ho1-3_safebank_solution.accdb (additional modifications)	• Create a Query Using a Wizard • Specify Simple Query Criteria • Change Query Data • Add a Table to a Query Using Design View and Sort a Query

From *Exploring Office 2007 Volume I*, Robert T. Grauer, Michelle Hulett, Cynthia Krebs, Maurie Wigman Lockley, Keith Mulbery, and Judy Scheeren. Copyright © 2007 by Pearson Education. Published by Prentice Hall.

CASE STUDY

National Conference

You received a work-study assignment to the Office of Student Life at your school. This morning, the dean of Student Affairs, Jackie Cole, invited you to come to her office. Dr. Cole returned from the National Conference of Student Service Providers yesterday. Thousands of educators participate in this conference annually. She volunteered your school to host the event next year. She explained that this is a wonderful opportunity to showcase your school to the rest of the education world, but that the conference details need to be planned carefully so that the scheduled events execute flawlessly. Then Dr. Cole explained that she selected you as the work-study student because of your Access skills. She explained that no one else in the office knew anything about Access. She noted that a project of this magnitude required a database to efficiently manage the data. Then she said, "We are depending on you to create and manage the database and make our school look good."

Dr. Cole asked the IT department to help you design the database. The IT staff has created a small database with a table for the speakers and a table that joins the speakers and sessions together. An Excel spreadsheet contains information about the sessions. You will need to import the Excel data into the Access file, connect it with the rest of the database, and update the data.

The IT staff did not think about the conference participants when they designed the database. You need to design a table that will hold the information about the conference participants. Think carefully about what information might be needed about each registrant. Then think about how to connect the registration information to the rest of the database. You need to establish the primary and foreign keys for the Registrant table as you plan the other fields in that table.

Your Assignment

- Copy the file named *chap2_case_natconf.accdb* to your production folder. Name the copy **chap2_case_natconf_solution.accdb**.
- Open each table and familiarize yourself with the data.
- Open the Relationships window and acquaint yourself with the tables, fields, and relationships among the tables in the database.
- Import the data contained in the Excel file, *chap2_case_sessions.xlsx*. As you create the import, think about which field will be the primary key and establish appropriate properties.
- Establish a relationship between the Sessions table and the other tables in the database. Remember that a relationship may only be formed on data of like type and size.
- Replace the first record in the Speakers table with information about you.
- Create a new record in the Speakers table. Add yourself as a speaker. Your area of expertise is Student Life.
- Create a new Session. Title it **Undergraduate Challenges**. Examine the session times and rooms and schedule this session so that it does not conflict with the other sessions.
- Create a query that will show the speaker's name, the session title, and the room number. Add parameters to limit the output to sessions conducted by **Davis, Kline**, and **you**. Print the query results.
- Create a table for conference participant's registrations. Carefully anticipate which fields need to be included. Participants must pay a $500 registration fee.
- Create a new record in the registration table. Add yourself as a participant.
- Capture a screenshot of the Relationships window. Paste the screenshot into a Word file. Save the file as **chap2_case_natconf_solution.docx**.
- Compact and repair your file. Back up the database as **chap2_case_natconf_solution_backup.accdb**.

Table Design, Properties, Views, and Wizards

Good database design provides the architectural framework supporting the work the database accomplishes. If the framework is flawed, the resulting work will always have flaws, too. You may remember the period leading to New Year's Eve in 1999, Y2K. Many people stocked up on groceries, withdrew cash from their checking accounts, and filled their gas tanks because they believed that the computer-operated grocery check-outs, automatic banking machines, and gasoline pumps would not function properly (if at all) on New Year's Day, 2000. These frightened people had legitimate reasons due to poor database design. Electronic data storage was (and remains) relatively expensive. Principles of good design dictate saving storage space when possible. As a space-saving measure, most dates in most computers prior to the mid-1990s stored the year as a two-digit number. For example, 1993 was stored as 93. The Information Systems and Computer Science professionals responsible for managing the databases in the world failed to anticipate the consequences of flawed database design.

Computers perform relatively simple arithmetic computations to measure time lapses. When subtracting 1993 from 1995, the computer knows that two years have passed. The results do not change when the dates are stored as 93 and 95. However, what would happen when the computer subtracted 99 from 01? You know that a two-year period has passed. But, the computer would believe that a *negative* 98 years had passed! Before New Year's Day, 2000, IS professionals worked extra hours correcting the design flaws in the way their systems handled and processed dates. On January 1, 2000, computerized grocery stores, ATMs, and gas pumps virtually all worked. The overtime hours combined with the new hardware and software required cost an estimated $21 billion globally to fix.

This chapter introduces the Safebank database case study to present the basic principles of table and query design. You use tables and forms to input data, and you create queries and reports to extract information from the database in a useful and organized way. The value of that information depends entirely on the quality of the underlying data, which must be both complete and accurate.

In this section, you learn about the importance of proper design and essential guidelines that are used throughout the book. After developing the design, you implement that design in Access. You create a table, and then refine its design by changing the properties of various fields. You will gain an understanding of the importance of data validation during data entry.

Designing Data

As a consumer of financial services, you know that your bank or credit union maintains data about you. Your bank has your name, address, phone number, and Social Security number. It knows if you have a credit card and what your balances are. Additionally, your bank keeps information about its branches. Think about the information your bank generates and then make a list of the data needed to produce that information. The key to the design process is to visualize the output required to determine the input needed to produce that output. Think of the specific fields you need and characterize each field according to the type of data it contains (such as text, numbers, or dates) as well as its size (length). Figure 1 shows one sample list of fields. Your list may vary. The order of the fields within the table and the specific field names are not significant. What is important is that the tables contain all necessary fields so that the system can perform as intended.

Table Design, Properties, Views, and Wizards

Customer's Last Name—Text
Customer's First Name—Text
Customer's Identification Number—Either text or number
Address—Text
City—Text
State—Text
Postal Code—Number
Phone—Text
Branch Identification—Either text or number
Branch Manager's Name—Text
Branch Manager's Start Date—Number date formatted
Branch Location—Text
Account Number—Either text or number
Balance—Number formatted as currency

Figure 1   Data Needed for a Bank Database

Figure 1 reflects the results of a careful design process based on six essential guidelines:

1. Include the necessary data.

2. Design for the next 100 years.

3. Design in compliance with Sarbanes Oxley.

4. Design in compliance with PNPI Regulations.

5. Store data in its smallest parts.

6. Avoid calculated fields in table data.

7. Design to accommodate date arithmetic.

The following paragraphs discuss these guidelines. As you proceed through the text, you will begin developing the experience necessary to design your own systems. Design is an important skill. You also must understand how to design a database and its tables to use Access effectively.

Include the Necessary Data

. . . ask yourself what information will be expected from the system, and then determine the data required to produce that information.

The best way to determine what data are necessary is to create a rough draft of the reports you will need, and then design tables that contain the fields necessary to create those reports. In other words, ask yourself what information will be expected from the system, and then determine the data required to produce that information. Consider, for example, the type of information that can and cannot be produced from the table in Figure 1:

- You can determine which branch a customer uses. You cannot, however, tell the customer with multiple accounts at different locations what the total balance of all accounts might be.

- You can calculate a total of all account balances by adding individual account balances together. You could also calculate the sum of all deposits at a branch. You cannot tell when a deposit was made because this small exercise does not store that data.

- You can determine who manages a particular branch and which accounts are located there. You cannot determine how long the customer has banked with the branch because the date that he or she opened the account is not in the table.

Whether these omissions are important depends on the objectives of the system. Of course, the data stored in a real bank's database is far more complex and much larger than the data you will use. This case has been simplified.

Design for the Next 100 Years

A fundamental law of information technology states that systems evolve continually and that information requirements change. Try to anticipate the future needs of the system, and then build in the flexibility to satisfy those demands. Include the necessary data at the outset, and be sure that the field sizes are large enough to accommodate future expansion. The *field size property* defines how many characters to reserve for a specific field.

The *field size property* defines how much space to reserve for each field.

When you include all possible elements of data that anyone might ever need, you drive up the cost of the database. Each element costs employee time to enter and maintain the data and consumes storage space. Computers have a finite amount of space. Good database design must balance the current and future needs of the system against the cost of recording and storing unnecessary data elements. Even with using data warehouses, the amount of data that we can store is limited.

> Good database design must balance the current and future needs of the system against the cost of recording and storing unnecessary data elements.

Suppose you are designing a database for your college. You would need to include students' on-campus and permanent addresses. It might be useful for someone to know other places a student might have lived or even visited during their lives. A worker in the Student Life office could help an international student connect with someone who used to live in or at least visited the international student's homeland. A student who had moved often or traveled extensively might need an extra page on his or her application form. Completing the application might take so long that the student might apply to a different college. A worker in the admissions office would need extra time to enter all the places of residence and travel into the database. The school's database file would grow and require additional storage space on the university computer system. The benefits provided to the international student from connecting him to someone who had been in his country may not justify the cost of entering, maintaining, and storing the additional data.

A *validation rule* checks the authenticity of the data entered in a field.

The data will prove useful only if they are accurate. You need to anticipate possible errors a data entry operator might commit. Access provides tools to protect data from user error. A *validation rule* restricts data entry in a field to ensure the correct type of data is entered or that the data does not violate other enforced properties, such as exceed a size limitation. The validation rule checks the authenticity of the data entered when the user exits the field. If the data entry violates the validation rule, an error message appears and prevents the invalid data from being stored in the field.

Design in Compliance with Sarbanes Oxley

Sarbanes Oxley Act (SOX) protects the general public and companies' shareholders against fraudulent practices and accounting errors.

Following the financial and accounting scandals involving Enron and World Com in 2002, the U.S. Congress passed the *Sarbanes Oxley Act (SOX)*. Its intent is to protect the general public and companies' shareholders against fraudulent practices and accounting errors. The Securities and Exchange Commission (SEC) enforces the act. Although primarily focused on the accounting practices followed by publicly traded companies, SOX permeates corporate Information Technology policies and practices. The act requires that all business records, including electronic messages, be saved for a period of five years and be made available to the SEC on request. Penalties for non-compliance include fines, imprisonment, or both. The IT department faces the challenge of archiving all the required information in a cost-effective and efficient way.

Design in Compliance with PNPI Regulations

Federal laws and regulations govern the safeguarding of personal, non-public information (*PNPI*), such as Social Security Numbers (SSNs), credit or bank account numbers, medical or educational records, or other sensitive, confidential or protected data (i.e., grades used in context with personally identifiable information such as name, address, or other easily traceable identifiers). Organizations must store your personal information in computer systems. For example, without your Social Security Number, the financial aid office cannot release scholarship money to pay your tuition. Your employer cannot cut a paycheck without knowing your Social Security Number. Your doctor cannot tell the student health service at your school whether you have been immunized against the measles without your written permission. The data must be stored with protected and restricted access. Congress has passed several laws to protect you from identity theft or other misuse of your private, personal information. The most important of these laws include the following:

- Family Educational Rights and Privacy Act (FERPA) [educational records]
- Gramm-Leach-Bliley Act (GLBA) [financial institution and customer data]
- Health Insurance Portability and Accountability Act (HIPAA) [health information]

Store Data in Their Smallest Parts

The design in Figure 1 divides a customer's name into two fields (first and last name) to reference each field individually. You might think it easier to use a single field consisting of both the first and last name, but that approach is inadequate. Consider this list in which the customer's name is stored as a single field:

- Allison Foster
- Brit Reback
- Carrie Graber
- Danielle Ferrarro
- Evelyn Adams
- Frances Coulter

The first problem in this approach is lack of flexibility: You could not easily create a salutation of the form *Dear Allison* or *Dear Ms. Foster* because the first and last names are not accessible individually. In actuality you could write a procedure to divide the name field in two, but that is beyond the capability of the Access novice.

A second difficulty is that the list of customers cannot be put into alphabetical order by last name very easily because the last name begins in the middle of the field. The names are already alphabetized by first name because sorting always begins with the left position in a field. Thus the "A" in Allison comes before the "B" in Brit, and so on. The proper way to sort the data is on the last name, which can be done more efficiently if the last name is stored as a separate field.

Think of how an address might be used. The city, state, and postal code should always be stored as separate fields. Any type of mass mailing requires you to sort on postal codes to take advantage of bulk mail. Other applications may require you to select records from a particular state or postal code, which can be done more efficiently if you store the data as separate fields. Often database users enter the postal code, and the database automatically retrieves the city and state information. You may need to direct a mailing to only a neighborhood or to a single street. The guideline is simple: Store data in their smallest parts.

Avoid Calculated Fields in Table Data

A *calculated field* is a field that derives its value from a formula that references one or more existing fields.

A *calculated field* produces a value from an expression—a formula or function that references an existing field or combination of fields. Although the information derived from calculations can be incredibly valuable to the decision maker, it is useful only at the moment the calculation is made. It makes no sense to store outdated data when recalculating; it will provide the decision maker with fresh, accurate information. Calculated fields should not be stored in a table because they are subject to change and waste space.

The total account balance for a customer with multiple accounts is an example of a calculated field because it is computed by adding the balances in all of the customer's accounts together. It is unnecessary to store the calculated sum of account balances in the Account table, because the table contains the fields on which the sum is based. In other words, Access is able to calculate the sum from these fields whenever it is needed, which is much more efficient than doing it manually.

Design to Accommodate Date Arithmetic

A *constant* is an unchanging value, like a birth date.

Date arithmetic is the process of subtracting one date from another.

A *date/time field* is a field that facilitates calculations for dates and times.

A person's age and date of birth provide equivalent information, as one is calculated from the other. It might seem easier, therefore, to store the age rather than the birth date to avoid the calculation. That would be a mistake because age changes continually and needs to be updated continually, but the date of birth remains *constant*—an unchanging value. Similar reasoning applies to an employee's length of service versus date of hire. Like Excel, Access stores all dates as a serial integer. You can use *date arithmetic* to subtract one date from another to find out the number of days, months, or years that have lapsed between them. Access provides a special data definition for *date/time fields* to facilitate calculations.

Design Multiple Tables

After listing all of the data items that you want to include in the database, you need to group them into similar items. Group the customer information into one table, the branch information into another, and the account information into a third table. A well-designed database provides a means of recombining the data when needed. When the design is sound, the **referential integrity** rules ensure that consistent data is stored in a related table. For example, the Customers and Account tables are linked by relationship. Referential integrity ensures that only valid customer IDs that exist in the Customers table are used in the Account table; it prevents you from entering an invalid customer ID in the Account table.

Data redundancy occurs when unnecessary duplicate information exists in a database.

Avoid *data redundancy*, which is the unnecessary inclusion of duplicate data among tables. You should never store duplicate information in multiple tables in a database. The information about a customer's address should only exist in a single table, the Customers table. It would be poor database design to also include the customer's address in the Account table. When duplicate information exists in a database, errors may result. Suppose the address data were stored in both the Customers and Account tables. You need to anticipate the consequences that may result when a customer moves. A likely outcome would be that the address would be updated in one but not both tables. The result would be unreliable data. Depending on which table served as the source for the output, either the new or the old address might be provided to the manager requesting the information. It is a much stronger design to have the address stored in only one table but tied to the rest of the database through the power of the relationships. See Figure 2.

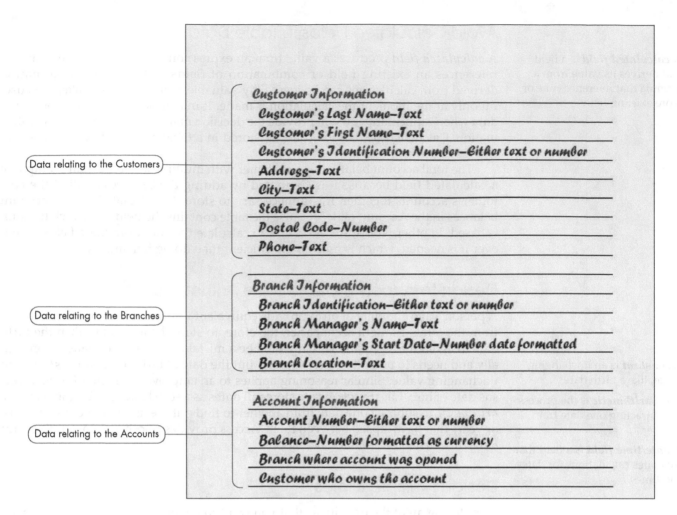

Figure 2 Bank's Database Data Grouped to Form a Table

Creating Tables

A table and all Access objects must be created within an Access file. To create a table, you must first create the file that will house it. Access works from storage, not memory. The other Microsoft Office programs work from memory: You create first and then save. With Access you must save a file first and then create its contents. You will open a new blank database and save it to a specific storage location before you can begin creating your tables.

Access provides several ways to create a table. You can create a table by entering the table data into a field. You also can import table data from another database or application, for example, Excel. Regardless of how a table is created, you can modify it to include a new field or to delete an existing field.

Every field has a field name to identify the data that is entered into the field. The field name should be descriptive of the data and can be up to 64 characters in length, including letters, numbers, and spaces. Actual databases employ *CamelCase notation* for fields, objects, and filenames. Instead of spaces in multi-word field names, use uppercase letters to distinguish the first letter of each new word, for example, ProductCost or LastName. Access is used frequently as a user-friendly means to connect to large databases stored on mainframes. Using Access, the manager can enter the organization's databases without needing courses in specialized computer languages. The manager then can find the data needed to make a decision and convert it to information. Most large databases and most mainframe computer systems will not accept spaces in field names.

Every field also has a *data type* that determines the type of data that can be entered and the operations that can be performed on that data. Access recognizes nine data types.

CamelCase notation uses no spaces in multi-word field names, but uses uppercase letters to distinguish the first letter of each new word.

A *data type* determines the type of data that can be entered and the operations that can be performed on that data.

Illustrations of Data Types and Uses | Reference

Data Type	Description	Example
Number	A **Number** field contains a value that can be used in a calculation, such as the number of credits a student has earned. The contents of a number field are restricted to numbers, a decimal point, and a plus or minus sign.	Height
Text	A **Text** field stores alphanumeric data, such as a student's name or address. It can contain alphabetic characters, numbers, and/or special characters (i.e., an apostrophe in O'Malley). Fields that contain only numbers but are not used in a calculation (i.e., Social Security Number, telephone number, or postal code) should be designated as text fields. A text field can hold up to 255 characters.	City
Memo	A **Memo** field can be up to 65,536 characters long. Memo fields are used to hold descriptive data (several sentences or paragraphs).	Library databases that store research papers
Date/Time	A **Date/Time** field holds formatted dates or times (i.e., mm/dd/yyyy) and allows the values to be used in date or time arithmetic.	March 31, 2008
Currency	A **Currency** field can be used in a calculation and is used for fields that contain monetary values.	Your checking account balance
Yes/No	A **Yes/No** field (also known as a Boolean or Logical field) assumes one of two values, such as Yes or No, True or False, or On or Off.	Dean's list
OLE	An **OLE** Object field contains an object created by another application. OLE objects include pictures, sounds, or graphics.	Excel workbook
AutoNumber	An **AutoNumber** field is a special data type that Access uses to assign the next consecutive number each time you add a record. The value of an AutoNumber field is unique for each record in the file, and thus AutoNumber fields are frequently used as the primary key. The numbering may be sequential or random.	Customer account number
Hyperlink	A **Hyperlink** field stores a Web address (URL). All Office documents are Web-enabled so that you can click a hyperlink and display the associated Web page.	www.UNCG.edu

Establish a Primary Key

The **primary key** is a unique field (or combination of fields) that identifies each record in a table. Access does not require that each table have a primary key. Good database design strongly recommends the inclusion of a primary key in each table. You should select infrequently changing data for the primary key. For example, a complete address (street, city, state, and postal code) may be unique but would not make a good primary key because it is subject to change when someone moves.

The *AutoNumber field* type assigns a unique identifying number to each record.

You probably would not use a person's name as the primary key because many people have the same name. A Customer Identification Number, on the other hand, is unique and is a frequent choice for the primary key, as in the Customers table in this chapter. The primary key emerges naturally in many applications, such as a part number in an inventory system, or the ISBN in the Books table of a bookstore or library. At your school you have a Student ID that uniquely identifies you. No other student has the same Student ID. When no primary key occurs naturally, you can create a new field with the *AutoNumber field* type, and Access will assign a unique identifying number to each new record. Figure 3 illustrates two types of table data. In the table shown at the top of the figure, the book's ISBN is the natural primary key because no two book titles have the same ISBN. It uniquely identifies the records in the table. The lower table depicts a table where no unique identifier emerged naturally from the data, so Access automatically numbered the records in order to distinguish them.

ISBN uniquely identifies the books in the bookstore

No natural unique identifier in this table, AutoNumber field

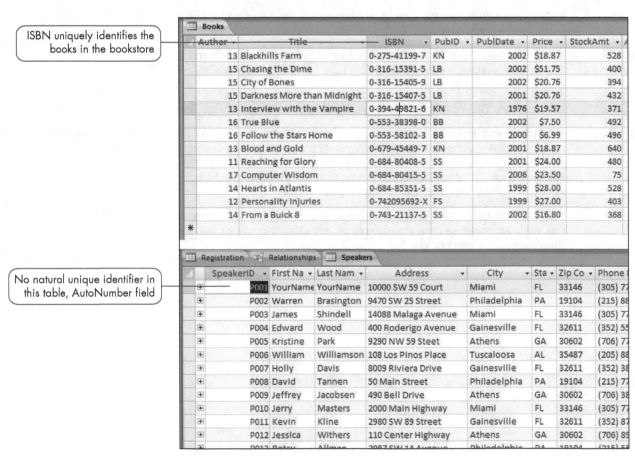

Figure 3 Tables Illustrating AutoNumbered and Naturally Emerging Primary Keys

Explore Foreign Key

A **foreign key** is a primary key from one table that is used in a different table as the basis for the relationship between the tables. The Customer ID may be the primary key in the Customers table. It serves to uniquely identify each customer. It often will appear as a foreign key in a related table. For example, the Order table may contain a field establishing which customer placed an individual order. Although a

Relational Databases and Multi-Table Queries

single Customer Identification Number can appear only one time in the Customers table, it may appear repeatedly in the Order table. A single customer may place multiple orders.

If you were the database administrator for the Youth Soccer League, you would assign a primary key to each player in the Players table and to each team in the Teams table. The Players table would have a field to show for which team the players play. The primary key in the Players table would uniquely identify the child with a PlayerID and also would show which team he or she played on using a TeamID (foreign key). Because each team has several players, you will find the TeamID repeated frequently in the Players table. Figure 4 depicts portions of the Players and Teams tables.

Figure 4 Tables Illustrating Primary and Foreign Keys

Use Table Views

The **PivotTable view** provides a convenient way to summarize and organize data about groups of records.

The **PivotChart view** displays a chart of the associated PivotTable View.

You may view your table in different ways. For example, you work in Datasheet view to add, edit, and delete records. The Datasheet view of an Access table resembles an Excel spreadsheet and displays data in rows (records) and columns (fields). In this chapter you will use the Design view to create and modify a table's structure, properties, and appearance. The **PivotTable view** provides a convenient way to summarize and organize data about groups of records. The **PivotChart view** displays a chart of the associated PivotTable view. Figure 5 displays a table in Datasheet view that corresponds to the table you saw in Figure 1. The Datasheet view displays the record selector symbol for the current record. It displays an asterisk in the record selector column next to the blank record at the end of the table.

Figure 5 Customers Table in Datasheet View

TIP Toggle between Datasheet and Design Views

To toggle from the Datasheet view to the Design view, click View in the Views group on the Home tab or right-click the table tab that appears above the datasheet and choose Design View from the menu. To toggle from the Design view to the Datasheet view, click View in the Views group on the Design tab or right-click the table tab that appears above the Design view grid and choose Datasheet View from the menu.

Work with Properties

A *property* is a characteristic or attribute of an object that determines how the object looks and behaves.

A *property* is a characteristic or attribute of an object that determines how the object looks and behaves. Every Access object (tables, forms, queries, and reports) has a set of properties that determine the behavior of that object. The properties for an object are displayed or changed in a property sheet. Each field has its own set of properties that determine how the data in the field are stored and displayed. The properties are set to default values according to the data type, but you can modify if necessary. The properties are displayed in the Design view and described briefly in the following paragraphs.

A *caption property* specifies a label other than the field name that appears at the top of a column in Datasheet view, forms, and reports.

Exclusively using CamelCase notation provides a consistent method to name your fields, but it may make the information difficult to read and understand. Therefore, you can use the *caption property* to create a more readable label that appears at the top of a column in Datasheet view and in forms and reports. For example, a field named ProductCostPerUnit can have the caption *Per Unit Product Cost*. The caption displays at the top of a table or query column in Datasheet view and when the field is used in a report or form. You use the formal field name, ProductCostPerUnit, in any expressions.

In the following hands-on exercise you begin by creating a database and entering data into a table. Then you switch to the Design view to add additional fields and modify selected properties of various fields within the table.

Before launching Access, use Windows Explorer to verify that you have a folder named **Your Name Access Production** on your storage device. Remember that you cannot run Access from a floppy or a Zip disk or a CD, even a CD-RW. The access speed of most USB thumb drives is adequate. Access runs best from the My Documents folder or a network drive.

Access Table Property Types and Descriptions | Reference

Property Type	Description
Field Size	The **Field Size** property adjusts the size of a text field or limits the allowable value in a number field. Microsoft Access uses only the amount of space it needs even if the field size allows a greater number. However, Access often connects to other database programs that reserve space for the specified field length. Good practice limits the field size to reduce system storage requirements.
Format	The **Format** property changes the way a field is displayed or printed, but does not affect the stored value.
Input Mask	The **Input Mask** property facilitates data entry by displaying literal characters that are displayed but not stored, such as hyphens in a Social Security Number or slashes in a date. It also imposes data validation by ensuring that the data entered by the user fits within the mask (i.e., it prevents typing an additional digit in a phone number).
Caption	The **Caption** property specifies a label other than the field name for forms and reports. It also displays on the table's Datasheet view. It permits a more user-friendly way to View the data.
Default Value	The **Default Value** property automatically enters a designated (default) value for the field in each record that is added to the table. If 90 percent of your customers lived in North Carolina, you might consider setting the default value for the State field to NC in order to save data entry time.
Validation Rule	The **Validation Rule** property rejects any record in which the data entered does not conform to the specified rules for data entry.
Validation Text	The **Validation Text** property specifies the error message that is displayed when the validation rule is violated.
Required	The **Required** property rejects any record that does not have a value entered for this field.
Allow Zero Length	The **Allow Zero** Length property enables text or memo strings of zero length.
Indexed	The **Indexed** property increases the efficiency of a search on the designated field. (The primary key in a table is always indexed.)
Unicode Compression	The **Unicode Compression** property is set to "Yes" by default for Text, Memo, and Hyperlink fields to store the data more efficiently.
IME Mode IME Sentence Mode	The **IME Mode and IME Sentence Mode** properties refer to the Input Method Editor for East Asian languages.
Smart Tags	The properties permit advanced users to add action buttons to a field. If you were using a database offering products for sale, a Smart Tag button embedded in a product name might open an inventory file and tell the database user what products are in stock.

Hands-On Exercises

1 | Table Design, Properties, Views, and Wizards

Skills covered: 1. Create a New Database **2.** Create a Table by Entering Data **3.** Change the Primary Key, Modify Field Properties, and Delete a Field **4.** Modify Table Fields in Design View **5.** Create a New Field in Design View **6.** Switch Between the Table Design and the Table Datasheet Views

Step 1 Create a New Database	Refer to Figure 6 as you complete Step 1. **a.** Start Microsoft Access. You should see the Welcome Window. **b.** Click **Blank Database** in the New Blank Database section of the *Getting Started with Microsoft Office Access* window. The lower right corner of the window displays the Blank Database section with file management tools. **c.** Click **Browse**—the little yellow folder. **d.** Click the **Save in drop-down arrow** and select the appropriate drive. Double-click the **Your Name Access Production** folder. You need to be intentional about where you save your database file. Otherwise you may have difficulty finding it again. **e.** Click in the **File name** box and select *Database1.accdb*. Type **chap2_ho1-3_safebank_solution.accdb** to name your database and click **OK**. Click the **Create command** in the Blank Database section of the *Getting Started with Microsoft Office Access* window. The Database window for the *chap2_ho1-3_safebank_solution.accdb* should appear. **TROUBLESHOOTING:** If you skipped the instructions in Step 1d, you may have problems finding your file. From the desktop right-click My Computer and select Explore from the shortcut menu. Click the Search tool. Select All Files or Folders. In the box type **chap2_ho1-3_safebank_solution.accdb.** When the search results return, copy the file, and then paste it into the appropriate folder. Open and work the remainder of the hands-on exercises from the appropriate folder.

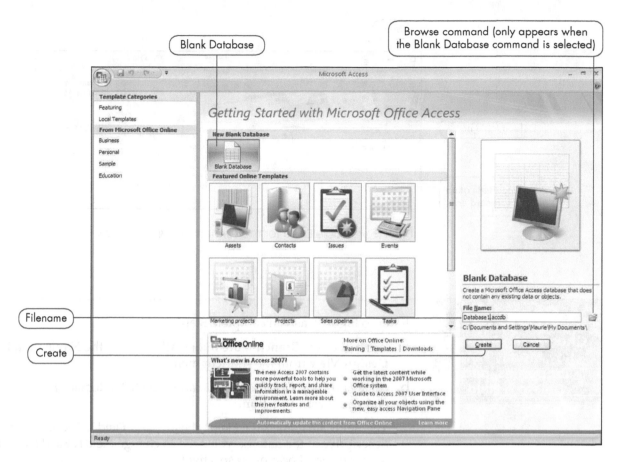

Browse command (only appears when the Blank Database command is selected)

Blank Database

Filename

Create

Figure 6 Welcome to Microsoft Office Access

Refer to Figure 7 as you complete Step 2.

a. Type **B1** in the gold bordered cell and press **Enter**. The insertion point moves to the right. You also may navigate between the cells in the table by pressing **Tab** or the **arrow keys**.

b. Type **Lockley** in the first row of the second column. Press **Enter** and type **Uptown** in the next column.

c. Click in the cell below B1 and type **B2**, **Weeks**, and **Eastern**.

If your ID numbers do not match those shown in Figure 7, do not be concerned. You will be deleting that field in a later step.

d. Enter the additional data for the new table as shown in Figure 7.

e. Click **Save** on the Quick Access Toolbar. Type **Branch** in the Save As dialog box and click **OK**.

Entering data provides an easy way to create the table initially. You can now modify the table in Design view as described in the next several steps.

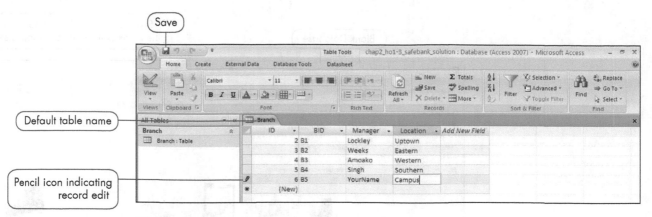

Figure 7 Table Data for the (Unnamed) Branch Table

Step 3

Change the Primary Key, Modify Field Properties, and Delete a Field

Refer to Figure 8 as you complete Step 3.

a. Right-click the **Branch table** under All Tables in the Navigation Pane and select **Design View** from the shortcut menu.

b. Click and Drag *Field1* to select it and type **BID**. Replace *Field2* with **Manager** and *Field3* with **Location.**

The fields are named ID, Field1, Field2, and Field3. These field names are not descriptive of the data, so you need to change Field1, Field2, and Field3 to BID, Manager, and Location, respectively.

c. Click the **row selector** to the left of the *BID* field. The entire row selects as shown in Figure 8.

d. Click **Primary Key** in the Tools group on the Design tab.

You changed the primary key in this table from the automatically generated one that Access created for you to the one you intended, the BID. As soon as you identified BID as the primary key, the Indexed property updated to Yes (No Duplicates). The primary key must be a unique identifier for each record.

TROUBLESHOOTING: A primary key must be a unique identifier for each record in the table. If you had trouble here, check to make sure the Indexed property is set to Indexed, Yes (No Duplicates). Return to Datasheet view and examine your data entry to ensure that you typed the correct values in the BID field.

e. Right-click the row selector to the left of the ID field. Select **Delete Rows** from the shortcut menu. Click **Yes** in the warning box instructing Access to permanently delete the selected field.

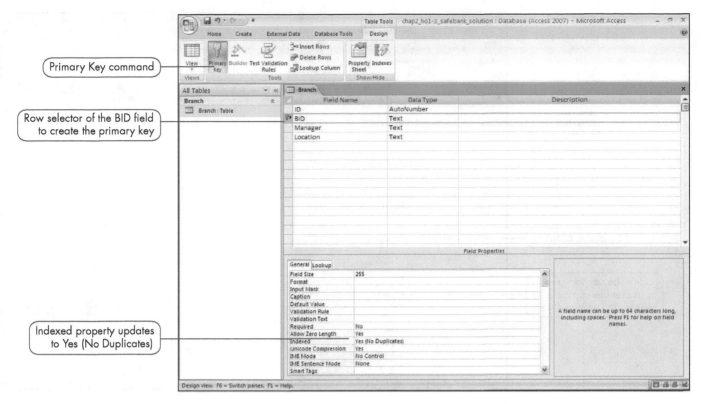

Primary Key command

Row selector of the BID field to create the primary key

Indexed property updates to Yes (No Duplicates)

Figure 8 Branch Table in Design View

Step 4

Modify Table Fields in Design View

Refer to Figures 8 and 9 as you complete Step 4.

a. Modify some of the properties of the **BID** field.

1. Click in the **BID** field in the top section of the design window.

2. Click in the **Field Size** property box in the Field Properties section and type **10**.

3. Click in the **Caption** property box and type **Branch ID**.

4. Check the **Indexed** property box to make sure it is **Yes (No Duplicates)**.

If you need to change it, click in the Indexed property box. A drop-down arrow displays on the right side of the box. Scroll to select **Yes (No Duplicates)** as shown in Figure 8.

For the next several tasks you will toggle between the top of the design screen and the Field Property box on the bottom of the design screen.

b. Click the **Manager** field name at the top of the window. Look in the Field Properties section. In the **Field Size** property box, replace *255* with **30**. In the **Caption** property box, type **Manager's Name**.

A caption provides a more descriptive field name. It will head the column in Datasheet view and describe data in other database objects, such as reports, forms, and queries.

c. Click the **Location** field name at the top of the window. In the **Field Size** property box, change *255* to **30**. In the **Caption** property, type **Branch Location**.

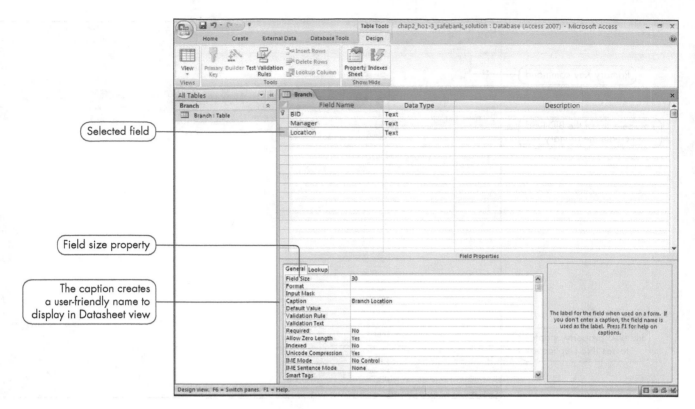

Selected field

Field size property

The caption creates a user-friendly name to display in Datasheet view

Figure 9 Change Field Properties to Increase Efficiency

Step 5
Create a New Field in Design View

Refer to Figure 10 as you complete Step 5.

a. Click the blank cell below the *Location* field name. Create a new field by typing the field name named **StartDate**.

b. Press **Tab** to move to the *Data Type* column. Click the **Data Type drop-down arrow** and select **Date/Time**.

c. Press **Tab** to move to the *Description* column and type **This date is the date the manager started working at this location.**

d. Click in the **Caption** property box and type **Manager's Start Date**.

e. Click the **Format property drop-down arrow** and select **Short Date** from the list of Date formats.

f. Click **Save** on the Quick Access Toolbar to save the Branch table within the *chap2_ho1-3_safebank_solution* database.

A warning dialog box opens to indicate that the size of the BID, Manager, and Location field properties were shortened. It asks if you want to continue anyway. Always read the Access warnings! In this case you are OK. You changed the size of the BID field from 255 to 10 in Step 4a. You did not need 255 characters to identify the BID. Your bank only has five locations. You changed the other two field sizes in Steps 4b and 4c.

g. Click **Yes** in the warning box.

The table Design view is useful to modify the structure of fields or to add fields to an existing table. However, tables cannot be populated in the Design view. The Datasheet view must be used to add data to a table.

TIP Keyboard Shortcut for Data Types

You also can type the first letter of the field type such as D for Date/Time, T for Text, or N for number. Click into the data type column in the field's row and, using the keyboard, type the first letter of the field type.

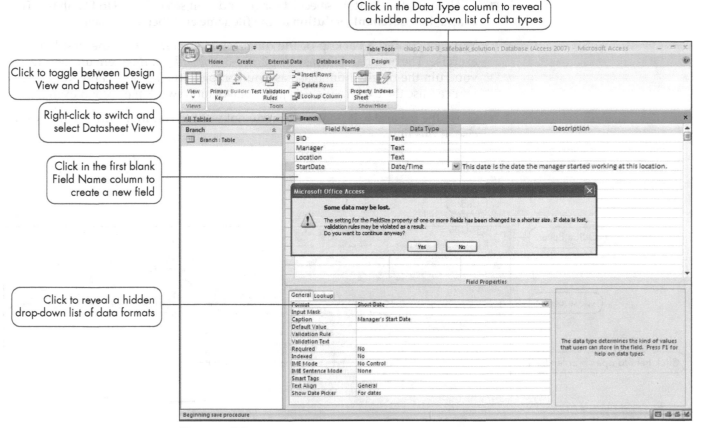

Figure 10 Change Field Properties to Increase Efficiency

Step 6

Switch Between the Table Design and the Table Datasheet Views

Refer to Figure 11 as you complete Step 6.

a. Right-click the gold tab shown in Figure 10 and select **Datasheet View** from the shortcut menu. (To return to the Design view, right-click the tab in Datasheet view and select Design View or click **View** in the Views group on the Design tab.)

b. Enter the dates each manager started work as shown in Figure 11.

After entering the date for yourself, you remember that you started work on October 11.

c. Click the **calendar command** and click the **October 11** date on the calendar.

d. Click the table's **Close command**. **Do not save the changes**.

e. Double-click the **Branch table** in the Navigation Pane to open the table. Check the start dates.

You did not save any changes you made; you closed the table without saving changes. The dates are correct because Access works from storage, not memory.

f. Click the **Office Button**, select **Print**, and then select **Quick Print**.

Most users do not print Access table data. Tables store and organize data and rarely generate output. People do not spend time formatting table data. Check with your instructor to see if you should submit a printed Branch table for feedback.

g. Click the **Office Button**, select **Manage**, and then select **Back Up Database**. Type **chap2_ho1_safebank_solution** as the filename and then click **Save**.

You just created a backup of the database after completing the first hands-on exercise. The original database *chap2_ho1-3_safebank_solution* remains onscreen. If you ruin the original database as you complete the second hands-on exercise, you can use the backup file you just created and rework the second exercise.

h. Close the file and exit Access if you do not want to continue with the next exercise at this time.

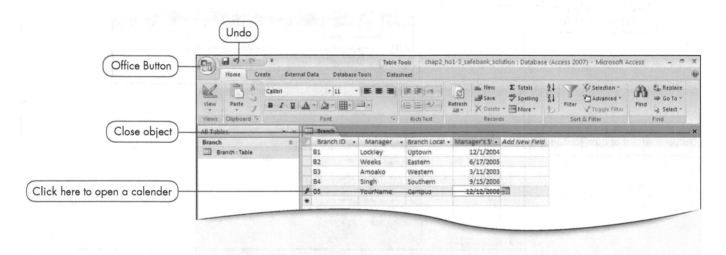

Figure 11 Calendar Facilitates Data Entry

Multiple Table Database

Earlier you designed a database and combined similar data items into groupings called tables. You have completed the first table in the database, the Branch table. If you re-examine your design notes and Figure 2, recall that you planned for two additional tables in the Safebank database. The power of a relational database lies in its ability to organize and combine data in different ways to obtain a complete picture of the events the data describe. Good database design connects the data in different tables through links. These links are the relationships that give relational databases the name. In your Safebank database one customer can have many accounts or can bank at any of the bank locations. That is, the customer's ID may be listed for many account numbers in the Accounts table, but the customer's ID is listed only one time in the Customers table. When the database is set up properly, database users can be confident that if they search for a specific customer identification number, they will be given accurate information about that customer's account balances, address, or branch preferences.

In this section, you learn about table relationships, referential integrity, indexing, and importing data from Excel.

Understanding Table Relationships

The relationship is like a piece of electronic string that travels throughout the database, searching every record of every table until it finds the events of interest. Once identified, the fields and records of interest will be tied to the end of the string, pulled through the computer, and reassembled in a way that makes the data easy to understand. The first end of the string was created when the primary key was established in the Branch table. The primary key is a unique identifier for each table record. The other end of the string ties to a field in a different table. You will include the Branch ID as a foreign field in the Accounts table. A foreign key is a field in one table that is also stored in a different table as a primary key. Each value of the Branch ID (BID) can occur only once in the Branch table because it is a primary key. However, the BID may appear multiple times in the account table because many different accounts are at the same branch.

Establish Referential Integrity

The relationships will be created using an Access feature that enforces referential integrity. Integrity means truthful or reliable. When referential integrity is enforced, the user can trust the threads running through the database and tying related items together. The Campus branch manager can use the database to find the names and phone numbers of all the customers with accounts at the Campus branch. Because referential integrity has been enforced, it will not matter that the branch information is in a different table from the customer data. The invisible threads keep the information accurately connected. Managers need organized and dependable data upon which they base decisions. The threads also provide a method of ensuring data accuracy. You cannot enter a record in the Account table that references a Branch ID or a Customer ID that does not exist in the system. Nor can you delete a record in one table if it has related records in other tables.

> As you work, ask yourself what the anticipated results should be and then verify. When you become skilled at anticipating output correctly, you are surprised less often.

If this were a real bank's data system, the files would be much larger and the data more sophisticated. However, the same design principles apply regardless of the database size. A small file gives you the ability to check the tables and see if your results are correct. Even though the data amounts are small, you need to develop the work practices to manage large amounts of data. With only a handful of records, you can easily count the number of accounts at the Campus branch. In addition to learning HOW to accomplish a task, you should learn to anticipate the computer's response to an instruction. Ask yourself what the anticipated results should be and then verify. When you become skilled at anticipating output correctly, you are surprised less often.

Multiple Table Database

Identify Cascades

Cascades permit data changes to travel from one table to another.

Cascades are an Access feature that helps update related data across tables. In databases *cascades* permit data changes to travel from one table to another. The database designer may establish cascades to update or delete related records. The string tying related items together can also make global changes to the data. If one bank branch closed and the accounts were not transferred to a different branch, the *cascade delete* feature would search the database and delete all of the accounts and customers who banked solely at the closed branch. (This may not be an optimal business practice, but it explains how the cascade delete feature works.) If a customer with an account at one branch opens a new account at a different branch, the *cascade update* will travel through the databases and connect the new account to the customer's address in the Customers table and the new account balance in the Accounts table.

Cascade delete searches the database and deletes all of the related records.

Cascade update connects any primary key changes to the tables in which it is a foreign key.

As a general rule, you do not want changes cascading through the database. An inattentive data entry clerk could, with the click of a mouse, delete hundreds of records in various tables throughout the database. However, you need the power of a cascade occasionally. Suppose your company and another firm merged. Your firm has always stored customer account numbers as a five-digit number. The other firm has always used a three-digit account number. In this case you would turn the cascade update feature on; open the Customers table; and change all of the three digit numbers to five digit ones. The new account numbers would cascade through the database to any records in any table related to the Customers table—for example, the Payments or Orders tables.

Retrieve Data Rapidly by Indexing

The **indexed property** is a list that relates the field values to the records that contain the field value.

In Hands-On Exercise 1 you created the Branch table and established the BID as the primary key. Access changed the *indexed property* to Yes (No Duplicates). Access uses indexing exactly like you would read a book on U.S. history. If you need to know who succeeded Van Buren as president, you could start on page 1 and read the book in order page by page. Alternatively, you could go to the index and discover where the information about Van Buren may be found and open directly to that page. Using the index in a book makes finding (retrieving) information quicker. Indexing a database field has the same effect; it greatly reduces retrieval time. The actual index is a list that relates the field values to the records that contain the field value. Without an index, each row in the database would need to be scanned sequentially, an inefficient search method. The increased search time would adversely affect the performance of the database. All primary keys must be indexed. Additional table fields also may be indexed.

Sharing Data with Excel

Many Access and Excel tasks overlap. Although you are learning the highly valuable skill of using Access, more people know how to use Excel than Access. Therefore, a lot of data resides within Excel spreadsheets. Often the data stored in those spreadsheets fits well into an Access database design. Therefore, you need to be able to integrate existing Excel spreadsheet data into the organization's database. Fortunately, Access provides you with wizards that facilitate data sharing with Excel. Access can both import data from Excel and export data to Excel easily.

Figures 12–18 show how to use the Get External Data – Excel Spreadsheet wizard. You launch the wizard by clicking the External Data tab. Table 1 lists and describes the four groups on the External Data tab.

Table 1 Access and Other Applications Share Data

Process	When Used
Get External Data	Used to bring data into an Access database. The data sources include Excel, Other Access files, XML, SharePoint Lists, and Text files.
Export Data	Used to send a portion of a database to other applications. You might use this to create a Mail Merge letter and envelopes in Word. You could create an Excel file for a co-worker who does not know how to use (or does not have) Access, or could share your data over the Internet via a SharePoint List.
Collect and Update	You could create an e-mail mail merge to send e-mails to your clients and then use Access to manage the clients' responses.
Offline SharePoint Lists	This process might be used when traveling, if an immediate Internet connection is not available.

Launch the wizard by clicking the Excel command in the Get External Data Group. Figure 12 shows the External Data tab that contains the Import Excel command. After you specify the data storage location, you can use the imported data to create a new table in Access, to *append* new records to an existing Access table, or to create a link between the Excel file and the Access table. When linked, any changes made to the Excel file will be updated automatically in the database, too.

You *append* records to an existing table by adding new records to the end of the table.

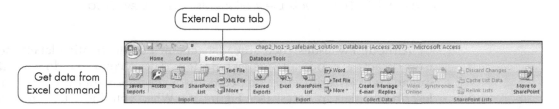

Figure 12 Select the Source and Destination for the Data

Figure 13 shows the Get External Data – Excel Spreadsheet dialog box. This feature controls where you find the data to import. It asks you to choose among three options governing what to do with the data in Access: place it in a new table, append the data to an existing table, or link the Access table to the Excel source.

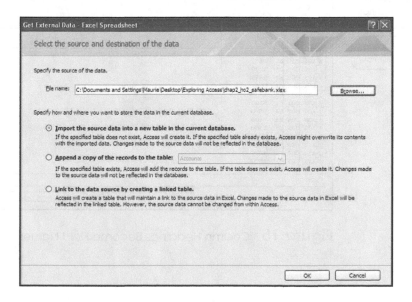

Figure 13 Select the Source and Destination of the Data

Relational Databases and Multi-Table Queries

After you select the Excel workbook, you see the Import Spreadsheet Wizard dialog box, which displays a list of the worksheets in the specified workbook (see Figure 14). Use the options to specify a worksheet, in this case, the Customers worksheet. The bottom of the Import Spreadsheet Wizard dialog box displays a preview of the data stored in the specified worksheet.

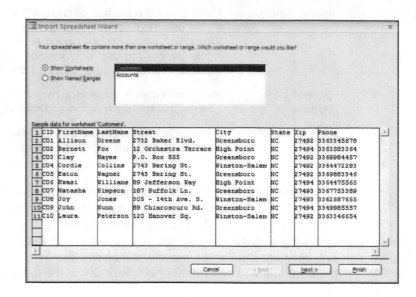

Figure 14 Show Available Worksheets and Preview Data

Although well-designed spreadsheets include descriptive labels, not all Excel users practice good spreadsheet design. The second window of the Import Spreadsheet Wizard dialog box contains a check box that gives you a chance to describe the data to Access (see Figure 15). When you find a label row in a spreadsheet, check the box. Access will use the Excel labels to generate the Access field names. When you find unlabeled data, do not check the box, and the data will import using Field1, Field2, and so on as field names.

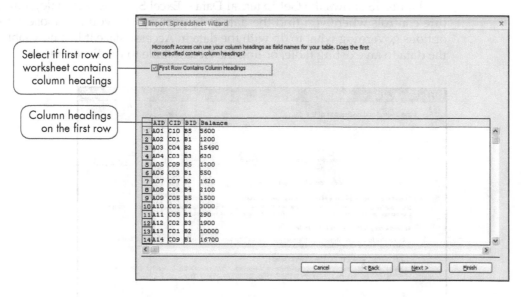

Select if first row of worksheet contains column headings

Column headings on the first row

Figure 15 Column Headings Become Field Names

The third window of the Import Spreadsheet Wizard dialog box enables you to stipulate field properties (see Figure 16). The AID field is shown in the figure. Because it will become this table's primary key, you need to set the Index Property to Yes (No Duplicates). Use the Field Name box to select other fields (columns) in the worksheet and establish their properties. Not all Access table properties are supported by the wizard. You will need to open the table in Design view after importing it and make some additional property changes.

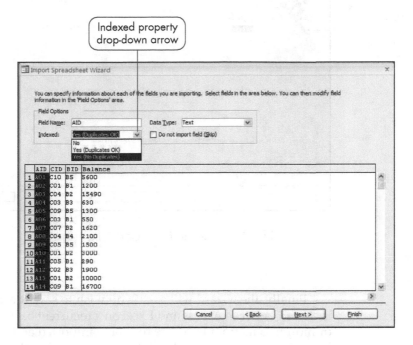

Figure 16 Field Options for Importing the Spreadsheet

The fourth window of the Import Spreadsheet Wizard dialog box enables you to establish the primary key before the import takes place (see Figure 17). If the option for *Let Access add primary key* is selected, Access will generate an AutoNumber field and designate it as the primary key. In the import described in the figure, the Excel data has a unique identifier that will become the table's primary key on import.

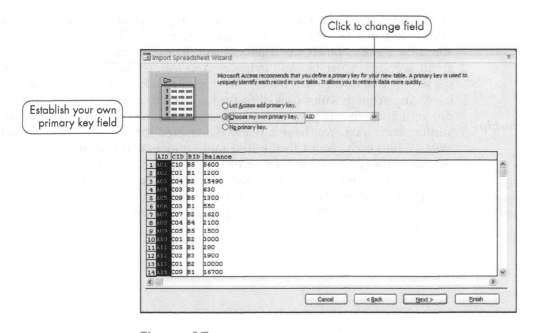

Figure 17 Primary Key Designation

Use the final window of the Import Spreadsheet Wizard dialog box prompts you to name the Access table. If the worksheet in the Excel workbook was named, Access uses the worksheet name as the table name (see Figure 18).

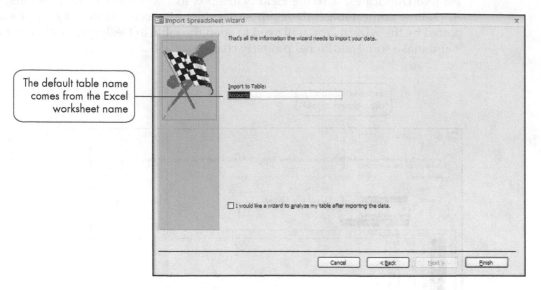

The default table name comes from the Excel worksheet name

Figure 18 Table Name for Import Spreadsheet

Finally, the wizard will ask if you wish to save the import steps. Frequently data is shared between Access and Excel on a recurrent basis. At the close of a day or week or month, data from Excel are routinely imported and updated in Access. Saving the import steps expedites the data re-importation the next time it is needed. The imported data become a permanent part of the Access file. Access will open a final dialog box asking if you want to save the import specifications. In your hands-on exercise, the data import is a one-time only event so you do not need to save the import parameters.

Establishing Table Relationships

A **one-to-many relationship** exists when each record in the first table may match one, more than one, or no records in the second table. Each record in the second table matches one and only one record in the first table.

You should store like data items together using a logical file management structure. The customer data are stored in the Customers table. The Branch table stores data about the bank's branch, management, and location. The Accounts table stores data about account ownership and balances. You learned earlier that relationships form the strings that tie the related table data together. When you tie something, you use a knot. Any scout or sailor uses different knots for different purposes. Just as you use different knots for differing tasks, Access provides several differing relationships for joining your data. You have already discovered that a **one-to-many relationship** exists when each record in the first table may match one, more than one, or no records in the second table. Each record in the second table matches one and only one record in the first table to establish a powerful knot or relationship. In a well-designed database you use this type of relationship most frequently. Table 2 lists and describes the different types of relationships you can form between Access tables.

Table 2 Relationship Types

Relationship Name	Definition
One-To-Many	This relationship is between a primary key in the first table and a foreign key in the second table. The first table must have only one occurrence of each value. That is: Each customer must have a unique identification number in the Customers table or each employee must have a unique employee identification number in the Employee table. The foreign key field in the second table may have recurrent values. For example, one customer may have many different account numbers, or one employee can provide service to many customers.
One-To-One	Two different tables use the same primary key. Sometimes security reasons require a table to be split into two related tables. For example, anyone in the company can look in the Employee table and find the employee's office number, department assignment, or telephone extension. However, only a few people need to have access to the employee's salary, Social Security Number, performance review, or marital status. Both tables use the same unique identifier to identify each employee.
Many-To-Many	This is an artificially constructed relationship giving many matching records in each direction between tables. It requires construction of a third table called a juncture table. For example, a database might have a table for employees and one for projects. Several employees might be assigned to one project, but one employee might also be assigned to many different projects. When Access connects to databases using Oracle or other software, you find this relationship type. When using Access as a stand-alone software, you would specify a Multivalue field and record multiple items as legitimate entries in a single field.

Establish a One-To-Many Relationship

When you click the Database Tools tab, you see the Show/Hide group (see Figure 19). The first command is the tool that opens the Relationship window. If this were a long established database, the Relationship window would be populated with the related tables in the database.

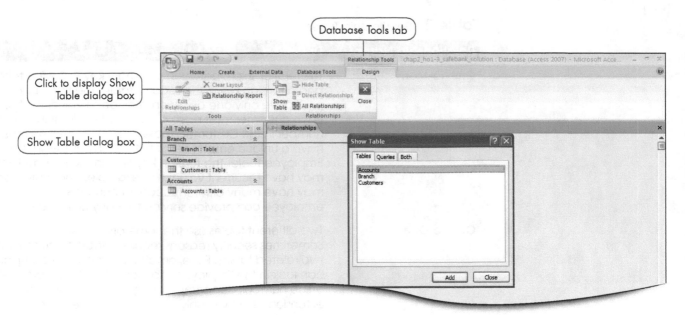

Figure 19 The Show/Hide Group and Show Table Dialog Box

Because the first time you will use the Relationship window you will be working in a newly created database, you must first use the Show Table dialog box to add the necessary tables to the Relationship window (see Figure 19). Select the tables you want to use in relation to other tables and add them to the Relationship window by clicking Add.

> ### TIP   Navigation Between the Relationship Window and a Table's Design
>
> When you right-click the table title bar in the Relationship window, the shortcut menu offers you a chance to open the table in Design View. Because relationships may be established only between data with the same definition, you have a chance to check how the data in different tables have been defined.

When possible, expand the table windows to display the complete list of field names shown in the table (see Figure 20). You may rearrange the tables by clicking and dragging the table window title bar.

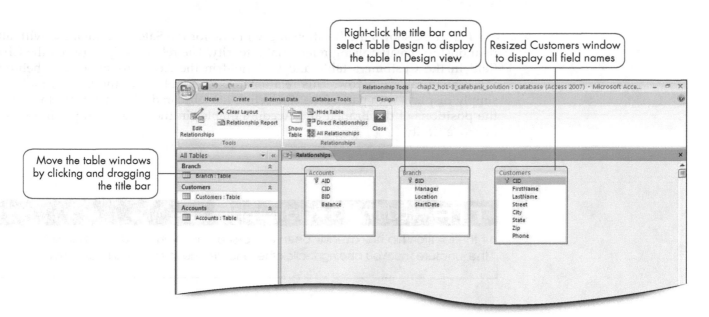

Figure 20 The Relationship Window with Resized Tables

Establish the relationships by clicking and dragging the field name from one table to the field name in the related table. When you release the mouse, the Edit Relationships dialog box opens (see Figure 21). Prior to establishing a relationship, Access runs through the table data to ensure that the rules you attempt to establish in the relationship can be met. For example, it checks to make sure that the branch identification number in the Accounts table (foreign key) exactly matches a Branch ID in the Branch table where it is the primary key. If all of the Branch IDs do not match exactly between the tables, Access cannot establish the relationship with referential integrity enforced. It will attempt to make a connection, but it will warn you that a problem exists with the data.

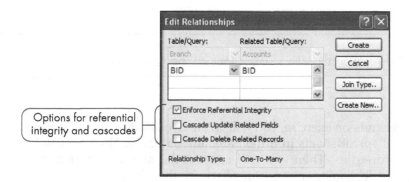

Figure 21 The Edit Relationships Dialog Box

Figure 22 shows the Relationship window for the Safebank database with all relationships created using referential integrity. The relationship between the CID field in the Customers table and CID field in the Accounts table runs behind the Branch table window. This relationship does not affect the Branch table; it simply displays with part of the connecting line obscured. You may want to switch the positions of the Branch and Accounts tables in the Relationship window to improve clarity.

TIP   Editing a Relationship

If the relationship has already been established and you need to edit it, right-click the juncture line. You also right-click the juncture line to delete a relationship.

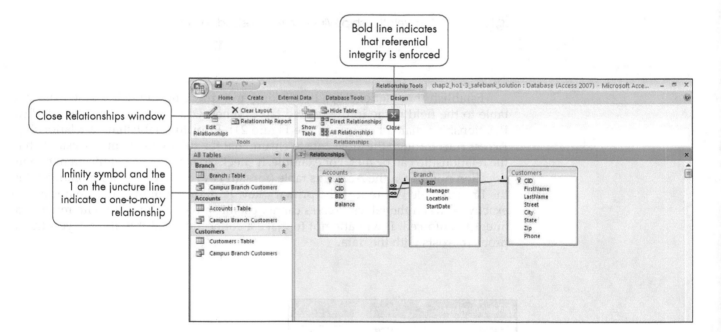

Figure 22 The Relationship Window Displaying One-to-Many Relationships

In the next hands-on exercise, you will create two additional tables by importing data from Excel spreadsheets into the Safebank database. You will establish and modify field properties. Then you will connect the newly imported data to the Branch table by establishing relationships between the tables.

Hands-On Exercises

2 | Imports and Relationships

Skills covered: 1. Import Excel Data Into an Access Table **2.** Import Additional Excel Data **3.** Modify an Imported Table's Design **4.** Add Data to an Imported Table **5.** Establish Table Relationships **6.** Understand How Referential Integrity Protects Data

---

Step 1

Import Excel Data into an Access Table

Refer to Figure 23 and Figures 13 through 18 as you complete Step 1.

a. Open the *chap2_ho1-3_safebank_solution.accdb* if necessary, then click **Options** on the Security Warning toolbar, click the **Enable this content option** in the Microsoft Office Security Options dialog box, and click **OK**.

   TROUBLESHOOTING: If you create unrecoverable errors while completing this hands-on exercise, you can delete the *chap2_ho1-3_safebank_solution* file, copy the *chap2_ho1_safebank_solution* database you created at the end of the first hands-on exercise, and open the copy of the backup database to start the second hands-on exercise again.

b. Click the **External Data tab** (see Figure 12). Click **Import Excel Spreadsheet** in the Import group to launch the Get External Data – Excel Spreadsheet wizard. Select the **Import the source data into a new table in the current database option**, if necessary, as shown in Figure 13.

c. Click **Browse** and go to your **Exploring Access folder**. Select the *chap2_ho2_safebank.xlsx* workbook. Click **OK**.

   The Import Spreadsheet Wizard activates. The first window shows all of the worksheets in the workbook. This particular workbook contains only two worksheets: Accounts and Customers. The Customers worksheet is active, and a list of the data contained in the Customers worksheet displays in the Wizard.

d. Click the **Customers worksheet** to preview the customer data. Return to the **Accounts worksheet** and click **Next** (see Figure 14).

e. Click in the **First Row Contains Column Headings check box** to tell Access that column heads exist in the Excel file (see Figure 15).

   The field names, AID, CID, BID, and Balance will import from Excel along with the data stored in the rows in the worksheet.

f. Click **Next**.

   The AID (Account ID) will become the primary key in this table. It needs to be a unique identifier, so we must change the properties to disallow duplicates.

g. Click the **Indexed Property drop-down arrow** and select **Indexed Yes (No Duplicates)**. Click **Next** (see Figure 16).

h. Click the **Choose my own primary key** option. Make sure that the **AID** field is selected. Click **Next** (see Figure 17).

   The final screen of the Import Spreadsheet Wizard asks you to name your table. The name of the Excel worksheet was Accounts and Access defaults to the worksheet name. It is an acceptable name (see Figure 18).

---

i. Click **Finish**.

A dialog box opens asking if you wish to save the parameters of this import to use again. If this were sales data that were collected in Excel and updated to the database on a weekly basis, saving the import would save time.

j. Click **Close**.

Saving these import parameters is not necessary. The new table displays in Datasheet view and resides in the Safebank database (see Figure 18).

k. Open the newly imported **Accounts table** in Datasheet view.

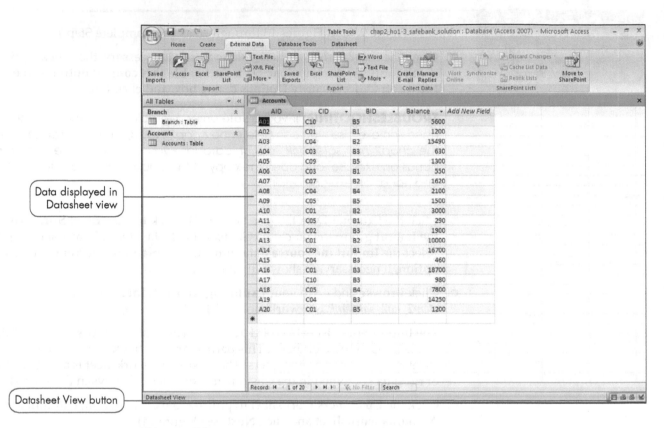

Figure 23 The Newly Imported Accounts Table

Step 2
Import Additional Excel Data

Refer to Figure 24 and Figures 13 through 18 as you complete Step 2.

a. Turn back to the beginning of Step 1 and repeat the instructions a through k.

b. Click on the **Customers worksheet** in Step 1d.

c. Change the index property of the **CID** field to **Yes (No Duplicates)** in Step 1f.

d. Identify the **CID** (Customer ID) as the primary key in Step 1g.

The default table name will be the Customers table. This is a good name so accept it.

e. Click **Finish** and click **Close**. The All Tables view will display three tables: Branch, Accounts, and Customers.

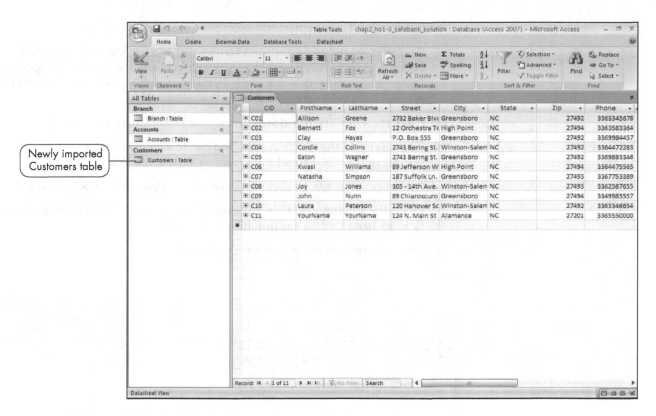

Figure 24 The Newly Imported Customers Table

Refer to Figure 25 as you complete Step 3.

a. Open the **Accounts table** in Design view and click the **AID** field if necessary.

b. Change the **AID** field size to **10**. Look at the bottom of the window in the Field Properties box.

The field size was set at 255. Importing data from Excel saves typing but does not always create an efficiently designed database.

c. Type **Account ID** in the **Caption** property box for the AID field.

d. Click the **CID** field in the top of the Design view window to activate the *Properties* for the CID field.

e. Type **10** in the **Field Size** property box for the CID field using the Field Properties box in the bottom of the window.

f. Type **Customer ID** in the **Caption** property for the CID field.

g. Click the **BID** field in the top of the Design View window to activate the Properties for the BID field.

h. Type **10** in the **Field Size** property box for the BID field in the Field properties box at the bottom of the window.

i. Type **Branch ID** in the **Caption** property box for the BID field.

j. Click the **Balance** field in the top of the Design view window to activate the Properties for the Balance field.

k. Click in the **Format** property box to see a drop-down arrow.

Access often hides drop-down arrows until the property is activated. As you become more familiar with the software, you will learn which properties contain these hidden drop-down arrows. In the meanwhile, develop the habit of clicking around each new screen.

l. Click the **Format drop-down arrow** and select **Currency** from the list.

m. Click **Save** on the Quick Access Toolbar to save the design changes you made to the Accounts table. **Read the Warning Box!** Click **Yes**.

In this case it is OK to click Yes because the size of three fields were shortened.

n. Open the **Customers table** in Design view. Change the **field size** of the **CID** field to **10** and add a **caption, Customer ID**.

o. Save the design changes to the Customers table.

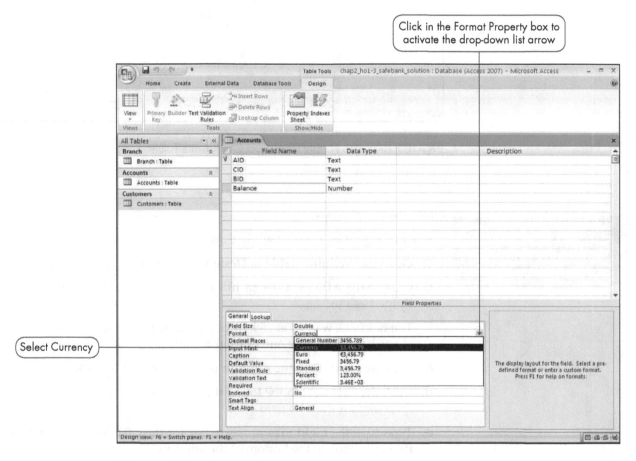

Figure 25 The Format Property of the Balance Field Set to Currency.

Step 4
Add Data to an Imported Table

Refer to Figure 26 as you complete Step 4.

a. Open the **Customers table** in Datasheet view.

The asterisk in the row selector area is the indicator of a place to enter a new record.

b. Click the **Customer ID** field in the record after C10. Type **C11**. Fill in the rest of the data using your information as the customer. You may use a fictitious address and phone number.

c. Open **Accounts table** in Datasheet view. Create a new account ID A21. Enter **C11** as the Customer ID and **B5** as the Branch ID. Use your course number and section for the Balance field value.

If you were a student in section 04 of ISM 210, you would enter 21004 as the Balance.

d. Close all of the tables; keep the database open.

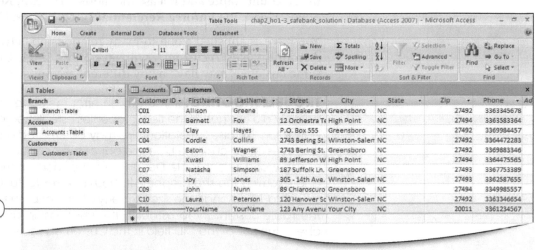

Figure 26 The Customers Table Displaying the New Account

Step 5
Establish Table Relationships

Refer to Figures 27 and 21 as you complete Step 5.

a. Click the **Database Tools tab**. Click **Relationships**.

The Relationship window opens to the Show Table dialog box.

TROUBLESHOOTING: If the Show Table dialog box does not open, click Show Table in the Relationships group on the Design tab.

b. Double-click each of the three tables to add them to the Relationship window. (Alternatively, click a table and then click **Add**.) Click **Close** in the Show Table dialog box.

The Accounts and Branch table boxes are large enough to display all of the field names. The Customers table has a scroll bar because it has too many fields to display in the small space.

TROUBLESHOOTING: If you duplicate a table, you may have gotten carried away clicking and adding. The duplicate table will display in the Relationship window with a number after its name, i.e. Branch1 or Customer2. Close the Show Table dialog box. Click the title bar of the duplicated table and press Delete. This procedure also works if you add the same table twice to a Query's design grid.

c. Run your mouse over the **blue line** at the bottom of the Customers table box until its shape changes to the **resize arrow**. With the double-headed arrow showing, click the left mouse button and drag down until all the field names display and the scroll bar disappears.

d. Click the **BID** field in the **Branch table**. Drag to the **BID** field in the **Accounts table** and release the mouse. The Edit Relationships dialog box opens. Check the **Enforce Referential Integrity** box. Click **Create**.

A thick black line displays joining the two tables. It has a 1 on the end near the Branch table signifying that it is connecting the primary key (unique identifier) to an infinity symbol on the end next to the Accounts table. You have established a one-to-many relationship between the Branch and Accounts tables.

e. Click the **CID** field in the **Customers table** to select it. Drag to the **CID** field in the **Accounts table** and release the mouse. The Edit Relationships dialog box opens. Check the **Enforce Referential Integrity** box. Click **Create**.

You have established a one-to-many relationship between the Customers and Accounts tables. A customer will have only a single Customer ID number. The same customer may have many different accounts: Savings, Checking, CDs, etc.

TROUBLESHOOTING: If you get an error message when you click Create, you possibly did not get all the field properties established correctly in Steps 3 and 4 of Hands-On Exercise 2. Relationships may be created only between like data types and sizes. Right-click the blue title bar of the Accounts window in the Relationship window and select Table Design from the shortcut menu. Click on the CID field and examine the size property. It should be set to 10. Click the BID field. It should be set to 10. Change the size property of one or both fields. Save your changes to the table design. Try to establish the relationship again. If it still does not work, check the size of the CID field in the Customers table. It should also be 10.

f. Click **Save** on the Quick Access Toolbar to save the changes to the Relationships. Close the Relationships window.

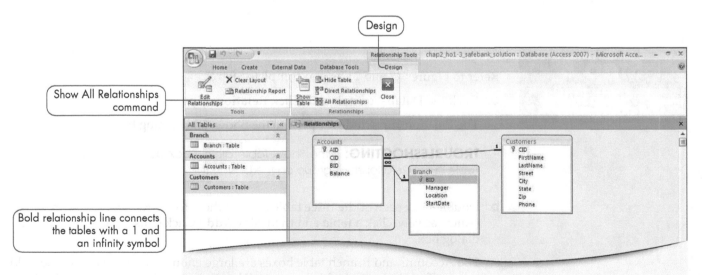

Figure 27 Properly Constructed Relationships Among the Tables

Step 6

Understand How Referential Integrity Protects Data

Refer to Figure 28 as you complete Step 6.

a. Open the **Accounts table** in Datasheet view. Add a new record: Account ID – A22; Customer ID – **C03** (Note, that is a zero, not a letter O); Branch ID – **B6**; Balance – **4000**. Press **Enter**.

A warning box appears. This bank has five branches. A sixth branch does not exist. In this case the warning message is telling exactly what is wrong. There is no related record for B6 in the Branch table. Access does not permit data entry of unconnected data. Referential integrity was enforced between the Branch ID in the Branch table and the Branch ID in the Accounts table. Access prevents the entry of an invalid Branch ID.

b. Click **OK**. Replace *B6* with **B5** and press **Enter**. As soon as you move to a different record, the pencil symbol disappears, and your data are saved.

You successfully identified a Branch ID that Access recognizes. Because referential integrity between the Accounts and Branch tables has been enforced, Access looks at each data entry item in a foreign key and matches it to a corresponding value in the table where it is the primary key. In Step 6a you attempted to enter a nonexistent Branch ID and were not allowed to make that error. In Step 6b you entered a valid Branch ID. Access examined the index for the Branch ID in the Branch table and found a corresponding value for B5.

c. Close the Accounts table. Reopen the **Accounts table** and you will find that the record you just entered for A22 has been saved.

d. Click the **Office Button**, select **Manage**, and then select **Back Up Database**. Type **chap2_ho2_safebank_solution** as the filename and click **Save**.

You just created a backup of the database after completing the second hands-on exercise. The original database *chap2_ho1-3_safebank_solution* remains onscreen. If you ruin the original database as you complete the third hands-on exercise, you can use the backup file you just created and rework the third exercise.

e. Close the file and exit Access if you do not want to continue with the next exercise at this time.

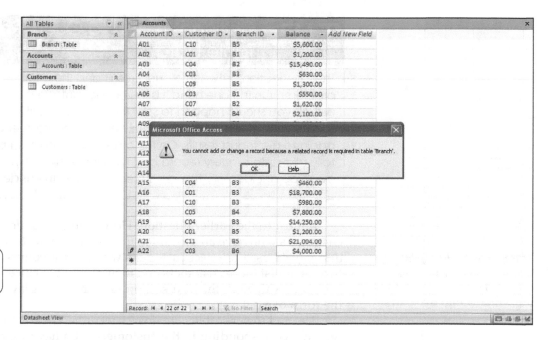

Figure 28 How Referential Integrity Works to Protect Data Accuracy

Queries

What if you wanted to see just the customers who bank at a specific branch or who have accounts with balances over $5,000? Perhaps you need to know the customers who have accounts at multiple branches. Maybe you will need a list of all the customers who bank with the branch managed by a specific manager. The manager's name is stored in the Branch table and the customer's name in the Customers table. In this small database, you could open both tables and mentally trace through the strings of the relationships and extract the information. But in a real world database with thousands of records, you would be unable to do this accurately. A query provides the ability to ask questions based on the data or a smaller grouping of data, and to find the answers to those questions.

A *query* permits you to see the data you want arranged in the sequence that you need. It enables you to select specific records from a table (or from several tables) and show some or all of the fields for the selected records. You can perform calculations to display data that are not explicitly stored in the underlying table(s), such as the amount of interest each bank account earned during the previous month.

In this section you use the Query Wizard to create a query. You set specific conditions to display only records that meet the condition. Finally, you learn about large databases.

A *query* enables you to ask questions about the data stored in a database and returns the answers from the records in the order that matches your instructions.

Creating a Query

Create a query either by using the *Query Wizard* or specifying the tables and fields directly in Design view. Like all of the Microsoft wizards, the Query Wizard is a method to automate your work. It facilitates new query development. The results of the query display in a *dataset*, which contains the records that satisfy the criteria specified in the query.

A dataset looks and acts like a table, but it is not a table; it is a dynamic subset of a table that selects, sorts, and calculates records as specified in the query. A dataset is similar to a table in appearance and, like a table, it enables you to enter a new record or modify or delete an existing record. Any changes made in the dataset are reflected automatically in the underlying table.

The *Query Wizard* is an Access tool that facilitates new query development.

A *dataset*, which contains the records that satisfy the criteria specified in the query, provides the answers to the user's questions.

TIP Changes Made to Query Results Overwrite Table Data

The connection between a query result and the underlying table data may create problems. On the one hand it is to your advantage that you can correct an error in data if you should happen to spot it in a query result. You save time by not having to close the query, open the table, find the record in error, fix it, and run the query again to get robust results. On the other hand, you must be careful not to accidentally click into a query record and type something. If you press Enter or Tab, whatever you accidentally typed is stored forever in the underlying table.

The *query design grid* displays when you select a query's Design view; it divides the window into two parts.

Return to the earlier question. How would you identify the names of all of the customers who have an account at the Campus branch? Figure 29 contains the *query design grid* used to select customers who have accounts at the Campus Branch and further, to list those customers and their account balances alphabetically. (The design grid is explained in the next section.) Figure 30 displays the answer to the query in the form of a dataset.

The Customers table contains 21 records. The dataset in Figure 30 has only six records, corresponding to the customers who have Campus branch accounts. The records in the table are ordered by the Customer ID (the primary key), whereas the records in the dataset are in alphabetical order by last name. Changing the order of data displayed in a query has no effect on the underlying table data.

TIP   Examine the Record Number

An experienced Access user always examines the number of records returned in a query's results. As you add additional criteria, the number of records returned should decrease.

Create a Select Query

A *select query* searches the underlying tables to retrieve the data that satisfy the query parameters.

The query in Figures 29 and 30 is an example of a select query, which is the most common type of query. A *select query* searches the underlying tables to retrieve the data that satisfy the query parameters. The data display in a dataset (see Figure 30), which can be modified to update the data in the underlying table(s). The specifications for selecting records and determining which fields will be displayed for the selected records, as well as the sequence of the selected records, are established within the design grid of Figure 29. The select query is one of many different query operations Access supports.

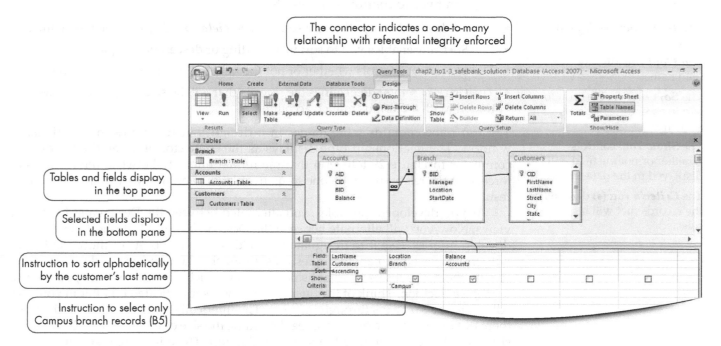

Figure 29 The Query Design View

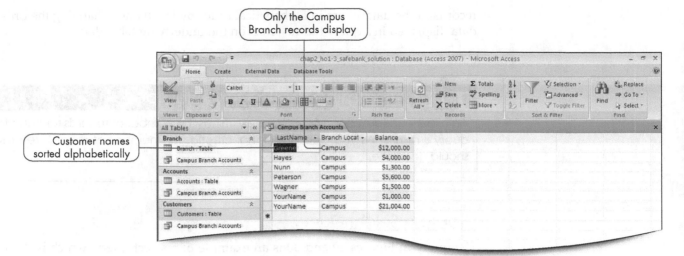

Figure 30 The Query Datasheet View

Use the Query Design Grid

The query design grid consists of two panes. The lower pane contains columns and rows. Each field in the query has its own column and contains multiple rows. The rows permit you to control query results.

The **Table row** displays the data source.

The **Field row** displays the field name.

The **Sort row** enables you to sort in ascending or descending sequence.

The **Show row** controls whether or not the field will be displayed in the dataset.

The **Criteria row(s)** determines the records that will be selected.

- The **Table row** displays the data source. The **Field row** displays the field name.
- The **Sort row** enables you to sort in ascending or descending sequence.
- The **Show row** controls whether or not the field will be displayed in the dataset.
- The **Criteria row(s)** determines the records that will be selected, such as customers with a Campus branch account.

The top pane contains table names in a design that resembles the relationship window. The relationship type displays as the connector between the tables. The connector in Figure 29 tells you that referential integrity between the tables is in force, that the relationship is a one-to-many relation, and that we can trust the query results.

As you developed the tables, you alternated between the Design and Datasheet views. Now you will alternate between the Design view and Datasheet view as you develop queries. Use it to designate the fields and the subsets of those fields that will empower you to answer questions about the data and make decisions. You specify the data subsets by establishing criteria, which are rules or tests you can use to make a decision. Think of the query criteria as a sophisticated oil filter in your car. All of the car's oil runs through the filter. The filter collects dirt particles and strains them out of the oil. The query criteria determine the size of the filter and allow you to sift through the data to find the records of interest. The criteria operate much like a filter in a table. The difference between a filter and a query is that the query becomes a permanent part of the database. A filter gives you a temporary method to view the data.

Specifying Criteria for Different Data Types

The field data type determines how the criteria are specified for that field. You need to enter criteria for a text field enclosed in quotation marks. To find only the records of customers with accounts at the Campus branch, you would enter "Campus" as the criteria under the Location field. You enter the criteria for number, *currency* (e.g., $3.00 in the United States), and counter fields as digits with or without a decimal point and/or a minus sign. (Commas and dollar signs are not allowed.) When the criterion is in a date field, you enclose the criterion in pound signs. You should enter date criteria in the mm/dd/yyyy format, such as #10/14/2008#. You enter criteria for a Yes/No field as Yes (or True) or No (or False).

Access accepts values for text and date fields in the design grid in multiple formats. You can enter the text with or without quotation marks, such as *Campus* or *"Campus."* You can enter a date with or without the pound signs, such as *1/1/2008* or *#1/1/2008#*. Access will enter the quotation marks or pound signs, respectively, for you when you move to the next cell in the design grid. Thus, text entries are always shown in quotation marks and dates in pound signs.

A **currency** is the medium of exchange; in the United States, currency formatted values display with a dollar sign.

Use Wildcards

Select queries recognize the question mark and asterisk wildcards that enable you to search for a pattern within a text field. A question mark stands for a single character in the same position as the question mark; thus *H?ll* will return *Hall*, *Hill*, and *Hull*. An asterisk stands for any number of characters in the same position as the asterisk; for example, *S*nd* will return *Sand*, *Stand*, and *Strand*. If you search a two-letter state code field for *?C*, Access will return *NC*, *SC*, and *DC*. If you search the same field with either **C* or *C**, Access will return *CA*, *CO*, *CT*, *DC*, *NC*, and *SC*.

Use Operands in Queries

An **operator** is a mathematical symbol, such as +, -, *, and /.

An **operand** is the portion of the mathematical expression that is being operated on.

A numeric field may be limited through standard numeric operators; **operators** such as plus, minus, equals, greater than, less than, multiply (*), divide (/), and not equals (<>). An **operand** is a portion of the mathematical expression that is being operated on, such as the value stored in a field. In Access, you use the field name as an operand, such as Date() - 30. Both the Date() field and 30 are operands. Table 4 shows sample expressions and discusses their results.

Table 4 Criteria Operands

Expression	Result
>10	For a Price field, items with a price over $10.00
<10	For a Price field, items with a price under $10.00
>=10	For a Price field, items with a price of at least $10.00
<=10	For a Price field, items with a price of $10.00 or less
=10	For a Price field, items with a price of exactly $10.00
<> 10	For a Price field, items with a price not equal to $10.00
!=10	For a Price field, items with a price not equal to $10.00
#2/2/2008#	For a ShippedDate field, orders shipped on February 2, 2008
'2/2/2008'	For a ShippedDate field, orders shipped on February 2, 2008
Date()	For an OrderDate field, orders for today's date
Between 1/1/2007 and 3/31/2007	For a specified interval between a start and end date
Between Date( ) And DateAdd ("M", 3, Date( ))	For a RequiredDate field, orders required between today's date and three months from today's date
< Date( ) – 30	For an OrderDate field, orders more than 30 days old
Year((OrderDate)) = 2005	For an OrderDate field, orders with order dates in 2005
DatePart("q", (OrderDate)) = 4	For an OrderDate field, orders for the fourth calendar quarter
DateSerial(Year ((OrderDate)), Month ((OrderDate)) + 1, 1) – 1	For an OrderDate field, orders for the last day of each month
Year((OrderDate)) = Year(Now()) And Month((OrderDate)) = Month(Now())	For an OrderDate field, orders for the current year and month

Work with Null and Zero-Length Strings

A ***null*** value is the formal, computer term for a missing value.

Sometimes finding what is *not* known is an important part of making a decision. For example, which orders have been accepted but not shipped? Are we missing phone numbers or addresses for some of our customers? The computer term for a missing value is *null*. Table 5 gives the following illustrations on how to use the Null criterion in a query.

Table 5 Establishing Null Criteria Expressions

Expression	Result
Is Null	For an Employee field in the Customers table when the customer has not been assigned a sales representative. (Some fields, such as primary key fields, can't contain Null.)
Is Not Null	For a ShipDate field, orders already shipped to customers
" "	For an E-mail field for customers who don't have an email address. This is indicated by a zero-length string. This is different from a Null value. Use this only when you know a customer has no e-mail, not when he or she has e-mail but you do not know what it is. You enter a zero-length string by typing two double quotation marks with no space between them (" ").

Understand Query Sort Order

The *query sort order* determines the order of items in the query Datasheet View.

The *query sort order* determines the order of items in the query Datasheet view. You can change the sort order of a query by specifying the sort order in the design grid. The sorts work from left to right. The leftmost field with a sort order specified will be the primary sort field; the next sort specified field to the right will be the secondary sort field, and so forth. Change the order of the query fields in the design grid to change the sort order of the query result. Alter the field order within the design grid by clicking in the Table row (the second row) of the design grid and specifying the table and then in the Field row and selecting a different field name. The table must be specified first because each field row drop-down list shows only the names of the fields in the specified table. You also may insert additional columns in the design grid by selecting the column, right-clicking the selection, and choosing Insert column from the shortcut menu. The inserted column will insert to the right of the highlighted column.

TIP   Reorder Query Fields

With a query open in Design view, move your mouse above a field name. The mouse pointer will change shape to a bold black arrow. When you see the bold black arrow, click the mouse. The field's column selects. Move your mouse slowly over the top of the selected area until the pointer shape changes to the move shape (a thick white arrow). When the white arrow shape shows, click and drag the field to a new position on the design grid. A thick black border moves with your mouse to tell you where the field will move. Release the mouse when the border moves to the desired position.

Establish And, Or, and Not Criteria

Until now all of the questions that you have asked the database to answer through queries have been relatively simple. Access adapts to more complex query specifications. What if you need a list of all of the customers who bank at the Campus branch and do not have accounts at any other branches? Which customers bank only at the Campus or Uptown branches? Are there customers of the Campus branch with deposits over $5,000? These questions involve multiple field interaction.

The **And operator** returns only records that meet all criteria.

The **Or operator** returns records meeting any of the specified criteria.

The **Not operator** returns the opposite of the specified criteria.

The moment you specify criteria in multiple fields, Access combines the fields using the And or the Or operator. When the expressions are in the same row of the query design grid, Access uses the **And operator**. This means that only the records that meet *all* criteria in all of the fields will be returned. If the criteria are positioned in different rows of the design grid, Access uses the **Or operator** and will return records meeting *any* of the specified criteria. The **Not operator** returns the *opposite* of the specification.

Figure 31 shows a query in Design view that specifies an And operator. It will return all of the Campus branch accounts with balances over $5,000. Both conditions must be met for the record to be included. Figure 32 shows a query in Design view that specifies an Or operator. It will return all of the Campus branch accounts with any balance plus all accounts at any branch with balances over $5,000. Either condition may be met for a record to be included. Figure 33 shows a query in Design view that specifies a Not operator. It will return all of the accounts at all of the branches excluding the Campus branch. You may combine And, Or, and Not operators to achieve the desired result. If you need a list of the accounts with balances over $5,000 at the Campus and Uptown branches, you set the criteria so that the >5000 expression is duplicated for each location specified (see Figure 34).

Field:	LastName	Location	Balance
Table:	Customer	Branch	Account
Sort:	Ascending		
Show:	☑	☑	☑
Criteria:		"Campus"	>5000
or:			

Figure 31 And Criterion—Only Records Satisfying Both Conditions Will Return

Field:	LastName	Location	Balance
Table:	Customer	Branch	Account
Sort:	Ascending		
Show:	☑	☑	☑
Criteria:		"Campus"	
or:			>5000

Figure 32 Or Criterion—Records Meeting Either Condition Will Return

Field:	LastName	Location	Balance
Table:	Customer	Branch	Account
Sort:	Ascending		
Show:	☑	☑	☑
Criteria:		Not "Campus"	
or:			>5000

Figure 33 Not Criterion—Any Record Except the Matching Will Return

Field:	LastName	Location	Balance
Table:	Customer	Branch	Account
Sort:	Ascending		
Show:	☑	☑	☑
Criteria:		"Campus"	>5000
or:		"Uptown"	>5000

Figure 34 And and Or Criteria—Records Meeting Both Conditions at Both Branches Return

Copying and Running a Query

After you create a query, you may want to duplicate it to use as the basis for creating similar queries. Duplicating a query saves time in selecting tables and fields for queries that need the same structure but different criteria. After you create and save one or more queries, you can execute them whenever you need them to produce up-to-date results.

Copy a Query

Sometimes you have one-of-a-kind questions about your data. Then you create and run the query, find the answer and close it. If you create the query with the wizard, you save and name it in the last step. If you create the query in Design view, it is possible for you to exit the query without saving changes. Most queries answer recurrent questions. What were sales last week in Houston, in Dallas, in Chicago? In cases like this, you set up the query for the dates and places of interest one time, then copy it, rename the copy and establish the parameters for a different city or date.

Frequently you will need to examine multiple subsets of the data. In Hands-On Exercise 3 you will create a query displaying the names and account balances of the customers who have accounts at the Campus branch. Should you need to know the same information about the customers who have Uptown accounts, you would select the query in the Navigation pane, and then copy and paste it to a blank space at the bottom pane. Right-click the copy and rename it Uptown. Open the newly created Uptown query in Design view and replace the Campus criterion with Uptown. When you run and save the query, the resulting dataset displays customers and account balances from the Uptown branch. Using this method takes you a few minutes to create branch specific queries for all five locations.

Run a Query

When you **run a query**, Access processes the query instructions and displays records that meet the conditions.

After you create the query by specifying criteria and save it, you are ready to run it. You **run a query** by clicking the Run command (the red exclamation point) to direct Access to process the instructions specified by the query. In our databases the queries run quickly. Even in the largest database you will use in the end of chapter exercises, no query will take more than a few seconds to run. As you learn how to work with these databases, keep in mind that real-world databases can be massive. Think through the query design carefully. Include all necessary fields and tables, but do not include fields or tables that are not necessary to answer the question. Unnecessary fields slow the query's run time.

Using the Query Wizard

You may create a query directly in Design view or by using the Query Wizard. Even if you initiate the query with a wizard, you will need to learn how to modify it in Design view. Often it is much faster to copy an existing query and make slight modifications to its design than it would be to start at the beginning of the wizard. You also will need to know how to add additional tables and fields to an existing query in case you failed to think through the design thoroughly and you omitted a necessary field. To launch the Query Wizard, click the Create tab and click Query Wizard in the Other group (see Figure 35).

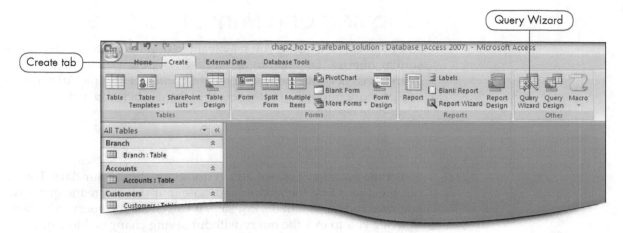

Figure 35 Launching the Query Wizard

Access produces many different kinds of queries. Here we will work with the most common query type, the select query. This is a powerful and sophisticated tool. Select the Simple Query Wizard in the first dialog box of the Query Wizard as shown in Figure 36.

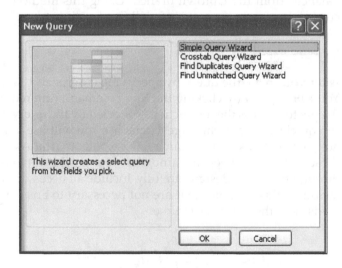

Figure 36 The Simple Query Wizard Step 1

In the second step of the Query Wizard dialog box you specify the tables and fields needed in your query. As soon as you click on the table in the Tables/Queries drop-down box, a list of that table's fields display in the Available fields box. See Figures 37 and 38.

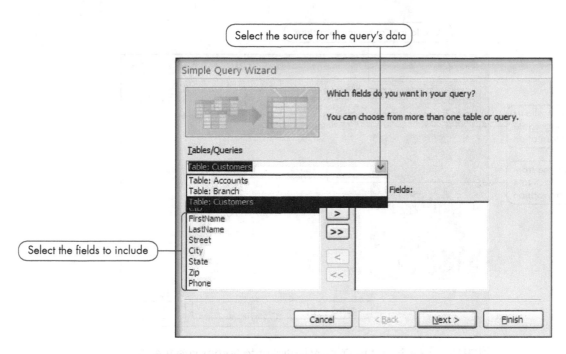

Figure 37 Specify which Tables or Queries to Use as Input

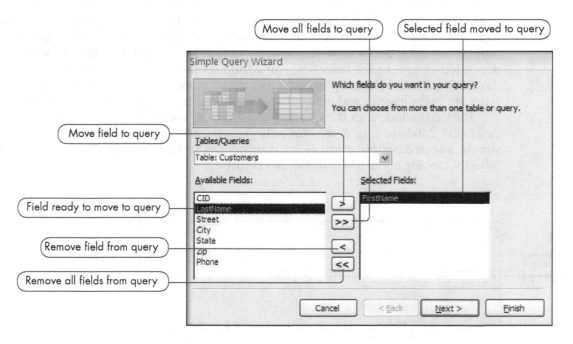

Figure 38 Specify the Fields for the Query

Select the necessary fields by clicking them to highlight and then using the navigation arrows described in Figure 39.

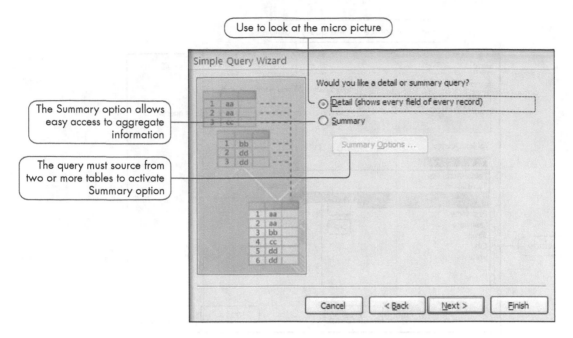

Figure 39 Select to Display Detail or to Summarize the Data

Aggregate means the collection of individual items into a total.

In the Query Wizard, you choose between a detailed or a summary query. The detail query provides every record of every field. The summary enables you to aggregate data and View only summary statistics. *Aggregate* means the collection of individual items into a total. If you were only interested in the total of the funds deposited at each of the branches, you would set the query to a summary and ask Access to sum the balances of all accounts in that branch. Some Access users summarize data in the queries and others do so in reports. Either approach is acceptable.

The final window in the Query Wizard directs you to name the query. A well-designed database might contain only 5 tables and 500 queries. Therefore, you should assign descriptive names for your queries so that you know what each contains by looking at the query name. See Figure 40.

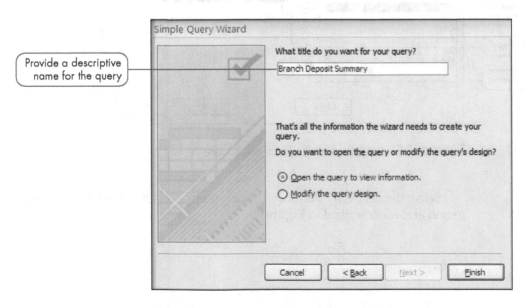

Figure 40 Name the Query Descriptively

Understanding Large Database Differences

Suppose you work for a large university. You need to identify all of the students at your university who are business majors, their advisor's names, and their specific majors. The Student table contains student names, identification numbers, majors, faculty advisor's identification number, class standing, addresses, and so on. The Faculty table contains faculty names, departmental affiliation, identification number, and rank. Your query needs to include fields for the student's name, major, and the advisor's name. You would not need the student's address or the faculty member's ID because those fields are unnecessary to answer the question. You need to establish criteria to select business majors: Accounting, Finance, Information Systems, Management, Marketing, and Economics.

Even if your computer is state-of-the-art, fast, powerful, and loaded with memory, this query might take up to 15 minutes to run. If you include unnecessary fields or tables, the run time increases. At the author's university, each additional table roughly doubles the query run time. As an Access beginner, your queries might contain too much or too little information. You will make frequent modifications to the query design as you learn. As you apply your database skills to work with large databases, you will learn to carefully design queries prior to running them to minimize the time to run the queries.

In addition to the earlier mentioned size difference between real world databases and those you will use in the class, real world databases involve multiple users. Typically the organization stores the database file on the network. Multiple people may simultaneously log into the database. Each user makes changes to tables or forms. At your school, thousands of users can extract data from the university's database. Prior to meeting your advisor, you check your transcript online. You enter a database to find out how many hours you have completed and whether or not you have met the prerequisites. You have permission to view your transcript but you do not have the necessary permission to change what is recorded there. Several hundred other users have more extensive privileges in your school's database. Your Access professor can enter and probably change your grade in this class. If the securities are appropriately set on the database, your Access professor is not able to change the grade that you earned in other courses.

Most large organizations employ database administrators and managers that ensure data security, efficacy, and integrity. These professionals are well paid to make sure that no one inside or outside the firm has access to classified data or can corrupt the data resident in the system. Additionally, SOX rules mandate backup and security measures.

The **front end** of a database contains the objects, like queries, reports, and forms, needed to interact with data, but not the tables where the record values reside.

The **back end** of the system protects and stores data so that users cannot inadvertently destroy or corrupt the organization's vital data.

These positions involve a great deal of responsibility. How does someone charged with this vital role do it? One common method involves splitting the database into front and back ends. Typically the *front end* of a database contains the objects, like queries, reports, and forms, needed to interact with data, but not the tables where the record values reside. The tables are safely stored in the *back end* system where users cannot inadvertently destroy or corrupt data. Most often the front and back ends of the database are stored on different systems placed in different locations to provide an extra security measure. Users within the organization are divided into groups by their data needs. Then the groups are assigned rights and privileges. For example, a professor has privileges to record grades for students registered in his or her classes but not for other professors' classes. The financial aid officer may look at student grades and financial records, but may not alter either. The dean may look at student grades, but probably not their financial records. The student health center physician may view a student's immunization records and update it when necessary, but cannot see the student's grades.

The next hands-on exercise introduces queries as a more useful way to examine data. You use the Query Wizard to create a basic query, and then modify that query by adding an additional field and an additional table, and performing simple query criteria specifications.

Hands-On Exercises

3 | Multiple-Table Query

Skills covered: 1. Create a Query Using a Wizard **2.** Specify Simple Query Criteria **3.** Change Query Data **4.** Add a Table to a Query Using Design View and Sort a Query

Step 1
Create a Query Using a Wizard

Refer to Figure 41 as you complete Step 1.

a. Open the *chap2_ho1-3_safebank_solution.accdb* database from Hands-On Exercise 2 (if necessary), click **Options** on the Security Warning toolbar and click the **Enable this content option** in the Microsoft Office Security Options dialog box, and click **OK**.

TROUBLESHOOTING: If you create unrecoverable errors while completing this hands-on exercise, you can delete the *chap2_ho1-3_safebank_solution* file, copy the *chap2_ho2_safebank_solution* database you created at the end of the second hands-on exercise, and open the copy of the backup database to start the third hands-on exercise again.

b. Click the **Create tab** and click **Query Wizard** in the Other group to launch the wizard.

The New Query Dialog box opens.

c. Select **Simple Query Wizard** and click **OK**.

d. Click the **Tables/Queries drop-down arrow** and select **Table: Customers**.

This step asks you to specify the tables and fields needed in the query. A list of the fields in the Customers table displays in the Available Fields box.

e. Double-click the **FirstName** field.

The FirstName field moves from the Available Fields box to the Selected Fields box. You can also double-click a field in the Selected Fields box to move it back to the Available box.

f. Click the **LastName** field and click the **Move Field to Query command** (see Figure 38).

g. Click the **Tables/Queries drop-down arrow** and select **Table: Accounts**.

h. From the list of fields in the Accounts table, select **BID** and **Balance** and move them one at a time to the Fields in Query box. Click **Next**.

Your query should have four fields: first and last names, BID, and Balance.

i. Select **Detail**, if necessary, to choose between a Detail and Summary Query. Click **Next**.

j. Name your query **Campus Branch Customers**. Click **Finish**.

This name describes the data that will eventually populate the query. The default name, Customers Query, comes from the first table selected when you started the query wizard.

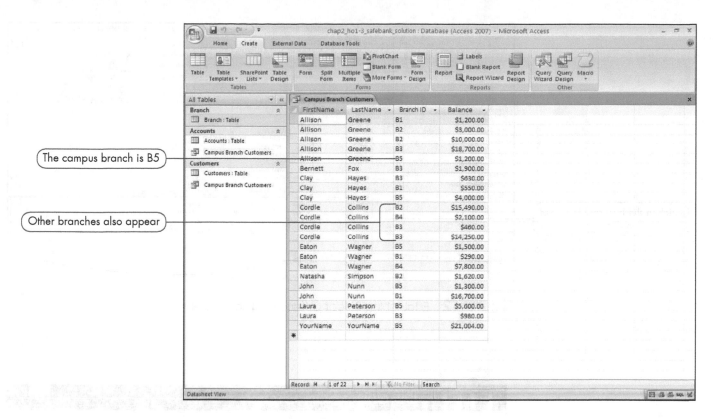

The campus branch is B5

Other branches also appear

Figure 41 Criteria Have Not Been Applied

Step 2	Refer to Figure 42 as you complete Step 2.
Specify Simple Query Criteria	**a.** Right-click the **Campus Branch Customers tab** and select **Design View** from the shortcut menu.

You have created the Campus Branch Customers query to view only those customers who have accounts at the Campus branch. However, other branch's accounts also display. You need to limit the query results to only the records of interest.

b. Click in the fifth row (the **criteria row**) under the **BID** field and type **b5**.

Access is not case sensitive but is frequently used to connect to larger databases for which case matters.

c. Click in the **Sort row** (third row) under the **LastName field** to activate the drop-down arrow. (This is another of the hidden arrows that only provides selections when the cell is active.) Select **Ascending** from the drop-down list.

d. Click **Run** in the Results group on the Design tab.

e. Save your query.

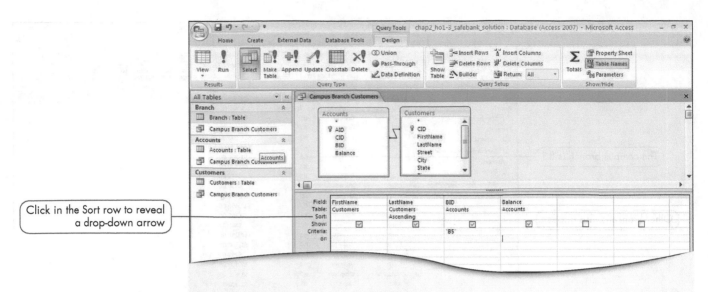

Click in the Sort row to reveal a drop-down arrow

Figure 42 Establishing Select Criteria and Sort Order

TIP Differing Sort Order

Your name is probably not **Your Name**. Unless your name begins with an X, Y, or Z, the sort order or your query will be different from that displayed in Figure 43. That is OK.

Step 3
Change Query Data

Refer to Figure 43 as you complete Step 3.

a. Click on the **Balance** field in the record for *Allison Greene's* account. Change **$1200** to **$12,000**. Press **Enter**. Close the query. Do *not* save your changes.

b. Open the **Accounts table**.

   Only one account shows a $12,000 balance. The Customer ID is C01.

c. Open the **Customers table**. Find the name of the customer whose Customer ID is **C01**.

   Allison Green's CID number is C01. The change you made in the query datasheet has permanently changed the data stored in the underlying table.

   TROUBLESHOOTING: Changes in query data change table data! As soon as you pressed Enter in Step 3a, the balance for Allison's account saved. (Remember Access works in storage, not memory.) A wise Access user is extremely careful about the position of the cursor and about typing stray characters while a table or query is open. As soon as you move to a different record, any edits are saved automatically, whether you intend the save or not!

d. Add a new record to the **Accounts table**. The Accounts table should be open. If not, open it now.

e. Type **A23**, **C11**, **B5**, and **1000**. Press **Enter**.

f. Open the **Campus Branch Customers query**. Click **Run** on the Design tab.

   You (as a bank customer) now show two accounts, one with a balance that matches your course and section number and one with a balance of $1,000.

Relational Databases and Multi-Table Queries

Because you closed and reopened the query, it re-ran prior to opening. Access reruns queries to ensure that the data the query returns is the most recent in the database.

g. Close the **Accounts table**.

You successfully created a multi-table query. It does almost everything that you intended. Because this bank is so small, everybody who works there (and probably most of the customers) knows that the Campus branch is B5. But what if this were the database for a real bank? How many thousands of branches does it have? (Remember you are designing your database for 100 years.) You decide that you want to display the branch name, not the ID number. The branch name is a field in the Branch table. The Campus Branch Customers query was based on the Accounts and Customers tables. In order to display the branch name, you need to connect the Branch table to the query.

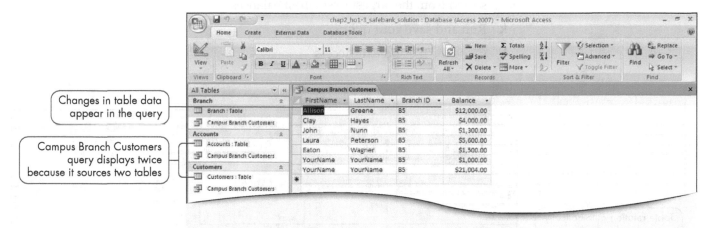

Figure 43 Campus Branch Customers Query Following Data Modifications

---

Step 4

Add a Table to a Query Using Design View and Sort a Query

Refer to Figure 44 as you complete Step 4.

a. Open the *Campus Branch Customers Query* if necessary. Right-click the query tab and select **Design View** from the shortcut menu.

b. Click the **Branch: table** under the **All Tables list** on the left-most window pane.

It will turn gold to indicate that it is selected.

c. Click and drag the selected **Branch table** to the **top pane** of the Query design grid.

Your mouse pointer shape will change to a Table as you drag.

d. Drop the **Branch table** next to the **Accounts table**.

The one-to-many relationship lines automatically connect the Branch table to the Accounts table. The query inherits the relationship specifications from the database design.

e. Click the **Location** field name in the Branch table and **drag** it down to the **first empty column**. It should be to the right of the Balance column.

f. Click the **Show row check box** under the **BID** field to hide this field.

The BID field is no longer needed because we have a more descriptive and easily understood name.

g. Remove the **b5** criterion by highlighting and then deleting it.

h. Type **Campus** as a criterion in the **Location** field.

The syntax actually requires that you enter text criteria within quotation marks, such as "Campus". Access will enter these quotes for you if you forget. If you use Access to get into large databases, you may need to remember the quotation marks while setting parameters for character fields.

i. Click the word *Location*. As soon as you leave the criteria row, Access adds the missing quotes for you.

j. Click in the **Sort row** of the **Balance** field to activate the drop-down list. Select **Descending**.

The query will still be sorted alphabetically by the customer's last name because that is the left-most sort field in the design grid. You have added an additional, or secondary, sort. Customers with multiple accounts will have their accounts sorted from the largest to smallest balances.

k. Run and save your query.

l. Close the file and exit Access.

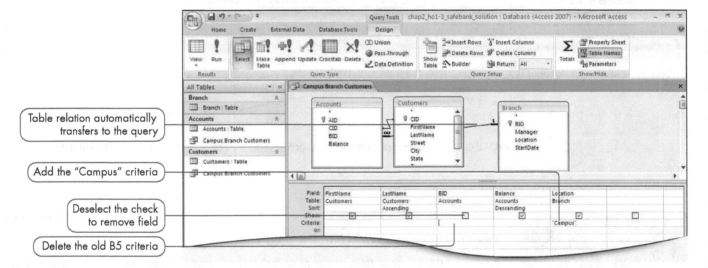

Figure 44 Drag and Drop the Branch Table to Add to the Query Design Grid

Summary

1. **Design data.** The architectural infrastructure that supports the database needs to be driven by the output the database will need to generate. You learned that good database design requires that you anticipate how the data will be used, both now and for a long time to come. Creating a database adds costs to the firm, and the designer must balance the costs of including data against the costs of needing it at some point in the future and not having it available. The Sarbanes Oxley Act governs how, where, and when publicly traded firms must store data. You learned that good design principles avoid making calculations in table data, that data should be stored in their smallest parts, and that like data should be grouped together to form tables.

2. **Create tables.** Access employs several ways to create a table. You can create a table yourself by entering the table data into a field. You also can import table data from another database or application, for example, Excel. You learned that each field needs a unique and descriptive name and were introduced to the CamelCase notation naming convention. Access accommodates many different types of data including: text, number, Date/Time, Yes/No, Memo, and others.

3. **Understand table relationships.** Data stored in different tables may be linked using the powerful tool of referential integrity enforcement. Typically, the primary key from one table (unique identifier) resides as a foreign key in another table. This becomes the means of creating the link.

4. **Share data with Excel.** Access facilitates data exchanges with Excel through imports and exports. You used the Import Wizard to import an Excel worksheet into an Access database table. The settings of the Import Wizard may be saved and reused when the import is recurrent.

5. **Establish table relationships.** You created links between tables in the database and attempted to enter an invalid branch number in a related table. You discovered that the enforcement of referential integrity prevented you from creating an account in a non-existent branch. Cascades give the database manager a powerful tool that facilitates updating or deleting multiple records in different tables simultaneously.

6. **Create a query.** You manipulated the data to display only those records of interest by creating a select query. Later you learned to add additional fields or tables to an existing query.

7. **Specify criteria for different data types.** Establishing criteria empowers you to see only the records that meet the criteria. Different data types require different criteria specifications. Date fields are enclosed in pound signs (#) and text fields with quote marks (""). Additionally you learned that there are powerful operators, And, Or, and Not, that return the results needed to answer complex questions. You established a sort order for arranging the query results. The Primary sort field needs to be in the left-most position in the query design grid. You may specify additional sort fields; their priority is determined by their left-to-right positions in the grid.

8. **Copy and run a query.** After specifying tables, fields, and conditions for one query, you can copy the query and modify only the criteria in the duplicate query. Copying queries saves time so that you do not have to select tables and fields again for queries that need the same structure but different criteria. After saving queries, you can run them whenever you need to display up-to-date results based on the query conditions.

9. **Use the Query Wizard.** An alternative to creating a select query is to use the Query Wizard. The wizard enables you to select tables and fields from lists. The last step of the wizard prompts you to save the query.

10. **Understand large database differences.** Large databases queries may take a long time to run. Therefore, you should think carefully about what fields and tables to include in the query prior to executing it. You learned that database administrators often split the database into front and back ends. Different users of a large database have different levels of access and privilege in order to protect the data validity.

Key Terms

Aggregate
And operator
Append
AutoNumber field
Back end
Calculated field
CamelCase notation
Caption property
Cascade delete
Cascade update
Cascades
Constant
Criteria row(s)
Currency
Data redundancy

Data type
Dataset
Date arithmetic
Date/time field
Field row
Field size property
Front end
Indexed property
Not operator
Null
One-to-many relationship
Operand
Operator
Or operator
PivotChart view

PivotTable view
PNPI
Property
Query
Query design grid
Query sort order
Query Wizard
Run a query
Sarbanes Oxley Act (SOX)
Select query
Show row
Sort row
Table row
Validation rule

Multiple Choice

1. When entering, deleting or editing table data

   (a) The table must be in Design view.

   (b) The table must be in Datasheet view.

   (c) The table may be in either Datasheet or Design view.

   (d) Data may be entered only in a form.

2. Which of the following is implemented automatically by Access?

   (a) Rejecting misspelled field entries in a record

   (b) Rejecting redundant field specifications among tables

   (c) Rejecting a record of a foreign key without a matching value in a related table

   (d) Rejecting a record in a primary key without a matching value in a related table

3. Social Security Number, phone number, and postal code should be designated as:

   (a) Number fields

   (b) Text fields

   (c) Yes/No fields

   (d) Any of the above depending on the application

4. Which of the following is true of the primary key?

   (a) Its values must be unique.

   (b) It must be defined as a text field.

   (c) It must be the first field in a table.

   (d) It can never be changed.

5. Social Security Number should not be used as a primary key because:

   (a) The Social Security Number is numeric, and primary key fields should be text.

   (b) The Social Security Number is not unique.

   (c) The Social Security Number is too long.

   (d) Using the Social Security Number may expose employees or customers to identity theft.

6. An illustration of a one-to-many relationship would be:

   (a) A unique city name relates to a single postal code.

   (b) A customer ID may be related to multiple account numbers.

   (c) A branch location may contain many branch identification numbers.

   (d) A balance field may contain many values.

7. Which of the following was not a suggested guideline for designing a table?

   (a) Include all necessary data

   (b) Store data in its smallest parts

   (c) Avoid calculated fields

   (d) Designate at least two primary keys

8. A query's specifications providing instructions about which fields to include must be entered

   (a) On the Show row of the query design grid

   (b) On the Sort row of the query design grid

   (c) On the Criteria row of the query design grid

   (d) On the Table Row of the query design grid

9. Which view is used to modify field properties in a table?

   (a) Datasheet view

   (b) Design view

   (c) PivotTable view

   (d) PivotChart view

10. Which of the following is true?

    (a) Additional tables may be added to a query only by restarting the Query Wizard.

    (b) Additional tables or fields may be added to a query by clicking and dragging in the query design grid.

    (c) Access does not permit the addition of additional tables or fields to an existing query.

    (d) Additional tables may be added by copying and pasting the fields from the table to the query.

11. In which view will you see the record selector symbols of a pencil and a triangle?

    (a) Only the Datasheet view of a table

    (b) Only the Datasheet view of a query

    (c) Neither the Datasheet view of a table nor query

    (d) Both the Datasheet view of a table nor query

12. You attempt to make a data edit in the Datasheet view of a query by changing an account balance and then press Enter.

    (a) The change also must be made to the underlying table for it to be a permanent part of the database.

    (b) The change must be saved for it to be a permanent part of the database.

    (c) An error message will display because queries are used only to view data, not edit.

    (d) The change is saved, and the underlying table immediately reflects the change.

...continued on Next Page

13. Data in a Name field is stored as Janice Zook, Zachariah Allen, Tom Jones, and Nancy Allen. If the field was sorted in ascending order, which name would be last?

(a) Janice Zook

(b) Zachariah Allen

(c) Tom Jones

(d) Nancy Allen

14. Which data type appears as a check box in a table?

(a) Text field

(b) Number field

(c) Yes/No field

(d) Name field

15. Which properties would you use to provide the database user with "user-friendly" column headings in the Datasheet View of a table?

(a) Field Size and Format

(b) Input Mask, Validation Rule, and Default Value

(c) Caption

(d) Required

16. Which of the following is true with respect to an individual's hire date and years of service, both of which appear on a query that is based on an employee table?

(a) Hire date should be a calculated field; years of service should be a stored field.

(b) Hire date should be a stored field; years of service should be a calculated field.

(c) Both should be stored fields.

(d) Both should be calculated fields.

17. What is the best way to store an individual's name in a table?

(a) As a single field consisting of the last name, first name, and middle initial, in that order

(b) As a single field consisting of the first name, last name, and middle initial, in that order

(c) As three separate fields for first name, last name, and middle initial

(d) All of the above are equally suitable.

18. Which of the following would not be a good primary key?

(a) Student Number

(b) Social Security Number

(c) An e-mail address

(d) A branch identification number

19. A difference between student database files and "real world" files is not:

(a) Split between front and back end storage.

(b) Many users add, delete, and change records in "real world" files.

(c) Student files tend to much smaller than "real world" files.

(d) Students work in live databases but "real world" files have multiple copies of the database on all user's desktops.

20. Your query has a date field. If you wanted the records for the month of March 2007 returned, how would you set the criteria?

(a) <3/31/2007

(b) between 3/1/2007 and 3/31/2007

(c) >3/31/2007

(d) = March 2007

Practice Exercises

1 Martha's Vineyard Bookstore—Creation

One of your aunt's friends, Jennifer Frew, owns and operates a tiny bookstore during the tourist season on Martha's Vineyard. Jennifer asked you to help her after your aunt bragged that you are becoming quite the computer whiz because of this class. You believe that you can help Jennifer by creating a small database. She has stored information about the publication companies and the books that she sells in Excel spreadsheets. You, in consultation with Jennifer, determine that a third table—an author table— also is required. Your task is to design and populate the three tables, establish appropriate linkages between them, and enforce referential integrity. This project follows the same set of skills as used in Hands-On exercises 1 and 2 in this chapter. If you have problems, reread the detailed directions presented in the chapter. Refer to Figure 45 as you complete your work.

a. Start Access and click **Blank Database** in the New Blank Database section of the *Getting Started with Microsoft Office Access* window. Click **Browse**, navigate to the Your Name Access Production folder, type **chap2_pe1_bookstore_solution.accdb**, and click **OK**. Then click **Create** in the Blank Database section of the *Getting Started with Microsoft Office Access* window.

b. Create a new table by entering data into what will become the Author table. Enter the following data.

Field1	Field2	Field3
11	Benchloss	Michael R.
12	Turow	Scott
13	Rice	Anne
14	King	Stephen
15	Connelly	Michael
16	Rice	Luanne

c. Click **Save** on the Quick Access Toolbar. Type **Author** in the Save As dialog box and click **OK**.

d. Right-click the **Author table** under All Tables in the Navigation Pane and select **Design View**. Access will automatically create a primary key; however, it is not the correct field for the primary key.

e. Click the row selector for the second row (Field1) and click **Primary Key** in the Tools group on the Design tab.

f. Check the properties of **Field1** to ensure that the *Indexed* property has been set to **Yes (No Duplicates)**, which is appropriate for a primary key. Select *Field1* and type **AuthorID** to rename the field, type **Author ID** as the caption, and select **Long Integer** as the field size.

g. Rename *Field2* as **LastName**, type **Author's Last Name** as the caption, and type **20** as the field size. Rename *Field3* as **FirstName**, type **Author's First Name** as the caption, and type **15** as the field size.

h. Click the **ID field row selector** to select the row and press **Delete** Click **Yes**.

i. Click **Save** on the Quick Access toolbar to save the design changes. It is safe to ignore the lost data warning because you did shorten the field sizes.

j. Click the **External Data tab** and click **Import Excel Spreadsheet** in the Import Group to launch the Get External Data Wizard – Get External Spreadsheet Wizard. Select the **Import the source data into a new table in the current database option**, click **Browse**, and go to your Exploring Access folder. Select the *chap2_pe1_bookstore.xlsx* workbook and click **OK**. This workbook contains two worksheets.

k. Select the **Publishers worksheet**. Use the **PubID** field as the primary key. Set the *Indexed Field Options* property box to **Yes (No Duplicates)**. In the next wizard screen, select the **PubID** as your primary key. Name the table **Publishers**. Do not save the import steps.

...continued on Next Page

l. Repeat the Import Wizard to import the **Books worksheet** from the same file into the Access database as a table named **Books**. Set the *Indexed Field Options* property box for the ISBN to **Yes (No Duplicates)**. Set the **ISBN** as the primary field. Do not save the import steps.

m. Open the **Books table** in Design view. Make sure the **PubID** field is selected, click in the *Field Size* property, box and type **2**. Change the **ISBN** *Field size* property to **15**. Change the **Price** field *Format* property to **Currency**. Change the **AuthorCode** field *Field Size* property to **Long Integer** to create the relationship later. Click **Save** on the Quick Access toolbar to save the design changes to the **Books table**.

n. Open the **Publishers table** in Design view. Make sure the **PubID** field is selected, click in the *Field Size* property box and type **2**, and click in the *Caption* property box and type **Publisher's ID**. For each of the following fields, click in the *Field Size* property box and type **50**: **PubName, PubAddress**, and **PubCity** fields. Set the *Field Size* property for **PubState** field to **2**. Change the *Pub Address* field name to **PubAddress** and change the *Pub ZIP* field name to **PubZIP** (without the spaces to be consistent with the other field names). Click **Save** on the Quick Access Toolbar to save the design changes to the **Publishers table**. Close all open tables.

o. Click the **Database Tools tab** and click **Relationships** in the Show/Hide group. Double-click each table name to add it to the Relationship window. Click and drag the **AuthorID** field from the **Author table** to the **AuthorCode** field in the **Books table**. Click the **Enforce Referential Integrity check box** in the Create Relationships dialog box. Then click **Create** to create a one-to-many relationship between the Author and Books tables.

p. Click and drag the **PubID** field from the **Publishers table** to the **PubID** field in the **Books table**. Click the three check boxes in the Create Relationships dialog box and click **Create** to establish a one-to-many relationship between the Publishers and Books tables.

q. Click **Save** on the Quick Access Toolbar to save the changes to the Relationship window. Press **PrintScreen** to capture a screenshot. Nothing seems to happen because the screenshot is saved to the Clipboard. Launch Microsoft Word. Type **your name and section number** and press **Enter**. Paste the screenshot into the Word file, save the file as **chap2_pe1_bookstore_solution.docx**, and print it. Close Word. The Access file should still be open.

r. Close the Relationship window. Click the **Office Button,** select **Manage**, and then select **Back Up Database**. Name the backup **chap2_pe1_bookstore_solution_backup.accdb**. Close the database.

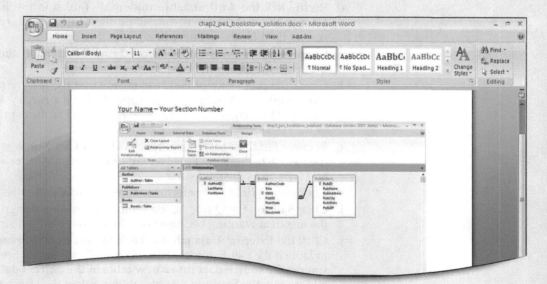

Figure 45 Word Screen Showing Capture of the Access Relationship Window

...continued on Next Page

2 Martha's Vineyard Bookstore— Querying

Your mother's friend is thrilled with the work that you have completed on the bookstore's database. She has received additional stock and asks you to update the file with the new information. Once updated she wants you to provide a printout of all of the books in stock that were published by Simon & Shuster. **You must work Exercise 1 before you can start this one.** This project follows the same set of skills as used in Hands-On exercise 3 in this chapter. If you have problems, reread the detailed directions presented in the chapter. Refer to Figure 46 as you complete your work.

a. Use Windows to copy *chap2_pe1_bookstore_solution.accdb*. Rename the copied database as **chap2_pe2_bookstore_solution.accdb**. Open *chap2_pe2_bookstore_solution*. Click **Options** in the Security Warning bar, click **Enable this content** in the Microsoft Office Security Options dialog box, and click **OK.**

b. Double-click the **Author table** in the All Tables pane to open the table in Datasheet view. Locate the new record indicator (the one with the * in the row selector) and click the first field. Enter data for the new record using **17** as Author ID and **your name** as the first and last names. Press **Enter.**

c. Open the **Books table** and click the **New (blank) record command.** Type **17** in the AuthorCode field, **Computer Wisdom** in the Title field, **0-684-80415-5** in the ISBN field, **KN** in the PubID field, **2006** in the PubDate field, **23.50** in the Price field, and **75** in the StockAmt field. Press **Enter.**

d. Click the **Create tab** and click **Query Wizard** in the Other group. Choose the **Simple Query Wizard**. From the **Author table** select the Author's **LastName** and **FirstName** fields. From the **Books table** select **Title**. Select the **PubName** field from the **Publishers table**. Name the query **Your Name Publishers, Books, and Authors**.

e. Open the query in Design view. Click in the criteria row of the PubName field. Type Knopf to create a criterion to limit the output to only books published by **Knopf**. Click **Run** in the Results group on the Design tab.

f. Return to Design view. Click the Sort row in the **LastName** field and select **Ascending**.

g. Move your mouse over the top of the **Title** field until the mouse pointer shape changes to a bold down arrow and then click. With the Title column selected, click and drag it to the left of the **LastName** field. Click the Sort row in the **Title** field and select **Ascending**. You will see sort commands on both the Title and LastName fields.

h. Click **Run** in the Results group on the Design tab. Save the query. Click the **Office Button**, select **Print**, and select **Quick Print**.

i. Click the **Office Button**, select **Manage**, and then select **Compact and Repair Database**.

...continued on Next Page

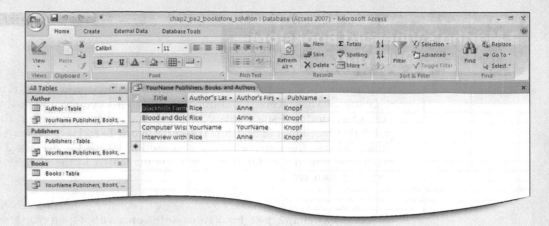

Figure 46 Sorted Query Results

3 Combs Insurance

The Comb's Insurance Company offers a full range of insurance services in four locations: Miami, Boston, Chicago, and Atlanta. Until now, they have stored all of the firm's Human Resource data in Excel spreadsheets. These files contain information on employee performance, salary, and education. Some of the files contain information on each of the company's job classifications, including education requirements and the salary range for that position. The firm is converting from Excel to Access to store this important data. There already is a database file containing two of the tables. You need to import the data for the third table from Excel. Once imported, you will need to modify field properties and connect the new table to the rest of the database. The Human Resources vice president is concerned that the Atlanta office ignores the salary guidelines published by the home office. He asks that you create a query to investigate the salary practices of the Atlanta office. This project follows the same set of skills as used in Hands-On Exercises 2 and 3 in this chapter. If you have problems, reread the detailed directions presented in the chapter. Refer to Figure 47 as you complete your work.

a. Copy the *chap2_pe3_insurance.accdb* file and rename it **chap2_pe3_insurance_solution**. Open the *chap2_pe3_insurance_solution* database, then open and examine the data stored in the **Location** and **Titles** tables. Become familiar with the field names and the type of information stored in each table. Pay particular attention to the number of different Position titles.

b. Click the **External Data tab** and click **Import Excel Spreadsheet** in the Import group to import the *chap2_pe3_employees.xlsx* file. Select the **Employees worksheet** and click the **First Row Contains Column Headings check box**. Set the *Indexed Field Options box* for the **EmployeeID** field to **Yes (No Duplicates)**. In the next wizard screen, select the **EmployeeID** as your primary key. Name the table **Employees.**

c. Open the **Employees table** in Design view. In the top of the design window position the insertion point on the **Location ID** field. Locate the *Field Size property* in the lower portion of the table Design view window and change the Field Size for the *Location ID* to **3**. Click in the *Caption* property box and type **Location ID**. In the top of the Design view

...continued on Next Page

window, position the insertion point on the **TitleID** field. Click in the *Field Size* property box in the lower portion of the table Design view window and type **3**. Click in the *Caption* property box and type **Title ID**. Save the design changes.

d. Switch the **Employees table** to the Datasheet view and examine the data. Click any record in the Title ID field and click **Descending** in the Sort & Filter group on the Home tab. How many different position titles are in the table? Does this match the number in the Titles table?

e. Locate the new record row, the one with the * in the row selector box. Click the first field. Add yourself as a new record. Your EmployeeID is **27201**. You are a **Trainee** (T03) in the **Atlanta** (L01) office earning **$27,350**, and your performance rating is **Good**. Press **Enter**.

f. Open the **Titles table** in Datasheet view and add the missing title. The *TitleID* is **T04**, the *Title* is **Senior Account Rep**. The rest of the record is **A marketing position requiring a technical background and at least three years of experience.** It requires a **Four year degree**. The minimum salary is **$45,000**. The maximum is **$75,000**. Do not type the dollar sign or comma as you enter the salary data. Close all open tables.

g. Click **Relationships** in the Show/Hide group on the Database Tools tab. Add the three tables to the Relationship window by double-clicking them one at a time (You may have to click the Show Table button to bring up the Show Table dialog box.) Close the Add Table dialog box.

h. Click the **LocationID** in the Location table and drag it to the **LocationID** in the Employees table. Drop it. In the Relationship dialog box click the **Enforce referential integrity check box**. Click the **TitleID** in the **Titles** table and drag it to the **TitleID** in the **Employees** table and drop it. In the Relationship dialog box, click the **Enforce Referential Integrity check box**. Save the changes to the relationships and close the Relationship window.

i. Click **Query Wizard** in the Other group on the Create tab. In the first screen of the Query Wizard, select **Simple Query Wizard**. Select **Table: Location** in the Tables/Queries list. Double-click **Location** to move it to the *Selected Fields* list. Select the **Employees table** in the Tables/Queries list. Double-click **LastName, FirstName,** and **Salary**. Select the **Titles** table in the Tables/Queries list. Double-click **MinimumSalary** and **MaximumSalary**. Click **Next**. Select the **Detail (shows every field of every record)** option and click **Next**. Type **Your Name Atlanta** as the query title and click **Finish**.

j. Open the **Your Name Atlanta query** in Design view. Click in the criteria row in the Location field. Type **Atlanta**. Click **Run** in the Results group on the Design tab. Check to ensure that the results display only Atlanta employees. Save and close the query.

k. Right-click the **Your Name Atlanta query** in the Navigation pane and select **Copy**. Right-click a white space in the All Objects pane and select **Paste**. In the Paste As window type **Your Name Boston** for the query name. Click OK.

l. Open the **Your Name Boston query** in Design view. Click in the criteria row in the Location field. Type **Boston**. Click **Run** in the Results group on the Design Tab. Check to ensure that the results display only Boston employees. Save and close the query.

m. Open the **Your Name Atlanta** query and the **Your Name Boston** query. *Your screen should appear similar to Figure 47*. Print both queries.

n. Click the **Office Button**, select **Manage**, and then select **Compact and Repair Database**.

...continued on Next Page

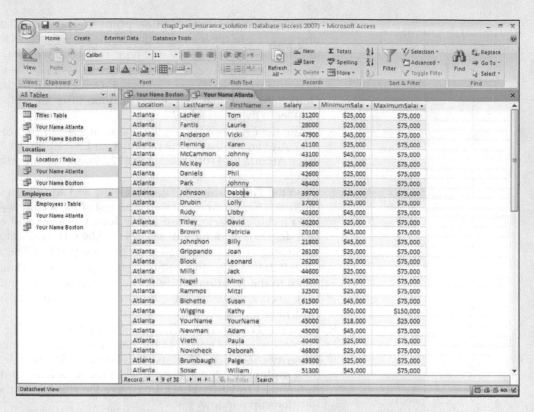

Figure 47 Atlanta Query Results

4 Coffee Service Company

The Coffee Service Company provides high-quality coffee, tea, snacks, and paper products to its customers. Most of the customers are offices in the area: IT firms, insurance offices, financial services. Coffee Service employees go to the customer location and restock the coffee, tea, and snacks supplied daily. A few accounts elect to pick up the merchandise at the Coffee Service Office. You have been asked to help convert the Excel files to an Access database. Once the database is set up, you need to use queries to help the owner do some market analysis. This project follows the same set of skills as used in Hands-On Exercises 2 and 3 in this chapter. The instructions are less detailed to give you a chance to practice your skills. If you have problems, reread the detailed directions presented in the chapter. Refer to Figure 48 as you complete your work.

a. Copy the *chap2_pe4_coffee.accdb* file. Rename the copy **chap2_pe4_coffee_solution. accdb**. Open the copied file, then open, enable the content, and examine the data stored in the tables. Become familiar with the field names and the type of information stored in each table.

b. Click the **External Data tab** and click **Import Excel Spreadsheet** in the Import group. Select the **Import the source data into a new table in the current database** option. Click **Browse**, select the *chap2_pe4_products.xlsx* workbook, and click **Open** then **OK**. Select the **Products worksheet** and click **Next**. Click the **First Row Contains Column Headings check box** and then click **Next**. Click the **Indexed property drop-down arrow** and select to **Yes** (No Duplicates). Make sure the ProductID field is active. Click **Next**. Click the **Choose my own primary** key **option** and select the **ProductID**. Click **Next**, type **Products** as the table name, and then click **Finish**.

c. Open the **Products table** in Design view. In the top of the design grid, click the **ProductID** field to select it. In the bottom portion of the window change the *Field size* property to **Long Integer**. Click in the *Caption* property box and type **Product ID**. Save the changes to the Products table. Close the Products table.

...continued on Next Page

d. Click the **Database Tools tab** and then click **Relationships** in the Show/Hide group. Click **Show Table** to open the Show Table dialog box. Double-click the **Products table** to add it to the Relationships window, if it is not already shown. Close the Show Table dialog box.

e. Click the **ProductID** in the **Products table** and drag and drop it on the **ProductID** in the **Order Details table**. The Edit Relationships dialog box opens. Click the **Enforce Referential Integrity check box**. Click **Create**. Save the changes to the Relationship window and close it.

f. Open the **Sales Reps table** and replace YourName in the *FirstName* and *LastName* fields with **YourName**.

g. Launch the **Query Wizard** in the Other group on the Create tab. Create a **Simple Select Query**. Select the **Sales Reps table** in the Tables/Queries list. Double-click the **LastName** and **FirstName** fields to move them to the Selected Fields list. Select the **Order Details table** in the Tables/Queries list. Double-click the **Quantity** field to move it to the query. Select the **Customers table** and double-click the **CustomerName** field. Select the **Products table** in the Tables/Queries list. Double-click the **ProductName**, **RefrigerationNeeded**, and **YearIntroduced** fields to move them to the query. This is a detail query. Name the query **Product Introduction**.

h. Open the **Product Information query** in Design view. Click in the sort row in the **YearIntroduced** field and select **Ascending**. Click the sort row of the **ProductName** field and select **Ascending**.

i. Click the criteria row in the LastName field and type **Your Last Name**. Click the criteria row in the FirstName field and type **YourName**. Click the criteria row in the YearIntroduced field and type **2004**. Click into the or row (the next row down) and type **2005**. Reenter your first and last name in the or criteria row for the FirstName and LastName fields. This establishes criteria so that only sales by you on products introduced in 2004 and 2005 display.

j. Click the **Design tab** and click **Run** in the Results group. Save the design changes to the query and close it. Right-click the query name in the Navigation pane and select **Rename**. Rename the query **2004–5 Product Introduction by YourName**. Print the query results.

k. Click the **Office Button**, select **Manage**, and then select **Compact and Repair Database**.

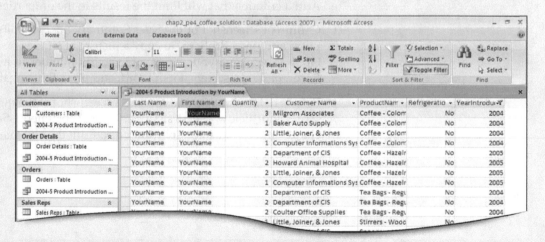

Figure 48 Sorted Product Introduction Query Results

You are an intern in a large, independent real estate firm that specializes in home sales. A database contains all of the information on the properties marketed by your firm. Most real estate transactions involve two agents—one representing the seller (the listing agent) and the other the buyer (the selling agent). The firm owner has asked that you examine the records of recent listings (real estate is listed when the home owner signs a contract with an agent that offers the property for sale) and sort them by subdivision (neighborhood) and the listing agent's name. The results need to include only the sold properties and be sorted by subdivision and the listing agent's last name. Refer to Figure 49 as you complete your work.

a. Locate the file named *chap2_mid1_realestate.accdb*; copy it to your working folder and rename it **chap2_mid1_realestate_solution.accdb**. Open the file and enable the content. Open the **Agents table.** Find and replace *Kia Hart*'s name with your name. Close the **Agents** table.

b. Create a detail query. You need the following fields: **LastName, FirstName, DateListed, DateSold, ListPrice, SellingAgent**, and **Subdivision**. Name the query **YourName Sold Property by Subdivision and Agent**. Run the query and examine the number of records.

c. In Design view enter the criteria that will remove all of the properties from the Water Valley Subdivision. Run the query and examine the number of records. It should be a smaller number than in Step b.

d. Rearrange the fields in the query so that the Subdivision field is in the leftmost column and the LastName field is the second from the left. Add the appropriate sort commands to the design grid to sort first by subdivision and then by LastName.

e. Add a criterion that will limit the results to the properties sold after October 31, 2008.

f. Capture a screenshot of the Sales Summary query results. Have it open on your computer and press **PrnScrn**. to copy a picture of what is on the monitor to the clipboard. Open Word, type your name and section number in a new blank document, press **Enter**, paste the screenshot in Word, and press **Enter** again.

g. Return to Design view and capture a screenshot of the query in Design view. Paste this screenshot below the first in the Word document. Save the Word document as **chap2_mid1_realestate_solution.docx**. Print the document.

...continued on Next Page

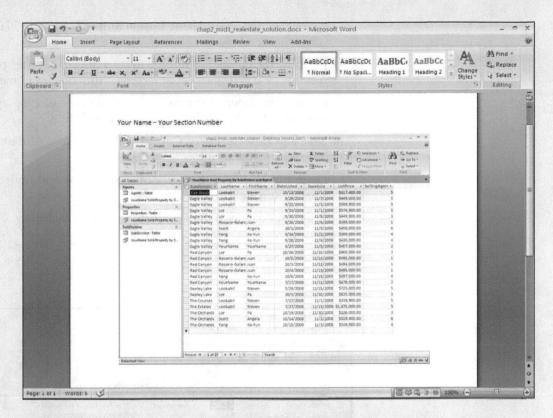

Figure 49 Sorted Product Introduction Query Results

2 Importing Excel Data, Creating, and Sorting a Query

The Prestige Hotel chain caters to upscale business travelers and provides state-of-the-art conference, meeting, and reception facilities. It prides itself on its international, four-star cuisines. Last year, it began a member rewards club to help the marketing department track the purchasing patterns of their most loyal customers. All of the hotel transactions are stored in the database. Your task is to help the manager of the Boston hotel identify the customers who used suites last year and who had more than two persons in their party. Refer to Figure 50 as you complete your work.

a. Copy the *chap2_mid2_memrewards.accdb* database and name the copy **chap2_mid2_ memrewards_solution.accdb.** Open and tour the newly copied file. Gain an understanding of the relationships and the data contained in the different tables. Specifically look for the tables and fields containing the information you need: dates of stays in Boston suites, the member's name, and the number in the party.

b. Import the Excel file *chap2_mid2_location.xlsx* into your database as a new table. Name the table as **Location.** Use the LocationID field as the primary key. Set the field size to Double.

c. Establish a relationship between the LocationID field in the **Location table** and the Location field in the **Orders table**. Enforce referential integrity.

d. Open the **Members table** and find Fred White's name. Replace Fred's name with your own first and last name. Now find *Karen Korte*'s name and replace it with your name.

e. Create a query that contains the fields you identified in Step a. Set a condition to limit the output to Boston, service from August–December 2007, and private parties greater than 2. Run the query and **sort** the results in descending order by the Service Date.

...continued on Next Page

Name the query **Your Name Boston Suites**. See Figure 50 if you need help figuring out which fields to select.

f. Examine the number of records in the status bar at the bottom of the query. It should display 23. If your number of records is different, examine the criteria.

g. Change the order of the query fields so that they display as **FirstName**, **LastName**, **ServiceDate**, **City**, **NoInParty**, and **ServiceName**.

h. Save and close the query. Copy it and in the Paste As dialog box, name the new query **YourName Miami Suites**.

i. Open the Miami Suites query in Design view and replace the Boston criterion with Miami. Run and save the changes.

j. Print your queries if directed to do so by your instructor. Compact, repair, and back up your file.

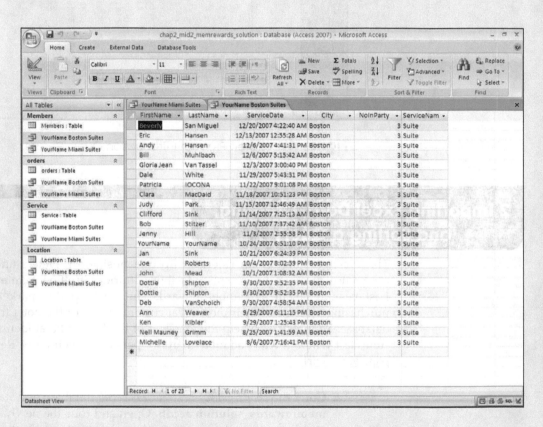

Figure 50 Boston Query Results

...continued on Next Page

3 Creating and Using Queries

Northwind Traders is a small, international, specialty food company. It sells products in eight different divisions: Beverages, Confections (candy), Condiments, Dairy Products, Grains and Cereals, Meat and Poultry, Produce, and Seafood. Although most of its customers are restaurants and gourmet food shops, it has a few retail customers, too. It purchases the merchandise from a variety of suppliers. All of the order information is stored in the company's database. The marketing department uses this database to monitor and maintain sales records. You are the marketing manager. Your task is to identify which customers purchase Chai (tea) and Chang (Chinese Beer) in 2007. It would be valuable for you to discover the order quantities and the countries where the orders ship. After you complete the query, you will copy it and add the salesperson's name field to the copy. Refer to Figure 51 as you complete your work.

a. Copy the *chap2_mid3_traders.accdb* file; rename the copy **chap2_mid3_traders_solution.accdb**. Open the newly copied file and enable the content. Tour the database Relationship window to gain an understanding of the relationships and the data contained in the different tables. As you tour, specifically look for the tables and fields containing the information you need, that is, orders shipped in **2007** for the **beverages Chai** and **Chang**, the quantities purchased, the date the order shipped, and the countries the purchases were shipped to. You are interested in all of the countries *excluding* the United States.

b. After you identify the necessary fields, create a query that includes the fields of interest. Name this query **YourName Shipping for Chai and Chang**.

c. Set the query criteria to select the records of interest—2007 orders of Chai and Chang shipped to all of the world except for the United States.

d. Sort the query results by the Company name (alphabetically) and then by the quantity ordered. (If the same company is listed twice, the largest quantity should be listed first.)

e. Print the query results. Save and close the query.

f. Copy the query and name the copy **YourName Chai and Chang Sales by Employee**.

g. Open the **Employees table** and replace *Andrew* Fuller's name with your own name.

h. Add the employee's First and Last Name fields to the newly copied query.

i. Rearrange the fields so that the employee last name field is the first in the design grid and the Employee's FirstName is the second. Sort the results by the Employee's LastName.

j. Run, save, and print the query. Compact, repair, and back up your file.

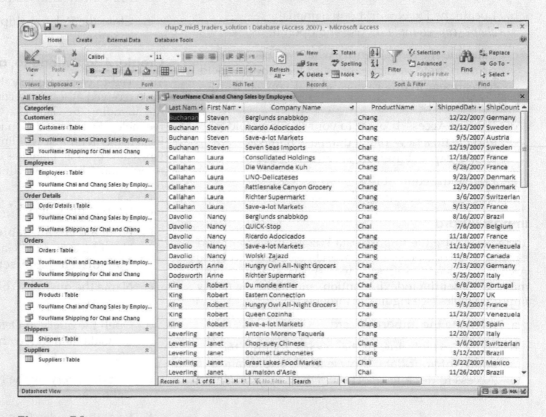

Figure 51 2007 Chai and Chang Sales by Employee

Capstone Exercise

The JC Raulston Arboretum at NC State University staff have been carefully saving their data in Excel for years. One particular workbook contains a worksheet that lists the names of all the Arboretum's "friends." This not-for-profit organization solicits contributions in the form of cash gifts, volunteer service, and "in-kind" gifts. An in-kind gift is a gift of a plant to the arboretum. Each year, one of the major fundraising events is the Gala. This is a formal event held on a delightful spring afternoon with cocktails, gourmet hors d'oeuvres, live music, and a silent auction featuring a plethora of unique plants and an eclectic array of many other distinctive items. As friends contribute service or funds to the Arboretum, another reward they receive are connoisseur plants. Connoisseur plants are rare new plants or hard-to-find old favorites, and they are part of the annual appeal and membership drive to benefit the Arboretum's many fine programs and its day-to-day operational expenses. These wonderful plants are sent to those who join the Friends of JC Raulston Arboretum at the Sponsor, Patron, Benefactor, or Philanthropist levels. The organization has grown. The files are too large to handle easily in Excel. Your task will be to begin the conversion of the files from Excel to Access.

Database File Setup

You need to open an Excel workbook that contains data on four named worksheets. Examine the data in the worksheets, paying attention to which fields will become the primary keys in each table and where those fields will appear as foreign keys in other tables in order to form the relationships.

a. Locate the Excel workbook named *chap2_cap_friends.xlsx* and open it.

b. Locate the Excel workbook named *chap2_cap_connplants.xlsx* and open it.

c. Examine the data, identify what will become the primary field in each table, and look for that field to reappear in other tables so that you can form relationships.

d. Launch Access, browse to your working folder, and create a new, blank database named **chap2_cap_arboretum_solution.accdb**.

e. Enable the content in *chap2_cap_arboretum_solution.accdb*.

Import Wizard

You need to use the Import Data Wizard twice to import each of the worksheets in the workbook from Excel into Access. You need to select the worksheets, specify the primary keys, set the indexing option, and name the newly imported tables (see Figures 12 through 18).

a. Activate the Import Wizard.

b. In the first window of the wizard, identify the source of your data. Browse to the Exploring Access folder and select the *chap2_cap_friends.xlsx* file.

c. The FriendID field will become the primary key. Set its indexing option to **Yes (No Duplicates)**.

d. When prompted, select the **FriendID** as the primary key.

e. Name the table **Friends**.

f. Import the *chap2_cap_connoisseur.xlsx* file, set the ID field as the primary key, and name the table as **Connoisseur**.

g. In Datasheet view, examine the newly imported tables.

Create Relationships

You need to create the relationship between the tables. Identify the primary fields in each table and, using the Relationships window, connect them with their foreign key counterparts in other tables. Enforce referential integrity.

a. Close any open tables and then display the Relationships window.

b. Add the two tables to the Relationship window with the Show Table dialog box. Then, close the Show Tables dialog box.

c. Drag the FriendID from the **Friends table** to the FriendNumber field in the **Connoisseur table**. Enforce Referential Integrity.

d. Print the Relationships window.

e. Close the Relationship window and save your changes.

Create, Add Criteria to, and Sort a Query

You need to create a query that identifies the people who have received at least one connoisseur plant and who are not attending the Gala. Use the Query Wizard to identify the tables, Friends and Connoisseur, and fields necessary. Establish criteria that will limit the results to only records where one or more plant has been sent and there is no Gala reservation. This query will need to be sorted by the last name field.

a. Launch the Query Wizard.

b. From the **Friends table** select the NameFirst, NameLast, and the Gala fields. From the **Connoisseur table**, select the SendPlant field.

c. Name the query as **YourName Gala No, Conn Plant Yes**.

d. Open the query in Design view and set criteria in the Gala field to **No** and in the SentPlants field to **>0**.

e. Sort the query by the NameLast field in alphabetical order.

f. Print the results. Compact, repair, and back up the file.

Mini Cases

Use the rubric following the case as a guide to evaluate your work, but keep in mind that your instructor may impose additional grading criteria or use a different standard to judge your work.

Employee Performance Review

GENERAL CASE

The chap2_mc1_insurance.accdb file contains data from a large insurance agency. Copy the *chap2_mc1_insurance.accdb* file, name it **chap2_mc1_insurance_solution.accdb**, and open the copied file. Use the skills from this chapter to perform several tasks. The firm's employee policy states that an employee needs to maintain a performance rating of good or excellent to maintain employment. If an employee receives an average or poor performance rating, she receives a letter reminding her of this policy and advising her to improve or suffer the consequences. You are the manager of the Atlanta office. You need to identify the employees who need a letter of reprimand. Once the query has been completed, it will be used to generate a form letter to be sent to the employees. You need to include fields for the letter that contain the employees' first and last names, their position titles, and their salary. You do not need to write the letter, only assemble the data for the letter to be written. The results need to be alphabetized by the employee's names. As you work, consider the order that the fields will need to be used in the letter and order the query fields accordingly.

Performance Elements	Exceeds Expectations	Meets Expectations	Below Expectations
Create query	All necessary and no unneeded fields included.	All necessary fields included but also unnecessary fields.	Not all necessary fields were included in the query.
Establish criteria	The query results correctly identified and selected records.	The query results correctly identified and selected records.	Incorrect criteria specifications.
Sorting	Query fields were logically ordered and appropriately sorted.	Query fields were appropriately sorted but not logically ordered.	Both the order and the sort were incorrect.
Query name	The query name described the content.	The query name partially described the content.	The query employed the default name.

Database Administrator Position

RESEARCH CASE

This chapter introduced you to the idea that employees who administer and manage databases receive high pay, but you have much more to explore. Use the Internet to search for information about database management. One useful site is published by the federal government's Bureau of Labor Statistics. It compiles an Occupational Outlook Handbook describing various positions, the type of working environment, the education necessity, salary information, and the projected growth. The Web site is **http://www.bls.gov/oco.** Your challenge is to investigate the position of Database Administrator. Use the BLS Web site and at least one other source. Write your instructor a memo describing this position. Use a memo template in Word, your most professional writing style, and specify the data sources.

Performance Elements	Exceeds Expectations	Meets Expectations	Below Expectations
Use online resources	Appropriate articles located and memo indicates comprehension.	Appropriate articles located but memo did not demonstrate comprehension.	Articles not found.
Extract useful information from the resources	Most major components of the position described accurately.	Many elements of the position described.	Many elements of the position missing or the description incomprehensible.
Summarize and communicate	Memo clearly written and free of misspellings.	Memo text indicates some understanding but also weaknesses.	Memo missing or incomprehensible.
Esthetics	Memo template correctly employed.	Template employed but signed in the wrong place or improperly used.	Memo missing or incomprehensible.

May and Beverage Queries

DISASTER RECOVERY

A co-worker called you into his office and explained that he was having difficulty with Access 2007 and asked you to look at his work. Copy the *chap2_mc3_traders.accdb* file to your working storage folder, name it **chap2_mc3_traders_solution.accdb**, and open the file. It contains two queries, May 2007 Orders of Beverages and Confections and 2007 Beverage Sales by Ship Country. The May 2007 Orders of Beverages and Confections query is supposed to only have information from May. You find other dates included in the results. Your challenge is to find and correct the error(s). The 2007 Beverage Sales by Ship Country returns no results. It needs to be ordered by country. It needs to be repaired and resorted. Print the Datasheet View of both queries.

Performance Elements	Exceeds Expectations	Meets Expectations	Below Expectations
Error identification	Correct identification and correction of all errors.	Correct identification of all errors and correction of some errors.	Errors neither located nor corrected.
May query	Correct criteria and sorted logically.	Correct criteria but inadequately sorted.	Incorrect criteria.
Beverage query	Correct criteria and sorted logically.	Correct criteria but inadequately sorted.	Incorrect criteria.

Access

Customize, Analyze, and Summarize Query Data
Creating and Using Queries to Make Decisions

bjectives

After you read this chapter you will be able to:

1. Understand the order of precedence.
2. Create a calculated field in a query.
3. Create expressions with the Expression Builder.
4. Create and edit Access functions.
5. Perform date arithmetic.
6. Create and work with data aggregates.

Hands-On Exercises

Exercises	Skills Covered
1. **CALCULATED QUERY FIELDS** **Open:** chap3_ho1-3_realestate.accdb **Save:** chap3_ho1-3_realestate_solution.accdb **Back up as:** chap3_ho1_realestate_solution.accdb	• Copy a Database and Start the Query • Select the Fields, Save, and Open the Query • Create a Calculated Field and Run the Query • Verify the Calculated Results • Recover from a Common Error
2. **EXPRESSION BUILDER, FUNCTIONS, AND DATE ARITHMETIC** **Open:** chap3_ho1-3_realestate.accdb (from Exercise 1) **Save:** chap3_ho1-3_realestate_solution.accdb (additional modifications) **Back up as:** chap3_ho2_realestate_solution.accdb	• Create a Select Query • Use the Expression Builder • Create Calculations Using Input Stored in a Different Query or Table • Edit Expressions Using the Expression Builder • Use Functions • Work with Date Arithmetic
3. **DATA AGGREGATES** **Open:** chap3_ho1-3_realestate.accdb (from Exercise 2) **Save:** chap3_ho1-3_realestate_solution.accdb (additional modifications)	• Add a Total Row • Create a Totals Query Based on a Select Query • Add Fields to the Design Grid • Add Grouping Options and Specify Summary Statistics

From *Exploring Office 2007 Volume I*, Robert T. Grauer, Michelle Hulett, Cynthia Krebs, Maurie Wigman Lockley, Keith Mulbery, and Judy Scheeren. Copyright © 2007 by Pearson Education. Published by Prentice Hall.

CASE STUDY

Replacements, Ltd.

(Replacements, Ltd exists. The data in the case file are actual data. The customer and employee information have been changed to ensure privacy. However, the inventory and sales records reflect actual transactions.)

Today is the first day in your new position as associate marketing manager at Replacements, Ltd. In preparation for your first day on the job you have spent hours browsing the Replacements Web site, www.replacements.com. There you learned that Replacements, Ltd. (located in Greensboro, N.C.) has the world's largest selection of old and new dinnerware, including china, stoneware, crystal, glassware, silver, stainless, and collectibles. Its 300,000-square-foot facilities (the size of five football fields!) house an incredible inventory of 10 million pieces in 200,000 patterns, some more than 100 years old. While interviewing for the position, you toured the show room and warehouses. You learned that Replacements provides its customers with pieces that exactly match their existing patterns of china, silver, crystal, etc. People who break a cup or accidentally drop a spoon in the disposal purchase replacement treasures.

You have been given responsibility for managing several different patterns of merchandise. You need to maintain adequate inventory levels. On the one hand you need to have merchandise available so that when a customer wishes to purchase a fork in a specific pattern, the customer service representatives can find it and box it for shipment. To accomplish this task, you need to closely monitor past sales in the various patterns in order to understand purchasing habits and product demand. On the other hand, the firm cannot afford to stock inventory of patterns no one wishes to purchase. You exchange information with the customer service representatives and monitor their performance. If you discover that one of the patterns you manage has excess inventory, you will need to direct the buyers to stop purchasing additional pieces in that pattern and encourage the customer service representatives to suggest the pattern to customers. You will determine if and when a pattern should be discounted or if an incentive program or contest should be implemented to reward the sales associates for successfully selling the overstocked merchandise.

Your Assignment

- Copy the *chap3_case_replacement.accdb* file to your production folder. Name the copy **chap3_case_replacement_solution.accdb**.
- Open the Relationships window and acquaint yourself with the tables, fields, and relationships among the tables in the database.
- You need to convert the data into useful information. To accomplish this task, you will need to create a query that identifies the revenue generated from sales in each of the patterns you manage.
- You also must determine which patterns customers purchase most often.
- Replacements encourages the customer service representatives by paying them bonuses based on the orders that they fill. You will calculate each customer service representative's total sales and calculate their bonuses. The bonus will be calculated based on ½% of the representative's total sales.
- Finally, you need to compare the inventory levels of each pattern piece with its sales volume. Careful monitoring of stock levels will prevent excessive inventory. For each item calculate the percent of the inventory level that was sold in the past month. For example, if there were 100 cups in a specific pattern in inventory at the beginning of the month and 18 of them were sold during the month, the sales-inventory ratio would be 18%. Set criteria so that the zero OnHandQuantity items are excluded from the calculation.

Customize, Analyze, and Summarize Query Data

Data Summary and Analysis

Practicing good database design discourages storing calculations as table data. Although storing calculated results in a table is not a good idea, Access *can* perform arithmetic calculations using formulae and functions much like Excel. However, the calculated results do not belong in tables. Instead, calculations needed to summarize and analyze data are found in three places: queries, forms, and reports. Professionals who use Access to develop applications within organizations have very different opinions about the most appropriate placement of calculations in Access. One group assembles and manipulates data inside a query. After you establish the calculations and criteria, the data are sent to an Access report to be cosmetically enhanced. (This is the practice that you will employ throughout the exercises in this book.) The other group does all of the calculations inside of forms and reports. This group uses fewer queries but creates far more sophisticated reports and forms.

In this section, you learn about the order of precedence and create a calculated field in a query.

Understanding the Order of Precedence

The *order of precedence* establishes the sequence by which values are calculated.

The *order of precedence* establishes the sequence by which values are calculated in an expression. Evaluate parenthetically expressed values, then exponents, multiplication and division, and, finally, addition and subtraction. Access calculates exactly what you tell it to calculate—even if your formulae are incorrect! Table 1 shows some examples of arithmetic order. You must have a solid understanding of these rules in order to "teach" the computer to generate the required output. Access, like Excel, uses the following symbols:

- Addition   +
- Subtraction   –
- Multiplication *
- Division   /
- Exponentiation ^

Creating a Calculated Field in a Query

You instruct Access to perform calculations in the Design view of the query. Create the calculated values in the first row of a blank column. You may scroll, if necessary, to find a blank column in the design grid or insert a blank column where you want

Table 1 Examples of Order of Precedence

Expression	Order to Perform Calculations	Output
= 2 + 3 * 3	Multiply first, and then add.	11
= (2 + 3) * 3	Add the values inside the parenthesis first, and then multiply.	15
= 2 + 2 ^ 3	Simplify the exponent first. $2^3 = 2*2*2$ or 8. Then add.	10
= (2 + 2) ^3	Add the parenthetical values first (2 + 2 = 4), and then raise the result to the 3rd power. $4^3 = 4*4*4$.	64
= 10/2 + 3	Divide first, and then add.	8
= 10/(2+3)	Add first to simplify the parenthetical expression, and then divide.	2
= 10 * 2 – 3 * 2	Multiply first, and then subtract.	14

the calculated value to appear. A formula used to calculate new fields from the values in existing fields is also known as an *expression*. An expression consists of a number of different items to produce the answers needed. The items used in an expression may include the following:

- Identifiers (the names of fields, controls or properties)
- Operators (arithmetic instructions about what to do with the identifiers like + or –)
- Functions (as in Excel, Access has built-in functions to perform routine calculations, like SUM or Average)
- *Constants* and values (numbers that may be used as a part of a calculation but are unlikely to change)

You may use the expression to perform calculations, retrieve a value from a field, set query criteria, verify data created, calculate fields or controls, and set grouping levels in reports. Access not only organizes and protects a firm's valuable data but also enables you to summarize, understand, and make decisions based on the data. Your value to an organization dramatically increases when you master the skills that surround expression building in Access.

Build Expressions with Correct Syntax

Enter the expression in the first row of the column. Using simple *syntax* rules you instruct the software to calculate the necessary values. You can create expressions to perform calculations using either field values or constants. You must correctly spell the field names for Access to find the appropriate values. You should assign descriptive names to the calculated fields. Access ignores spaces in calculations. The general syntax follows:

CalculatedFieldName: [InputField1] operand operator [InputField2] operand

Although this is the most appropriate format, Access enters the brackets for you if it recognizes the field name. Remember that an **operator** is a symbol, such as *, that performs some operation, such as multiplication. An **operand** is the value that is being manipulated or operated on. In calculated fields in Access, the operand is either a literal value or a field name. Figure 1 shows a calculated field named Interest. The calculated field first calculates the monthly interest rate by dividing the 3.5% (0.035) annual rate by 12. The monthly interest rate is then multiplied by the value in the Balance field to determine the amount of interest owed.

_sion is a formula
calculate new fields
the values in existing
ds.

A **constant** refers to a value that does not change.

Syntax is the set of rules by which the words and symbols of an expression are correctly combined.

Enter expression here

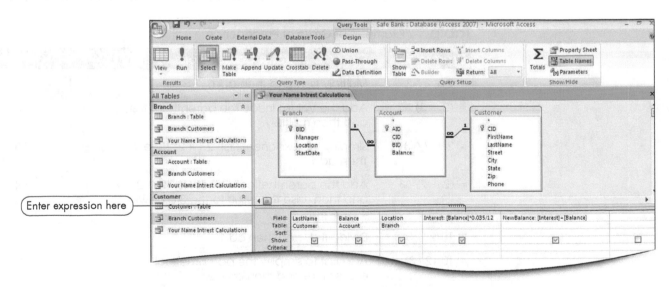

Figure 1 The Correct Location for a Calculated Query Expression

Customize, Analyze, and Summarize Query Data

To help reinforce how calculated fields work, suppose you need to calculate the revenue from a purchase order. Revenue is the name of the calculated field. The following expression generates the calculated field by multiplying the unit price by the quantity ordered:

Revenue:Price*Quantity

Access enters the brackets for you and converts the expression to the following:

Revenue: [Price]*[Quantity]

For a final example of calculated fields, suppose you need to calculate a 10% price increase on all products you sell. NewPrice is the name of the calculated field. The following expression multiplies the old price by 110%:

NewPrice:Price*1.1

Access enters the brackets for you and converts the expression to the following:

NewPrice: [Price]*1.1

When you run the query, the calculated results display in the query's Datasheet view. Using the above example, Access goes to the table(s) where the prices and order quantities are stored, extracts the current data, loads it into the query, and uses the data to perform the calculation. When you direct Access to collect fields that are stored in related tables, Access uses the "strings" that form the relationship to collect the appropriate records and deliver them to the query. For example, suppose you create a query that retrieves customers' names from the customer table and the dates that the orders were placed from the Order table. The Customers table might contain 50,000 customer records. The query will return only those customers who ordered something because the relationship integrity will limit the output to only the records of interest. After the data are assembled, you can manipulate the data in each record by entering expressions. After you run the query, you need to examine the calculated results to verify that the output is what you need. Access has the ability to process a lot of numbers very quickly. Unfortunately, Access can also return incorrectly calculated results equally quickly if the formula you create is incorrect. Remember and avoid *GIGO*—Garbage In; Garbage Out!

(GIGO—Garbage In; Garbage Out!)

Verify Calculated Results

After your query runs, look at the values of the input field and then look at the calculated results returned. Ask yourself, "Does this answer make sense?" Use a pocket calculator or the Windows calculator to perform the same calculation using the same inputs and compare the answers. Alternatively, you can use Excel to check your calculated results. Copy and paste a few records into Excel. Repeat all of the calculations and compare the answers. The Access calculated field, the calculator, and the Excel calculations should return identical results.

After verifying the calculated results, you should save the query to run the next time you need to perform the same calculations.

Save a Query Containing Calculated Fields

Saving a query does *not* save the data. It saves only your instructions about what data to select and what to do with it once it is selected. Think of a query as a set of instructions directing Access to deliver data and the form the data are to assume at delivery. Writing a query is like placing an order with a restaurant server. You may order a medium rare steak, a baked potato, and tossed salad with blue cheese dressing. Your server writes the order and any special instructions and delivers it to the kitchen. In the kitchen the cook fills the order based on your instructions. Then the server delivers the ordered food to you. The data in a database is like the raw food in the kitchen. It is stored in the freezer or refrigerator or the cupboard (the tables). Data from the query (server's order) are assembled and "cooked." The big difference is that in the restaurant, once your steak is delivered to you, it is no longer available to other diners to order. The data in a database are *never* consumed. Data can be ordered simultaneously by multiple queries in a multiple user database environment. The data physically reside in the tables and never move from their storage location. Running the query collects the field values in the records of interest. The query contains only the instructions governing how Access selects and interacts with the data. If you type over a data item in a query table view, the new value automatically replaces the old one in the table.

After you run, verify, and save the query, you can use the newly created calculated fields in subsequent calculations. You may use a calculated field as input for other calculated fields. However, you must first save the query so that the calculation's results will be available.

In the next exercise you will create calculated expressions, practice verification techniques, and generate and recover from a common error.

Hands-On Exercises

1 | Calculated Query Fields

Skills covered: 1. Copy a Database and Start the Query **2.** Select the Fields, Save, and Open the Query **3.** Create a Calculated Field and Run the Query **4.** Verify the Calculated Results **5.** Recover from a Common Error

---

Step 1 Copy a Database and Start the Query	Refer to Figure 2 as you complete Step 1.

a. Use Windows Explorer to locate the file named *chap3_ho1-3_realestate.accdb*. Copy the file to your production folder and rename the copied file as **chap3_ho1-3_realestate_solution.accdb**.

b. Open the *chap3_ho1-3_realestate_solution.accdb* file.

c. Click **Options** on the Security Warning toolbar and then click **Enable this content** in the Microsoft Office Security Options dialog box, and click **OK**.

d. Click the **Create tab** and then click **Query Wizard** in the Other group.

e. Select **Simple Query Wizard** in the New Query dialog box. Click **OK**.

The Simple Query Wizard dialog box displays so that you can specify the table(s) and fields to include in the query design.

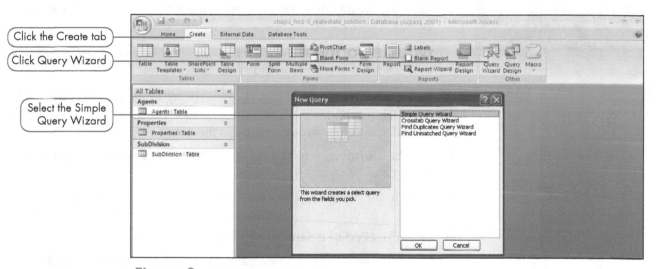

Click the Create tab
Click Query Wizard
Select the Simple Query Wizard

Figure 2 New Query Dialog Box

Step 2 Select the Fields, Save, and Open the Query	Refer to Figure 3 as you complete Step 2.

a. Click the **Tables/Queries drop-down arrow** and select **Table: Agents**. Double-click the **FirstName** and **LastName** fields in the **Available Fields list** to select them.

b. Click the **Tables/Queries drop-down arrow** and select **Table: Properties**. Double-click the following fields to select them: **DateListed, DateSold, ListPrice, SalePrice, SqFeet,** and **Sold**.

c. Compare your selected fields to those shown in Figure 3 and then click **Next**.

d. Verify that the **Detail (shows every field of every record) option** is selected in the *Would you like a detail or summary query?* screen in the Simple Query Wizard dialog box. Click **Next**.

e. Type **YourName Sale Price per SqFt** for the query title. Click **Finish**.

The results of the query appear in the Datasheet view.

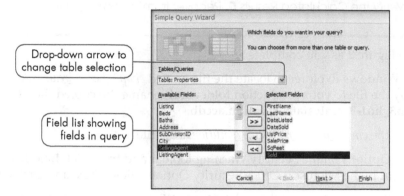

Figure 3 Select Fields for the Query

Step 3

Create a Calculated Field and Run the Query

Refer to Figure 4 as you complete Step 3.

a. Click the **Home tab** and click **View** in the View group to toggle to the Design view.

> **TROUBLESHOOTING:** If you click View and Access does not toggle to the Design view, click the View arrow and select Design View.

This query was based on two tables, so the upper half of the Design view displays the two tables, Agents and Properties. The lower portion of the Design view displays the fields currently in the query.

b. Use the horizontal scroll bar to scroll the design grid to the right until you see a blank column.

c. Click in the first row of the first blank column to position your insertion point there.

d. Type **PricePerSqFt: SalePrice/SqFeet** and press **Enter**.

This expression creates a new calculated field named PricePerSqFt by dividing the values in the SalePrice field by the values in the SqFeet field. In this calculated field, the operator is the division symbol (/), and the operands are the SalePrice and SqFeet fields. Look at Figure 4 if you need help with the syntax for the expression.

TIP Increasing Width of Columns

To increase the column width so that you can see the entire calculated field expression, double-click the vertical line in the gray area above the field names between the calculated field column and the blank column.

---

e. Right-click the field text box in the design grid that contains the PricePerSqFt calculated field. Select **Properties** from the shortcut menu. Click the **Format drop-down arrow** in the Property Sheet window and select **Currency**. Click the X to close the Property Sheet window.

f. Click the **Design tab**, if needed, and then click **Run** in the Results group.

When you run the query, Access performs all of the calculations and opens in the table view to display the results.

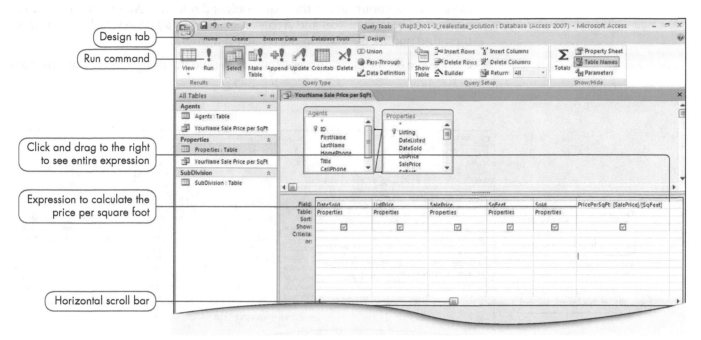

Figure 4 Expression Syntax

Step 4
Verify the Calculated Results

Refer to Figure 5 as you complete Step 4.

a. Examine the results of the calculation. Ask yourself if the numbers make sense to you.

TROUBLESHOOTING: Are you having a problem? You may wish to read Step 5 now. Often a typo entered in a calculated field will result in a parameter box opening. Step 5 discusses how to recover from this error.

Look at the fourth record. The sale price is $155,000, and the number of square feet is 1,552. You can probably verify these results by dividing the values in your head. The result is about $100. The PricePerSqFt field in Figure 5 displays $99.87.

b. Use the row selectors to select the first four records by clicking and dragging. After you select the four records, right-click them and select **Copy** from the shortcut menu.

c. Launch Excel, activate **cell A1** of a blank workbook, and paste the Access records into Excel.

The field names appear in the first row, and the four records appear in the next four rows. The fields are located in Columns A–I. The calculated field results are pasted in Column I as values rather than as a formula.

TROUBLESHOOTING: If you see pound signs (#####) instead of numbers in an Excel column, that means the column is too narrow to display the values. Position the mouse pointer on the vertical line between the column letters, such as between D and E, and double-click the vertical line to increase the width of column D.

d. In **cell J2**, type **=F2/G2** and press **Enter**.

The formula divides the sale price by the square feet. Compare the results in the I and J columns. The numbers should be the same. If the numbers are the same, close Excel without saving the workbook and return to Access. If the values differ, look at both the Excel and Access formulae. Determine which is correct and then find and fix the error in the incorrect formula.

e. Click **Save** on the Quick Access Toolbar to save the design modifications made to the *Your_Name Sale Price per SqFt* query.

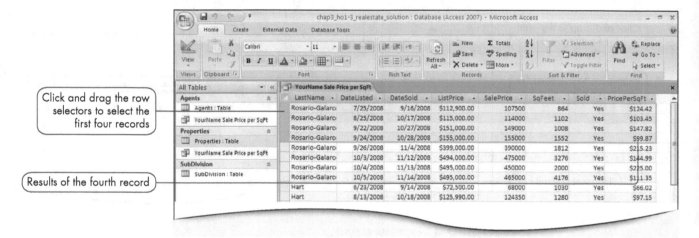

Figure 5 Examine Calculated Results

Refer to Figure 6 as you complete Step 5.

a. In the *YourName Sale Price per SqFt query*, click **View** in the Views group to switch to Design view. Scroll to the first empty column and click in the first row to position the insertion point.

Because Access users occasionally make a typing error when creating an expression, it is useful to learn how to recover from this type of error. You will intentionally misspell a field name used in a calculation by typing the field name SalePrice as SaleSPrice and SqFeet as SqRFeet.

b. Type **WrongPricePerSqFt: SaleSPrice/SqRFeet**.

Be sure that you added the extra *S* and *R* to the field names. You are making intentional errors to learn how Access will respond.

c. Click the **Design tab** and click **Run** in the Results group.

You should see the Enter Parameter Value dialog box. Examine the dialog box. What is it asking you to do? The dialog box indicates that Access could not find a value for SaleSPrice in the first record. This error occurs because the table does not contain a SaleSPrice field. Because Access is asking you to supply a value, you will type in a value.

TROUBLESHOOTING: You should carefully read the contents of a warning box or a parameter box when one appears. Access tries to tell you what is wrong. As your experience builds, the messages will become clearer to you.

d. Type **100000** in the parameter box. Before you click OK, try to anticipate what the software will do next. You intentionally misspelled *two* field names. Press **Enter** or click **OK**.

Another Enter Parameter Value dialog box displays, asking that you supply a value for SqRFeet. This error occurs because the table does not contain a SqRFeet field.

e. Type **1000** and press **Enter**.

The query has the necessary information to run and returns the results in Datasheet view.

f. Scroll right and examine the results of the calculation for WrongPricePerSqFt.

All of the records show 100. This result occurs because you entered the values 100000 and 1000, respectively, in the Enter Parameter Value dialog boxes, which used those literal values in the expression. The result of 100 appears for all records.

g. Return to Design view and correct the errors in the WrongPricePerSqFt field by changing the formula to **WrongPricePerSqFt: SalePrice/SqFeet**.

h. Right-click the field text box in the design grid that contains the WrongPricePerSqFt calculated field. Select **Properties** from the shortcut menu. Click the **Format drop-down arrow** in the Property Sheet window and select **Currency**. Click the X to close the Property Sheet window.

i. Run and save the query again.

The calculated values in the last two columns should be the same.

j. Click the **Office Button**, select **Manage**, and then select **Backup Database**. Enter the filename **chap3_ho1_realestate_solution** (note *ho1* instead of *ho1-3*) and click **Save**.

You just created a backup of the database after completing the first hands-on exercise. The original database *chap3_ho1-3_realestate_solution* remains onscreen. If you ruin the original database as you complete the second hands-on exercise, you can use the backup file you just created.

k. Close the file and exit Access if you do not want to continue with the next exercise at this time.

TIP   Learning Software

Following step-by-step instructions is a way to begin learning application software. If you want to become proficient in software, you must learn how to recover from errors. As you work through the rest of the Hands-On Exercises in this book, follow the instructions as presented and save your work. Then go back a few steps and make an intentional error just to see how Access responds. Read the error messages (if any) and learn from your mistakes in a safe environment.

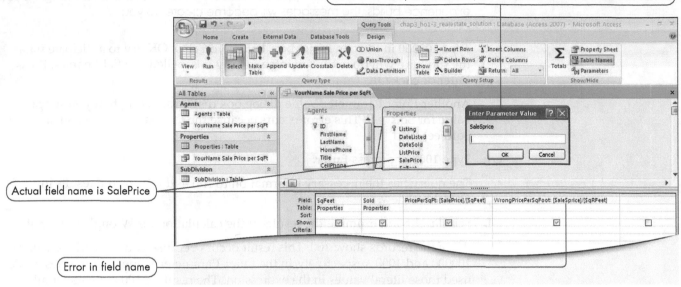

Figure 6 Error Recovery

Expression Builder

Before people used electronic database programs, decision makers were hampered because they could not find valid, timely, and accurate data to base decisions on. In today's world data remains a problem for decision makers; however, the nature of the problem has changed. The data are current, accurate, and authentic. But because so much data are available, managers can become overwhelmed. In the last hands-on exercise, you calculated a price per square foot for real estate listings. That simple calculation can assist a decision maker to ascribe value to a property. It is a useful way to examine a complex transaction in a simplified fashion. Access enables you to calculate the value, but typing (and spelling correctly) all of those field names in the calculation is a lot of work. Fortunately, you can use the *Expression Builder* as an alternative, easier method to perform calculations. When you create an expression in the field text box, you must scroll to see the entire expression. The Expression Builder's size permits you to see even long, complex formulae and functions in their entirety.

The *Expression Builder* is a tool to help you create a formula that performs calculations easily.

In this section, you learn how to create expressions with the Expression Builder. You then learn how to create and edit functions. Finally, you perform date arithmetic.

Creating Expressions with the Expression Builder

You can use the Expression Builder in a query design grid to assist you in properly crafting the appropriate syntax. It is a blend of a calculator and a spreadsheet. You also can use the Expression Builder in other Access objects where calculations are needed. These objects include the control properties in forms and reports and table field properties. The Expression Builder requires some practice for you to learn how to use it effectively. Once you master the Expression Builder, you may use it to create a formula from scratch, or you can use it to select some pre-built expressions or functions. Additionally, the Expression Builder enables you to include useful items such as page numbers and the current date or time.

(The Expression Builder . . . is a blend of a calculator and a spreadsheet.)

Access automatically assigns placeholder names to all expressions created with the Expression Builder as Expr1, Expr2, Expr3. You need to develop the habit of running the query, verifying the calculation results and then returning to the design grid and replacing Exp1 with a descriptive field name. Good work habits will save you hours and hours when you return to your calculations in six weeks or six months.

After you save the query, the newly calculated field and descriptively named field are available to use in subsequent calculations.

Launch the Expression Builder

Open the query in Design view and display the Design tab. The Builder command is found in the Query Setup group. Figure 7 shows the components of the Expression Builder. The middle column contains a list of fields available in the current query. Occasionally, you may need to use a field as a calculation input that is not contained in the current query. Everything in the database is available to you through the builder. If you click the plus sign to the right of the Tables or Queries folder in the left column, the folder will open and reveal the other tables and fields in the database. This is a wonderful feature for someone who forgot to include a needed field in a query.

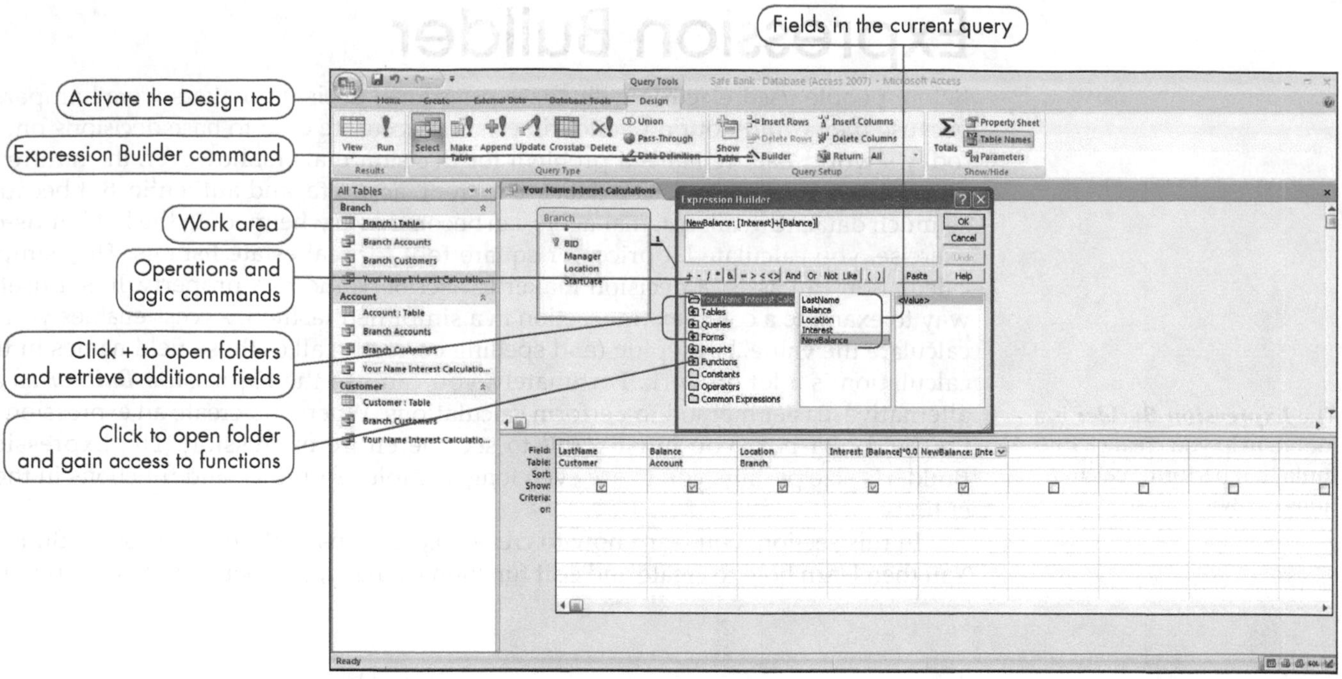
Fields in the current query
Activate the Design tab
Expression Builder command
Work area
Operations and logic commands
Click + to open folders and retrieve additional fields
Click to open folder and gain access to functions

Figure 7 Expression Builder

The work area is the large rectangle at the top of the dialog box. Just as in Excel, an Access expression created using the Expression Builder begins with an equal sign. You may either type it or click the equal sign in the logic and operands area under the work area. When you need a field entered, find the field (look first in the middle column) and double-click it to add it to the expression. The field is added with the syntactically appropriate brackets inserted. Type or click operands (+, –, *, /) as needed and add additional fields to complete the expression. When you finish the expression, click OK.

Creating and Editing Access Functions

An ***Access function*** performs an operation using input supplied as arguments and returns a value.

An ***argument*** is a necessary input component required to produce the output for a function.

An *Access function* calculates commonly used expressions using "canned" instructions and input values to return a calculated value. You must know the function's name and provide it arguments in order to use it. Access functions work much like Excel functions. You identify the function by its name (e.g., Average, Sum, PMT) and enter the required ***arguments***—what input values should be averaged, added, or calculated as a payment. They are grouped into categories of similar functions: Math, Financial, Date/Time, General, etc.

Calculate Payments with the PMT Function

The ***PMT function*** calculates a periodic loan payment given a constant interest rate, term, and original value.

Figure 8 shows the ***PMT function***, which calculates a periodic loan payment given a constant interest rate, specific term of the loan, and the original value of the loan. To use this function, you need to fill in values from data stored in fields from underlying tables or supply constants in the formula.

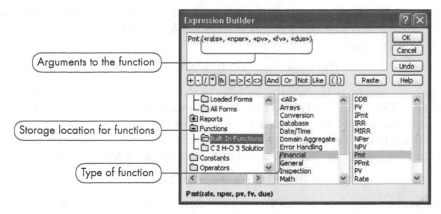

Figure 8 Access Function Shown in Expression Builder

The following syntax is required for the PMT function. Table 2 lists and describes the arguments for the PMT function.

Pmt(*rate, nper, pv, fv, type*)

Pmt(.065/12, 4*12, 12500,0,0)

Table 2

Part	Description
( )	Everything inside the parentheses is an argument to the function. The arguments are separated by commas. This function requires three arguments.
rate	Required. Expression or value specifying interest rate per period. (The period is the term of the loan payment, such as monthly or quarterly. For example, a car loan at an annual percentage rate (APR) of 6.5% with monthly payments gives the rate per period (month) of 0.065/12, or 0.005417).
nper	Required. Expression or integer value specifying total number of payment periods in the annuity. For example, monthly payments on a four-year car loan gives a total of 4 * 12 (or 48) payment periods.
pv	Required. Expression or value specifying present value (or how much you borrow) that a series of payments to be paid in the future is worth now. For example, the loan amount is the present value to the lender of the monthly car payments.
fv	Optional. Value specifying future value or cash balance you want after you've made the final payment. For example, most loans have a future value of $0 because that's what is owed after the final payment. However, if you want to save $50,000 over 18 years for your child's education, then $50,000 is the future value.
type	Optional. Value (0 or 1) identifying when payments are due. Use 0 if payments are due at the end of the payment period (the norm), or 1 if payments are due at the beginning of the period.

Execute Actions with the Iif Function

The Iif function evaluates a condition and executes one action when the condition is true and an alternate action when the condition is false.

Another useful function is the **IIf function**, which evaluates a condition and executes one action when the expression is true and an alternate action when the condition is false. The condition must evaluate as true or false only. For example, if balance >=10,000 or if City = "Chicago" illustrate appropriate conditions. Access evaluates the expression, determines whether it is true or false, and performs alternative actions based on the determination. For example, accounts with balances over

$10,000 earn a 3.5% interest rate, while accounts with balances below $10,000 earn only 2.75% interest. The following syntax is required for the IIf function:
IIf(expr,truepart,falsepart)

$$IIf(Balance >= 10000, .035, .0275)$$

Suppose you want to calculate the number of vacation weeks an employee is eligible to receive. The firm gives two weeks of vacation to employees with five or fewer years of employment and three weeks to employees who have worked more than five years for the firm. Your query has a field showing the number of years worked, YearsWorked. The proper syntax to calculate vacation weeks is the following:

$$WksVacation:IIf([YearsWorked]>5, 3,2)$$

This expression evaluates each record and determines if the number of years worked is more than five. When the number of years is greater than 5 (true), the expression returns the number 3 in the WksVacation field, indicating that the employee receives three weeks of vacation. If the years worked are not greater than 5 (false), the expression returns 2 in the WksVacation field, indicating that the employee receives two weeks of vacation. It is important that you write the expression so that it returns only a value of True or False for every record because Access cannot deal with ambiguities. The expression always evaluates both the true and false parts for each record. When the expression, the truepart, or the falsepart references a character string (words instead of numbers), you must type the return string (the true or false parts) inside of quotation marks.

TIP   Structure IIf Logic Carefully

Even experienced Access users get surprised sometimes when using IIf functions because the false part is evaluated even when the expression is true. Occasionally this false part evaluation will result in a *divide by zero* error. You can prevent this error by rewriting the expression and reversing the inequity. For example, change > to <=. You also must reverse the truepart and falsepart actions.

When you complete the expression, click OK. The Expression Builder dialog box closes, but nothing seems to happen. You have written the instruction in a form the computer understands, but you have not yet given the command to the computer to execute your instructions. The next step is to force an execution of your command by clicking Run. Your newly calculated result displays in the Datasheet view of the table. The column heading shows the default name, Expr1. Examine and verify the results of the calculation. When you are satisfied that the results are correct, return to Design view. In the design grid, double-click <Expr1> to select it, type over <Expr1> with a descriptive field name, run, and save the query.

TIP   Calculated Field Availability

A calculated query field will not be available to use in subsequent calculations until after you save the query. When you need to make multiple-step calculations, you must author the steps one at a time, then run, verify, and save after each step.

Using the Expression Builder Steps | Reference

1.	Open the query in Design view.
2.	Position the insertion point in a blank column.
3.	Select the Design tab.
4.	Click the Builder icon to launch the Expression Builder.
5.	When entering a formula, type (or click) an equal sign, =.
6.	Double-click field names to add to the expression.
7.	Type or click the icons for operators.
8.	Double-click the Functions folder and select the type of function needed, then from the right column select the individual function.
9.	Click OK to exit the Builder box.
10.	Run the query.
11.	Examine and verify the output.
12.	Return to the Design view.
13.	Highlight <Expr1> in the design grid and rename the field with a descriptive field name.
14.	Run the query and save it.

Performing Date Arithmetic

Access, like Excel, stores all dates as serial numbers. You may format the stored dates with a format that makes sense to you. In Europe, the date *November 20, 2008*, might be formatted as *20-11-2008* or *20.11.2008*. In the United States, the same date might be formatted as *11/20/2008*, and in South Asia, the date might be formatted as *20/11/2008*. **Date formatting** affects the date's display without changing the serial value. All dates and times in Access are stored as the number of days that have elapsed since December 31, 1899. For example, January 1, 1900, is stored as 1, indicating one day after December 31, 1899. If the time were 9:00 PM on November 20, 2008, no matter how the date or time is formatted, Access stores it as 39772.857. The 39772 represents the number of days elapsed since December 31, 1899, and the .857 reflects the fraction of the 24-hour day that has passed at 9:00 PM. This storage method may seem complicated, but it affords an Access user power and flexibility when working with date values. For example, because dates are stored as sequential numbers, you can calculate the total numbers of hours worked in a week if you record the starting and ending times for each day. Using **date arithmetic** you can create expressions to calculate an age in years from a birth date, or tell a business owner how many days past due an invoice is.

Date formatting affects the date's display without changing the serial value.

Using **date arithmetic** you can create expressions to calculate lapsed time.

Identify Partial Dates with the DatePart Function

You can look at entire dates or simply a portion of the date that is of interest. If your company increases the number of weeks of annual vacation from two weeks to three weeks after an employee has worked for five or more years, then the only part of the date of interest is the time lapsed in years. Access has a function, the **DatePart function**, to facilitate this. Table 3 shows the DatePart function parameters.

The **DatePart function** enables users to identify a specific part of a date, such as only the year.

$$DatePart("yyyy",[Employees]![HireDate])$$

Don't let the syntax intimidate you. After you practice using the DatePart function, the syntax will get much easier to understand.

Useful date functions are:

- **Date**—Inserts the current date into an expression.
- **DatePart**—Examines a date and returns only the portion of interest.
- **DateDiff**—Measures the amount of time elapsed between two dates. This is most often today's date as determined by the date function and a date stored in a field. For example, you might calculate the number of days a payment is past due by comparing today's date with the payment DueDate.

Table 3 Using the DatePart Function

Function Portion	Explanation
DatePart	An Access function that examines a date and focuses on a portion of interest.
"yyyy"	The first argument, the interval, describes the portion of the date of interest. We specified the years. It could also be "dd" or "mmm".
(Employees)!(HireDate)	The second argument, the date, tells Access where to find the information. In this case, it is stored in the Employee Table in a field named HireDate.

Hands-On Exercises

2 | Expression Builder, Functions, and Date Arithmetic

Skills covered: 1. Create a Select Query **2.** Use the Expression Builder **3.** Create Calculations Using Input Stored in a Different Query or Table **4.** Edit Expressions Using the Expression Builder **5.** Use Functions **6.** Work with Date Arithmetic

---

Step 1

Create a Select Query

Refer to Figure 9 as you complete Step 1.

a. Open the *chap3_ho1-3_realestate_solution* file if necessary, click **Options** on the Security Warning toolbar and click the **Enable this content option** in the Microsoft Office Security Options dialog box, and click **OK**.

TROUBLESHOOTING: If you create unrecoverable errors while completing this hands-on exercise, you can delete the *chap3_ho1-3_realestate_solution* file, copy the *chap3_ho1_realestate_solution* backup database you created at the end of the first hands-on exercise, and open the copy of the backup database to start the second hands-on exercise again.

b. Open the **Agents table** and replace **Angela Scott's** name with your name. Close the Agents table.

c. Click the **Create tab** and click **Query Wizard** in the Other group. Select **Simple Query Wizard** and click **OK**.

d. Select the fields (in this order) from the Agents table: **LastName** and **FirstName**. From the Properties table select **DateListed, DateSold, ListPrice, SalePrice**, and **SqFeet**. From the SubDivision table select the **Subdivision** field. Click **Next**.

You have selected fields from three related tables. Because relationships exist among the tables, you can trust that the agent's name that returns when the query runs will be the agent associated with the property.

e. Check to make sure that the option for a detail query is selected and click **Next**.

f. Name this query **YourName Commissions** and click **Finish**.

The query should run and open in Datasheet view. An experienced Access user always checks the number of records when a query finishes running and opens. This query should have 54 records. See Figure 9.

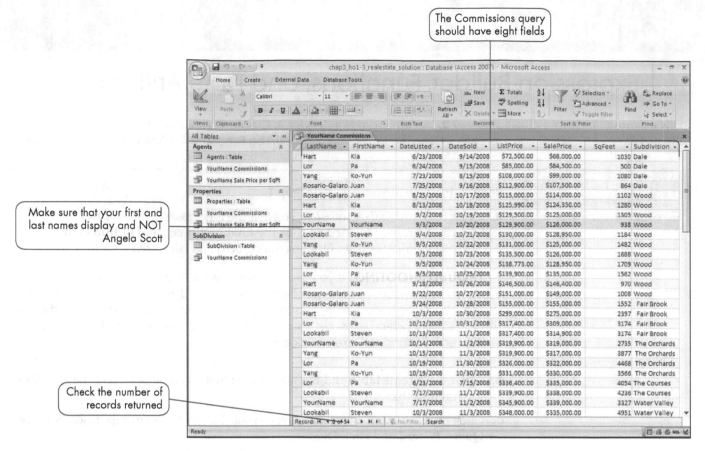

The Commissions query should have eight fields

Make sure that your first and last names display and NOT Angela Scott

Check the number of records returned

Figure 9 Datasheet View of the YourName Commissions Query

Step 2
Use the Expression Builder

Refer to Figure 10 as you complete Step 2.

a. Click the **Home tab** and switch to Design view. Scroll to the right to locate the first empty column in the design grid and position your insertion point in the first row.

b. Verify that the Design tab is selected and click **Builder** in the Query Setup group.

The Expression Builder dialog box opens. You may click the title bar and reposition it to a more convenient location if necessary.

c. Repeat the PricePerSqFt calculation from Hands-On Exercise 1 by using the Expression Builder. Click or type **=**.

d. Locate the list of fields in the Commissions query in the middle column and double-click the **SalePrice** field.

The work area of the Expression Builder dialog box should now display **= [SalePrice]**. The Expression Builder adds the **brackets** and always spells the field names correctly.

e. Click or type the divide operator (the forward slash, **/**) and then double-click the **SqFeet** field name in the middle column.

Now the work area of the expression builder will display **= [SalePrice] / [SqFeet]**.

f. Click **OK**. Run the query. Scroll right in the Datasheet view to find the newly calculated field, which is named Expr1.

g. Verify the results of the calculation.

The fifth record has values that can be rounded more easily in your head—$114,000 and 1102 Sq. Ft. That should return a result slightly higher than $100. The actual result is 0103.44. Once you are satisfied with the accuracy of the calculation, continue with the next step.

h. Activate the **Home tab** (if necessary) and change the view to Design view.

TIP Switching Between Design and Datasheet Views

An easy way to alternate views for an Access object is to right-click the object window's title bar and select the appropriate view from the shortcut menu. You can also click the views buttons in the bottom-right corner of the Access window. In this case, the object title bar says YourName Commissions. See Figure 10 for instructions on where to right-click.

i. Double-click **Expr1** in the field row of the right column. Type **PricePerSqFt**.

j. Right-click the field text box in the design grid that contains the PricePerSqFt calculated field. Select **Properties** from the shortcut menu. Click the **Format drop-down arrow** in the Property Sheet window and select **Currency**. Click the X to close the Property Sheet window.

k. Run the query. Click **Save** (or press **Ctrl + S**) and return to Design view.

l. Click the insertion point in the Field row of the first empty column and activate the Expression Builder. Look in the middle column that shows the list of available fields in this query. The last listed field should be the newly saved PricePerSqFt.

TROUBLESHOOTING: Sometimes you need to edit an expression created using the Expression Builder. When you open the Expression Builder to make the edits, you will find that Access adds <Expr1> to any unsaved expressions. Locate and double-click the <Expr1> to select it and delete it prior to making the necessary edits to the expression.

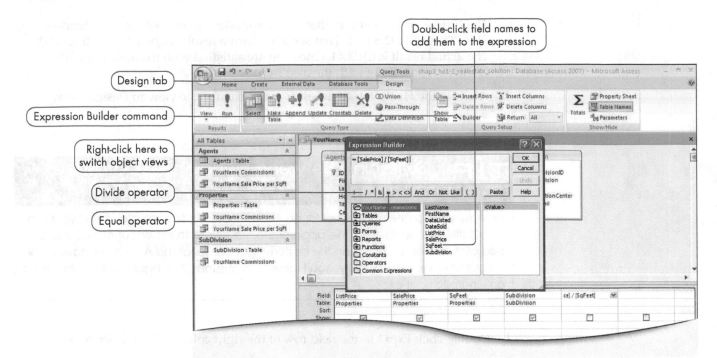

Figure 10 Working with the Expression Builder

Step 3
Create Calculations Using Input Stored in a Different Query or Table

Refer to Figure 11 as you complete Step 3.

a. Type = (equal sign) in the work area of the Expression Builder. Double-click **SalePrice** in the middle column to add it to the expression. Type or click / (divide symbol). Your formula in the work area should be = **[SalePrice]/.**

In addition to calculating the price per square foot, you decide that it would be helpful if you knew the price of the sold properties per bedroom, but you did not include a field for the number of bedrooms in the query. You have two options. One, you can cancel the expression, add the missing field to the query, and then restart the expression. Two, you also can use a field in a calculation that is not resident in the query. You need only tell Access where the field is stored.

b. Click the **Tables folder** in the left column of the Expression Builder.

The Tables folder expands to reveal the table objects in the database. Because you have not yet selected a table, the middle and right columns of the Expression Builder dialog box are empty.

c. Click the **Properties table**.

The middle column is populated with the names of the fields available from the Properties table. You will use this data to calculate the per bedroom sale price of the homes in the database.

d. Double-click the **Beds field**. Your expression will look like this:

= **[SalePrice] / [Properties]![Beds].**

This expression gives Access the instruction to go to the Properties table, locate the values of the number of bedrooms for each of the records in the Commissions query, and use that value to calculate a price per bedroom value. The appropriate number of bedrooms will be returned in each calculation because relationships exist between the tables. The query will inherit the referential integrity from the tables it sources.

e. Click **OK.** Click **Run.** Verify the calculated results.

f. Return to Design view. Double-click **Expr1** in the design grid to select it and type **PricePerBR.**

You have renamed Expr1, but the name change does not become permanent until you save the query design.

g. Right-click the PricePerBR calculated field. Select **Properties** from the shortcut menu. Click the **Format drop-down arrow** in the Property Sheet window and select **Currency.** Click the X to close the Property Sheet window.

h. Save the query.

i. Position the insertion point anywhere in the Field row in the PricePerBR column.

j. Click **Builder** in the Query Setup group on the Design tab.

The Expression Builder dialog box displays the renamed calculated field, PricePerBR, and a colon at the beginning of the expression without the equal sign (see Figure 11).

k. Click **OK** to close the Expression Builder dialog box.

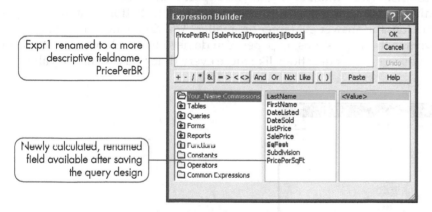

Expr1 renamed to a more descriptive fieldname, PricePerBR

Newly calculated, renamed field available after saving the query design

Figure 11 A Completed Expression

Step 4
Edit Expressions Using the Expression Builder

Refer to Figure 12 as you complete Step 4.

a. Click and drag to select the entire **PricePerBR** expression in the design grid. Right-click the selected expression and select **Copy.**

Be careful that you select and copy the entire expression. You need the new field name, all of the input fields, and the operands.

TROUBLESHOOTING: You cannot click into the next field in the design grid while the Expression Builder dialog box is open. Generally, any open dialog box in a Microsoft product is assigned top priority, and you must first deal with the dialog box before you can do anything anywhere else in the file. Close the Expression Builder dialog box if it is open.

b. Right-click in the field box of the first blank column and select **Paste.**

Your next task is to edit the copied formula so that it reflects the price per bathroom.

c. Position the insertion point anywhere in the copied formula and click **Builder.**

d. Move the I-beam pointer over any portion of the word *Beds* in the formula. Double-click.

The entire portion of the formula, [Properties]![Beds], should highlight.

e. Double-click the **Tables folder** in the left column, and then click the **Properties table** to open the folder and table, respectively.

Make sure that the middle column displays the field names of the available fields in the Properties table.

f. Double-click the **Baths field**.

The edited expression now displays **PricePerBR: [SalePrice] / [Properties]! [Baths]**.

g. Drag to select the **BR** in the *PricePerBR*. Replace BR with **Bath**.

The edited expression is **PricePerBath: [SalePrice] / [Properties]! [Baths]**.

h. Click **OK**. Click **Run**. Click **Save** and then return to Design view.

i. Right-click the PricePerBath calculated field. Select **Properties** from the shortcut menu. Click the **Format drop-down arrow** in the Property Sheet window and select **Currency**. Click the X to close the Property Sheet window.

j. Run the query. Examine the calculated results in the Datasheet view.

Do your results make sense? Which field has larger numbers in it, the price per bedroom or the price per bathroom? Do most houses have more bedrooms or bathrooms? Which number would you expect to be larger? Remember, you are dividing in these calculations. As the number on the bottom of a fraction gets larger, does the answer get larger or smaller? You do not need to write the answers to these questions on paper. You do need to develop a critical eye and force yourself to ask questions like these every time you calculate a value.

k. Click **Save**.

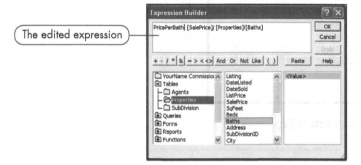

The edited expression

Figure 12 The Correctly Edited Formula

Step 5
Use Functions

Refer to Figures 13 and 14 as you complete Step 5.

a. Position the insertion point in the field row of the first blank column of the query in Design view.

You are going to use a financial function to calculate an estimated house payment for each of the sold properties. You make the following assumptions: 90% of the sale price financed, a 30-year period, monthly payments, and a fixed 6.5% annual interest rate. The first task is to calculate the amount financed. Assume a 10% down payment means that there will be 90% of the purchase price remaining to finance.

b. Right-click in the field box of the first blank column and select **Build** from the shortcut menu to display the Expression Builder dialog box. Type the formula = **[SalePrice] * .9** and click **OK**.

You will need to use this calculated value in subsequent calculations.

c. Run and save the query, return to Design view, double-click **Expr1,** and type **AmountFinanced**. Save the query.

d. Position the insertion point in the field row of the next available column. Launch the Expression Builder.

e. Double-click the **Functions folder** in the left column. Click **Built-In Functions folder**.

f. Look in the middle column. Click the **Financial** function category.

g. Look in the right column. Double-click the **Pmt function**.

The builder work area displays
    Pmt(<<rate>>,<<nper>>,<<pv>>,<<fv>>,<<due>>).

We are assuming monthly payments at a 6½% interest rate over 30 years with no balloon payment at the end of the 30-year period and that the finance charges are calculated at the end of each period.

h. Double-click each formula argument to select it. Substitute the appropriate information:

Argument	Replacement Value
<<rate>>	0.065/12
<<nper>>	30*12
<<pv>>	(AmountFinanced)—Click the YourName Commissions folder to display a list of field names available to use in the query.
<<fv>>	0
<<due>>	0

TROUBLESHOOTING: If you do not see the AmountFinanced field in the list of available field names, you probably forgot to save the query after running it. Press Esc to close the Expression Builder dialog box. Click Save or press Ctrl+S to save the query design changes and re-work steps d through h.

i. Examine Figure 13 to make sure that you have entered the correct arguments. Click **OK**. Run the query.

The payments are all negative numbers. That is normal. You will edit the formula to return positive values.

j. Return to Design view. Click in the Payment calculated field and open the Expression Builder. Position the insertion point to the left of the left bracket, [, and type a hyphen, –. Double-click **Expr1** and type **Payment**. The expression will now be:

Payment: Pmt(0.065/12, 30*12, –[AmountFinanced], 0,0). Click **OK**.

k. Right-click the Payment calculated field. Select **Properties** from the shortcut menu. Click the **Format drop-down arrow** in the Property Sheet window and select **Currency**. Click the **X** to close the Property Sheet window.

l. Run and save the query.

The calculated field values now appear as positive, rather than negative, values.

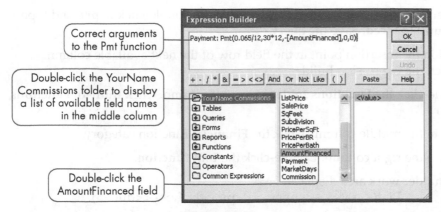

Correct arguments to the Pmt function

Double-click the YourName Commissions folder to display a list of available field names in the middle column

Double-click the AmountFinanced field

Figure 13 The Payment Function Arguments

Step 6
Work with Date Arithmetic

Refer to Figure 14 as you complete Step 6.

a. Position the insertion point in the field row of the first blank column of the query in Design view. Launch the Expression Builder.

You are going to calculate the number of days that each property was on the market prior to its sale.

b. Enter the formula **= [DateSold] – [DateListed]**. Run the query. Return to Design view and replace Expr1 with **MarketDays**. Save the query. Open the Property Sheet window and *format* the field as **Fixed** and set the *Decimal Places* to **0**.

Because Access stores all dates as serial numbers, the query returns the number of days on the market. The first property was placed on the market on June 23, and it sold on September 14. Look at your query result. This property was for sale all of July, all of August, and for parts of June and September. This is about three months. Does the query result reflect about three months?

c. Use the Expression Builder to multiply the SalePrice field by the commission rate of 7%. The formula in the Expression Builder is **= [SalePrice] * .07.** Run the query and replace Expr1 with **Commission**. Save the query.

The Commission calculated field calculates the total commission. The agent earns 7% of the sale price. The first agent's commission is 4760.

d. Right-click the Commission calculated field. Select **Properties** from the shortcut menu. Click the **Format drop-down arrow** in the Property Sheet window and select **Currency**. Click the **X** to close the Property Sheet window.

The values in the Commission calculated field now appear in Currency format. The first agent's commission displays as $4,760.00.

e. Click the **Office Button**, select **Manage**, and then select **Back Up Database**. Enter the filename **chap3_ho2_realestate_solution** (note *ho2* instead of *ho1-3*) and click the **Save button** on the Quick Access Toolbar.

You just created a backup of the database after completing the second hands-on exercise. The original database *chap3_ho1-3_realestate_solution* remains onscreen. If you ruin the original database as you complete the third hands-on exercise, you can use the backup file you just created.

f. Close the file and exit Access if you do not want to continue with the next exercise at this time.

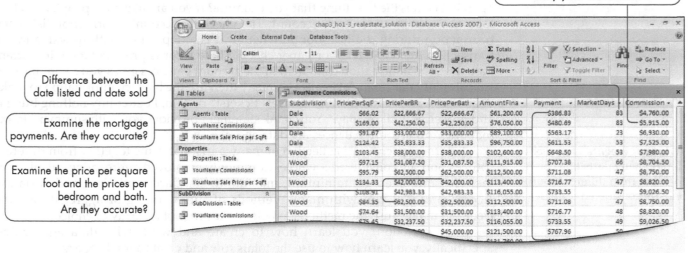

Figure 14 Verify, Verify, Verify!

Data Aggregates

Assume that you have an old-fashioned bank that still sends paper statements at the end of the month through the mail. Your statement arrives at your mailbox, and you open it. What is the first thing that you examine? If you are like most people, you first look at the balance for each account. The checking account information lists each transaction during the last month, whether it is a deposit or withdrawal, and the transaction method—ATM or paper check. These records provide vitally important data. But, the information contained in the account balances gives you a summarized snapshot of your financial health. You may then use the balance information to make decisions. "Yes, I can buy those concert tickets!" or "No, I better buy nothing but gas and groceries until payday." Your bank statement provides you with summary information. Your account balances are data aggregates.

A *data aggregate* is a collection of many parts that come together from different sources and are considered a whole. Commonly employed aggregating calculations include sum, average, minimum, maximum, standard deviation, and variance. Access provides you with many methods of summarizing or aggregating data. Decision makers use the methods to help make sense of an array of choices.

In this section, you learn how to create and work with data aggregates. Specifically, you learn how to use the totals row and create a totals query.

A *data aggregate* is a collection of many parts that come together from different sources and are considered a whole.

Creating and Working with Data Aggregates

Aggregates may be used in a query, table, form, or report. Access provides two methods of adding aggregate functions to a query. A *total row* displays as the last row in the Datasheet view of a table or query and provides a variety of summary statistics. The first method enables you to add a total row from the Datasheet view. This method is quick and easy, works in the Datasheet view of a table, and has the additional advantage that it provides the total information without altering the object design. You will recall that some databases are split into front and back end portions. Different users have different levels of privileges when interacting with the database. Adding a total row to a query or table can be accomplished by the lowest-privilege-level employee because it does not alter the structure of the object. The second method enables you to alter the query design and create a totals query. This method has the advantage of permitting you to group your data into relevant subcategories. For example, you can subtotal all houses sold in a specific subdivision or by each salesperson. After the summary statistics are assembled, you can employ them to make decisions. Who is the leading salesperson? In which neighborhood do houses sell most often or least often? This method requires that the user have rights to alter the design of a query. In a large, split database, a front-end user may not be afforded the rights to create or alter a query design. The query design is generally restricted to back-end users—the IT professionals only.

A *total row* displays as the last row in the Datasheet view of a table or query and provides a variety of summary statistics.

Data aggregation gives the decision maker a powerful and important tool. The ability to summarize and consolidate mountains of data into a distilled and digestible format makes the Access software a popular choice for managerial users. You already have learned that data aggregates may be created in queries. Access also permits aggregation in reports. In the first section you learned that some users calculate all of their expressions in queries, whereas others perform needed calculations in forms and reports. The positioning of data aggregates also may be accomplished in a variety of ways. Some users aggregate and calculate summary statistics in queries, others in reports. You will need to learn both methods of aggregation because the practices and procedures governing database use differ among firms. Some firms allow users relatively free access to both the front and rear ends of the database; other firms grant extremely limited front-end rights only.

Create a Total Row in a Query or Table

Figure 15 illustrates adding a total row to the Datasheet view. Access can total or average numeric fields only. Begin by positioning your insertion point in a numeric or currency field of any record. Then click Totals in the Records group on the Home tab. The word Total is added below the new record row of the query. The highlighted numeric field shows a box with an arrow in the Total row. You may choose from several different aggregate functions by clicking the arrow. This method works in the same way if you want to add a total row to a numeric field in a table.

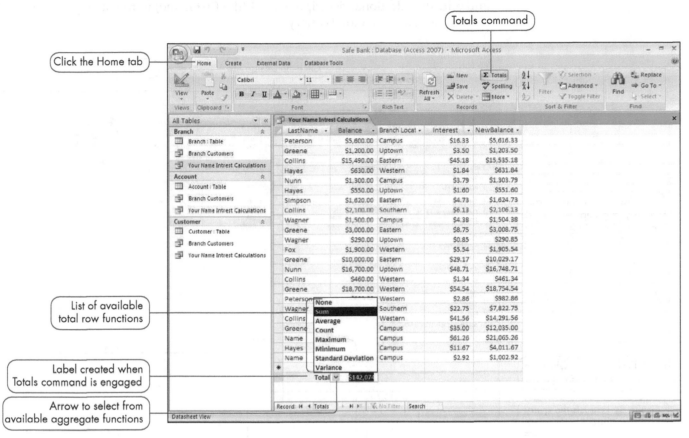

Figure 15 Adding a Total Row to a Query in Datasheet View

Group Totals in a Totals Query

The Total row, when added to a query, provides the decision maker with useful information. However, it does not provide any method of subtotaling the data. The total row is useful when a decision maker needs to know the totals or averages of all the data in a query or table. Sometimes knowing only the total is insufficient. The decision maker needs to know more detail. For example, knowing the total sales of houses during a period is good information. Knowing subtotals by salespeople would be more useful. Knowing subtotals by subdivision also would be useful information. Instead of using a total row, you can create a *totals query* to organize the results of a query into groups to perform aggregate calculations. It contains a minimum of two fields. The first field is the grouping field, such as the salesperson's last name. The second field is the numeric field that the decision maker wishes to summarize, such as the sale price of the homes. You may add other numeric fields to a totals query to provide additional information. The totals query in Access helps you provide a more detailed snapshot of the data.

> A ***totals query*** organizes query results into groups by including a grouping field and a numeric field for aggregate calculations.

Let's say you have created a SafeBank database for a bank with five branch locations. If you need to know the total deposits by location, you would create a totals query. The two fields necessary would be the Location field in the Branch table and

> (A totals query can only include the field or fields that you want to total and the grouping field.)

the Account Balance field in the Accounts table. After you create and run the query, you may add parameters to limit the totals query to a specific data subset. The process of adding criteria in a totals query is identical to any other query. Remember that a totals query can include only the field or fields that you want to total and the grouping field. No additional descriptive fields are allowed in the totals query. If you need to see the salesperson's last name, the sale price of the house, *and* the salesperson's first name, you would need to create two queries. The first query would be the totals query summarizing the sales data by last name. Then you would need to create a second query based on the totals query and add the additional descriptive field (the first name) to the new query. Figure 16 shows the setup for a totals query.

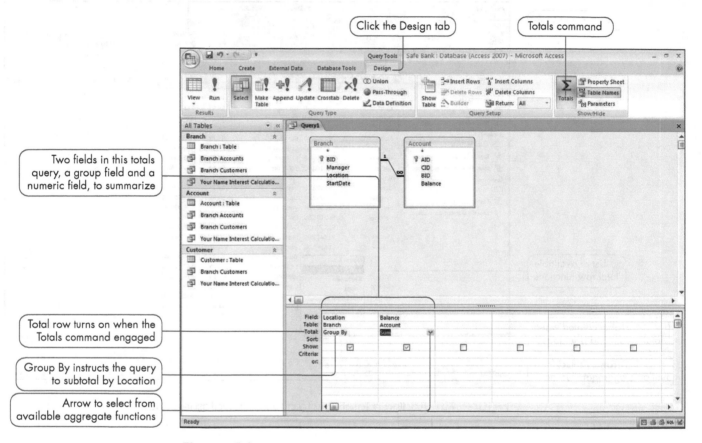

Figure 16 Constructing a Totals Query

Customize, Analyze, and Summarize Query Data

Hands-On Exercises

3 | Data Aggregates

Skills covered: 1. Add a Total Row **2.** Create a Totals Query Based on a Select Query **3.** Add Fields to the Design Grid **4.** Add Grouping Options and Specify Summary Statistics

Step 1	Refer to Figure 17 as you complete Step 1.
Add a Total Row	

a. Open the *chap3_ho1-3_realestate_solution* file if necessary, click **Options** on the Security Warning toolbar and click the **Enable this content option** in the Microsoft Office Security Options dialog box, and click **OK**.

> **TROUBLESHOOTING:** If you create unrecoverable errors while completing this hands-on exercise, you can delete the *chap3_ho1-3_realestate_solution* file, copy the *chap3_ho2_realestate_solution* backup database you created at the end of the first hands-on exercise, and open the copy of the backup database to start the second hands-on exercise again.

b. Open the **YourName Commissions query** in the Datasheet view.

c. Click the **Home tab** and click **Totals** in the Records group.

Look at the last row of the query. The Totals command is a toggle: Click it once to display the Total row. Click it again to hide the Total row. You need the Total row turned on to work the next steps.

d. Click in the cell that intersects the **Total row** and the **SalePrice** column.

This is another place in Access that when selected, a drop-down list becomes available. Nothing indicates that the drop-down menu exists until the cell or control is active. You need to remember that this is one of those places in order to aggregate the data.

e. Click the **drop-down arrow** and select **Sum** to calculate the total of all the properties sold. Widen the SalePrice field if you can't see the entire total value.

The total value of the properties sold is $19,936,549.00.

f. Scroll right, locate the **Subdivision field,** and click in the Total row to activate the drop-down list.

The choices from the total list are different. You may have the summary statistics set to None or Count. Subdivision is a character field. Access recognizes that it cannot add or average words and automatically limits your options to only tasks that Access is able to do with words.

g. Select **Count** from the drop-down list in the Total row for the Subdivision field.

h. Click in the **Total row** in the **PricePerSqFt** field. Click the **drop-down arrow** and select **Average**.

i. Click in any record of any field. Close the query.

A dialog box opens that asks if you wish to save the changes to the *layout* of the YourName Commissions query. It does NOT ask if you wish to save the changes made to the design. Toggling a Total row on and off is a layout (cosmetic) change only and does not affect the architectural structure of the query or table design.

j. Click **Yes**. The query saves the layout changes and closes.

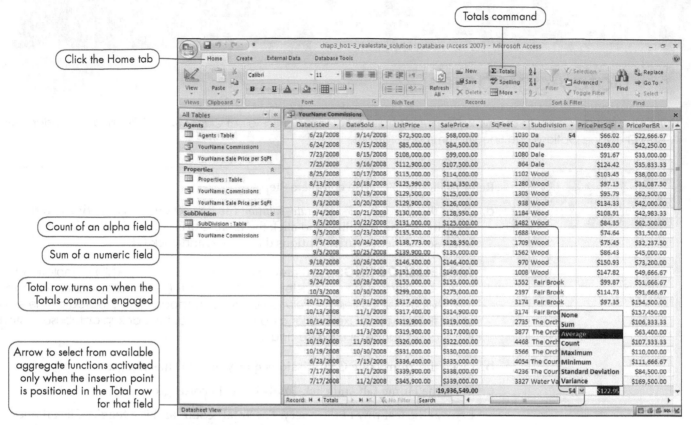

Figure 17 Add a Total Row to the Query Datasheet View

Step 2

Create a Totals Query Based on a Select Query

Refer to Figure 18 as you complete Step 2.

a. Click the **Create tab** and click **Query Design** in the Other group.

The Show Table dialog box opens. You could source this query on the tables. However, because you already have made many useful calculations in the Commissions query, it will save you time to source the Totals query on the Commissions query.

b. Click the **Queries tab** in the Show Table dialog box.

c. Select the **YourName Commissions query** and click **Add**.

d. Click **Close**.

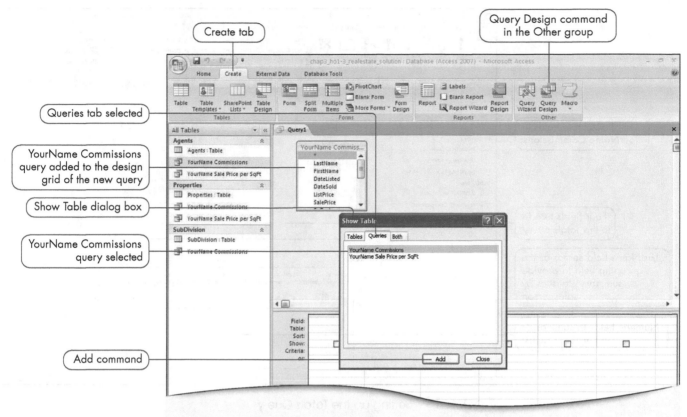

Figure 18 Create a Totals Query

Refer to Figure 19 as you complete Step 3.

a. Locate the **LastName** field in the YourName Commissions field list box.

You may add fields from the YourName Commissions query to the new query by clicking and dragging them to the design grid or by double-clicking.

b. Double-click the **LastName** field to add it to the grid.

You will create summary statistics based on each salesperson's activities. The LastName field is the grouping field in this totals query.

TROUBLESHOOTING: If you attempt to double-click a field name and the computer "beeps" at you, you probably forgot to close the Show Table dialog box.

c. Double-click the **SalePrice** field to add it to the grid.

d. Scroll down in the list of available fields box and double-click **MarketDays** to add it to the new query.

e. Add the **Commission** field to the new query.

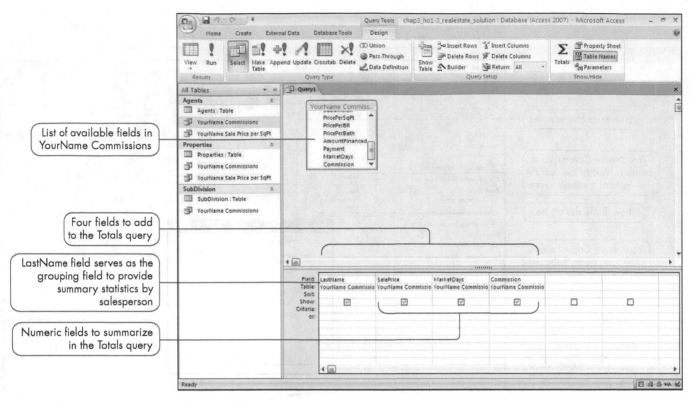

Figure 19 Setting up the Totals Query

Step 4
Add Grouping Options and Specify Summary Statistics

Refer to Figures 20 and 21 as you complete Step 4.

a. Click **Totals** in the Show/Hide group on the Design tab.

Look at the lower part of the design grid. The Totals command toggles a new row between the Table and Sort rows of the design grid. When the Totals command is activated, all fields are set to Group by. You only want one Group by field, the LastName field.

b. Click in the **Total row** for the **SalePrice** field. Click the **drop-down arrow** and select **Sum** from the list.

Here is another of those hidden drop-down lists. As you gain experience, you will learn where to look for them. For now, simply memorize that one will show up in the Total row.

c. Click in the **Total row** of the **MarketDays** field. Click the **drop-down arrow** and select **Avg**.

d. Click the **Total row** in the **Commission** field and select **Sum**.

e. Run the query. Return to Design view and set the properties of the SalePrice and Commission fields as **Currency**. Set the Format property of the DaysOnMarket field to **Fixed**. Set the Decimal Places property to **0**.

f. Verify results of the calculated summaries. Save the query as **YourName Commission Summary**.

g. Close the *chap3_ho1-3_realestate_solution* file.

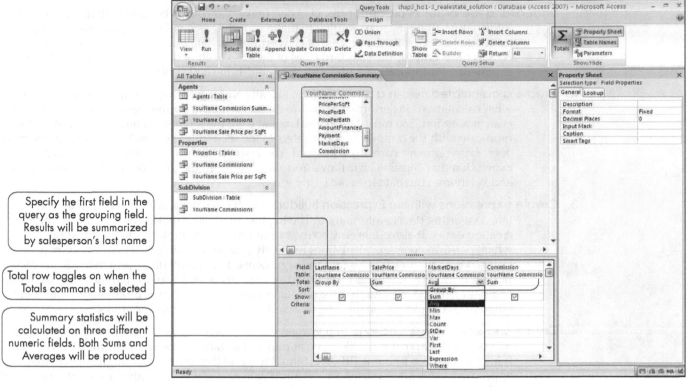

Totals command located in the Show/Hide group on the Design tab

Specify the first field in the query as the grouping field. Results will be summarized by salesperson's last name

Total row toggles on when the Totals command is selected

Summary statistics will be calculated on three different numeric fields. Both Sums and Averages will be produced

Figure 20 Specify Grouping Field and Summary Statistics

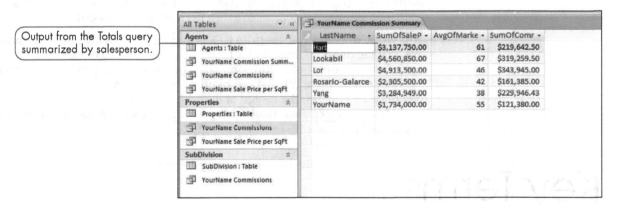

Output from the Totals query summarized by salesperson.

Figure 21 Specify Grouping Field and Summary Statistics

Summary

1. **Understand the order of precedence.** Decision makers are overwhelmed with data. They need information that they may employ to make sound decisions. Access provides many powerful tools that expedite the process of converting raw data into useful information. The Access tools employ the standard rules of order in arithmetic calculations: parentheses, exponents, multiplication and division, and addition and subtraction.

2. **Create a calculated field in a query.** Access, like all computer software, must be instructed in what calculations to perform and how to do the work. The formal name for those instructions is an expression. You must "speak the language" of the software in order to accurately communicate with the computer. Syntax refers to the set of rules by which the words and symbols of an expression are correctly combined. You learned that you can write a syntactically correct expression that contains logic flaws. You also developed the practice of critically examining and verifying your data to avoid costly errors.

3. **Create expressions with the Expression Builder.** The chapter introduced powerful tools that facilitate converting data to information. The Expression Builder makes the logistics of formula creation easier. It also offers easy access to a number of pre-built formulae, called functions, which perform complex calculations relatively painlessly. Using Access functions requires the user to know the function's name and arguments. The arguments appear in the Expression Builder enclosed in symbols (<<XXX>>) as a visual cue that you need to substitute a constant or a field name. Access can use the output of earlier calculations as input to subsequent calculations, but the expression must be renamed and the query saved prior to subsequent use.

4. **Create and edit Access functions.** You learned that Access, like Excel, has a variety of functions that can perform complex tasks in an automated fashion. You employ the functions by identifying the function by name (IIf, Avg, Sum, Pmt) and then entering the arguments in the appropriate order. Arguments are the input data Access uses to create the output. They may be field names or values.

5. **Perform date arithmetic.** Dates in Access are stored as serial numbers based on the number of days that have elapsed from an arbitrarily chosen base date, December 31, 1899. Access provides several functions to facilitate date handling. Additionally, you can simply subtract one date from another or add a number to a date to create a different date.

6. **Create and work with data aggregates.** Data aggregates provide powerful means to summarize and analyze data. You may add a Total row to the Datasheet view of a table or query and select from a number of useful summary options including count, sum, average, minimum, and maximum. These calculations require only a few mouse clicks to create. Additionally, they have no effect on the design of the table or query. When a more robust summary is needed, you may create a Totals query. This permits you to establish grouping levels for the data to make summaries more meaningful.

Key Terms

Access function
Argument
Constant
Data aggregate
Date arithmetic

Date formatting
DatePart function
Expression
Expression Builder
IIf function

Order of precedence
PMT function
Syntax
Total row
Totals query

Multiple Choice

1. Which statement most accurately describes the differences between a table field and a calculated field?

   (a) All data entries to a table field are permanently stored, but calculated field data do not exist in the database. They appear in the datasheet, form, or report but are not a part of the dataset.

   (b) A calculated field is permanently stored in the dataset when the query, table, form, or report design is saved. Only the properties governing the data are saved when a table is saved.

   (c) Query data and Table data are dynamic, and no data are permanently stored.

   (d) None of the above

2. Which of the following correctly identify the rules of order of arithmetic operations?

   (a) Exponentiation, Parenthesis, Addition, Subtraction, Multiplication, Division

   (b) Parenthesis, Exponentiation, Addition, Subtraction, Multiplication, Division

   (c) Parenthesis, Exponentiation, Multiplication, Division, Addition, Subtraction

   (d) Addition, Subtraction, Multiplication, Division, Exponentiation, Parenthesis

3. Which set of parenthesis is unnecessary in the following expression?
   $- (3 * 5) + (7 / 2) - (6\wedge2) * (36 *2)$

   (a) (3 * 5)

   (b) (7 / 2)

   (c) (6^2)

   (d) (36 *2)

   (e) All of the above

4. Which statement about saving a query is true?

   (a) Data are extracted from the source table and saved in query form.

   (b) Data are duplicated from the source table and saved in query form.

   (c) Data created using expressions are saved when the query is saved, but the source data stays in the original table.

   (d) No data are saved in a query.

5. The Expression Builder icon may be found in the:

   (a) Manage group on the Databases Tools tab

   (b) Query Setup group on the Design tab

   (c) Database Management group on the Design tab

   (d) Design group on the Query Setup tab

6. Your database contains a Price field stored in the Products table and a Quantity field stored in the Orders table. You have created a query but forgot to add the Price field in the design. Now you need to use the price field to calculate the total for the order. The correct syntax is:

   (a) OrderTotal:(Quantity)*(Products)!(Price)

   (b) OrderTotal=(Quantity)*(Products)!(Price)

   (c) OrderTotal:[Quantity]*[Products]![Price]

   (d) OrderTotal=[Quantity]*[Products]![Price]

7. Which of the following is true about a select query?

   (a) It may reference fields from more than one table or query.

   (b) It may reference fields from a table, but not a query.

   (c) It may reference fields from either a table or a query but not both.

   (d) It may reference fields from a form.

8. You correctly calculated a value for the OrderAmount using an expression. Now you need to use the newly calculated value in another expression calculating sales tax. The most efficient method is to:

   (a) Run and save the query to make OrderAmount available as input to subsequent expressions.

   (b) Create a new query based on the query containing the calculated Order amount and then calculate the sales tax in the new query.

   (c) Close the Access file, saving the changes when asked; reopen the file and reopen the query; calculate the sales tax.

   (d) Create a backup of the database, open the backup and the query, then calculate the sales tax.

9. If state law requires that wait staff be over age 21 to serve alcohol and you have a database that stores each employee's birthdate in the Employee table, which of the following is the proper syntax to identify the employees' year of birth.

   (a) Age:DatePart("yyyy",[Employee]![BirthDate])

   (b) Age=DatePart("yyyy",[Employee]![BirthDate])

   (c) Age:DatePart("yyyy",[BirthDate]![Employee])

   (d) Age=DatePart("yyyy",[BirthDate]![Employee])

...continued on Next Page

10. You want to add a Totals row in a query Datasheet view. Where will you find the Totals command?

   (a) In the Data group on the Home tab

   (b) In the Home group on the Data tab

   (c) In the Records group on the Home tab

   (d) In the Home group on the Records tab

11. Which statement about a Totals query is true?

   (a) A Totals query may contain only one descriptive field but several aggregating fields.

   (b) A Totals query may contain several descriptive fields but only one aggregating field.

   (c) A Totals query has a limit of only two fields, one descriptive field, and one aggregating field.

   (d) A Totals query can aggregate data, but to find a grand total, you must create a new query based on the Totals query and turn on the Total row in the new query.

12. You built a query expression and clicked Run. A parameter dialog box pops up on your screen. Which of the following actions is the most appropriate if you expected results to display and do not want to enter an individual value?

   (a) Click OK to make the parameter box go away.

   (b) Read the field name specified in the parameter box and look for that spelling in the calculated expression.

   (c) Type numbers in the parameter box and click OK.

   (d) Close the query without saving changes. Re-open it and try running the query again.

13. A query contains fields for StudentName and Address. You have created and run a query and are in Datasheet view examining the output. You notice a spelling error on one of the student's names. You correct the error in the query Datasheet view.

   (a) The name is correctly spelled in this query but will be misspelled in the table and all other queries based on the table.

   (b) The name is correctly spelled in the table and in all queries based on the table.

   (c) The name is correctly spelled in this query and any other queries, but will remain misspelled in the table.

   (d) You cannot edit data in a query.

14. Which of the following is not available as an aggregate function within a query?

   (a) Sum

   (b) Min

   (c) Division

   (d) Avg

15. Which of the following is not true about the rows in the query design grid?

   (a) The Total row can contain different functions for different fields.

   (b) The Total row can source fields stored in different tables.

   (c) The Total row is located between the Table and Sort rows.

   (d) The Total row can be applied only to numeric fields.

Practice Exercises

1 Comfort Insurance—Salaries and Bonuses

The Comfort Insurance Agency is a midsized company with offices located across the country. Each employee receives a performance review annually. The review determines employee eligibility for salary increases and the annual performance bonus. The employee data are stored in an Access database, which is used by the human resource department to monitor and maintain employee records. Your task is to calculate the salary increase for each employee and his or her performance bonuses (if any). You are the human resource department manager. If you correctly calculate the employee salaries and bonuses, you will receive a bonus. Work carefully and check the accuracy of the calculations. This project follows the same set of skills as used in Hands-On Exercises 1 and 2 in this chapter. The instructions are less detailed to give you a chance to practice your skills. If you have problems, reread the detailed directions presented in the chapter. Compare your results to Figure 22.

a. Copy the partially completed file *chap3_pe1_insurance* to your production folder. Rename it **chap3_pe1_insurance_solution**, open the file, and enable security.

b. Click the **Database Tools tab** and then click **Relationships** in the Show/Hide group. Examine the table structure, relationships, and fields. Once you are familiar with the database, close the Relationships window.

c. Click the **Create tab** and click **Query Wizard** in the Other group. Select **Simple Query Wizard** in the first screen of the dialog box. Click **OK**.

d. From the **Employees table** select the **LastName, FirstName, Performance**, and **Salary** fields to add fields to the query. From the **Titles table** select the **2008Increase** field. Click **Next**. This needs to be a detail query. Name the query **YourName Raises and Bonuses**. Click **Finish**.

e. Right-click the query window title bar or the Query tab and select **Design View** from the shortcut menu to switch to Design view.

f. Position the insertion point in the first blank column in the Field row. Type **NewSalary:[Salary]*[2008Increase]+[Salary]** to create an expression.

g. Click **Run** in the Results group on the Design tab to run the query. (If you receive the Enter Parameter Value dialog box, check your expression carefully for typos.) Look at the output in the Datasheet view. Verify that your answers are correct. If they are, use the Property Sheet window to format the **NewSalary** field as **Currency**, save the query.

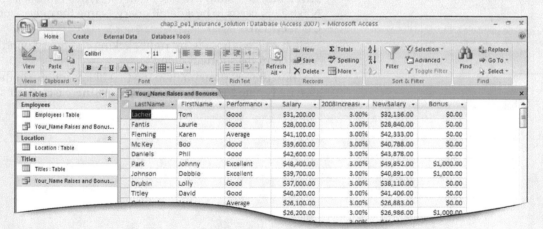

Figure 22 Raises and Bonuses

...continued on Next Page

h. Return to Design view. Position the insertion point in the first blank column in the Field row. Click **Builder** in the Query Setup group on the Design tab. In the **left column**, open the folder for **functions**. Open the **Built-In Functions** folder. Scroll the **right column** to locate the **IIf function**. Double-click to insert the function.

i. Double-click **<<expr>>** and replace it with **[Performance] = "Excellent"**; double-click **<<truepart>>** and replace it with **1000**; double-click **<<falsepart>>** and replace it with **0**. (That is zero, not the letter O.)

j. Run the query. Return to the Design view and double-click **Expr1** in the field row of the last column. Type **Bonus**. Run and save the query. Close the database.

2 Comfort Insurance—Vacation

The Comfort Insurance Agency is a midsized company with offices located across the country. The human resource office is located in the home office in Miami. Each year, each employee receives a performance review. The review determines employee eligibility for salary increases and the annual performance bonus. The employee data are stored in an Access database. This database is used by the human resource department to monitor and maintain employee records. Your task is to calculate the salary increase for each employee, the number of years they have worked for the firm, and the number of vacation days they are eligible to receive. You are the human resource department manager. If you correctly calculate the employee salaries and vacations, you will receive a bonus. Work carefully and check the accuracy of the calculations. This project follows the same set of skills as used in Hands-On Exercises 1 and 2 in this chapter. The instructions are less detailed to give you a chance to practice your skills. If you have problems, feel free to reread the detailed directions presented in the chapter. Compare your results to Figure 23.

a. Copy the partially completed file *chap3_pe2_insurance.accdb* to your production folder. Rename it **chap3_pe2_insurance_solution.accdb**, open the copied file, and enable the security content.

b. Click the **Database Tools tab** and then click **Relationships** in the Show/Hide group. Examine the table structure, relationships, and fields. Once you are familiar with the database, close the Relationships window.

c. Create a new query using the Query Wizard. Click the **Create tab** and click **Query Wizard** in the Other group. Select **Simple Query Wizard** in the first screen of the dialog box. Click **OK**.

d. Add fields to the query. From the **Employees table** select the **LastName, FirstName, HireDate**, and **Salary** fields. From the **Titles table** select the **2008Increase** field. Click **Next**. This needs to be a detail query. Name the query **Your_Name Raises and Tenure**. Click **Finish**.

e. Switch to Design view by right-clicking the query window tab and selecting **Design View** from the shortcut menu.

f. Position the insertion point in the first blank column in the Field row. Create an expression by typing **2008Raise:[Salary]*[2008Increase]**. Format it as **Currency**.

...continued on Next Page

g. Click **Run** in the Results group on the Design tab. Look at the output in the Datasheet view. Verify that your answers are correct. If they are, save the query.

h. Return to Design view. Position the insertion point in the first blank column in the Field row. Click **Builder** in the Query Setup group on the Design tab. In the left column, open the folder for functions. Open the Built-In Functions folder. Scroll the right column to locate the **DatePart** function. Double-click to insert the function to the work area.

i. Double-click *<<interval>>* in the function in the work area of the Expression Builder dialog box. Type, **"yyyy"**. Double-click *<<date>>* and replace it with **[HireDate]**. Delete the rest of the arguments and commas but do not delete the closing parenthesis. Your expression should look like this:

DatePart ("yyyy", [HireDate])

j. Run and verify the output. Return to Design view and replace Expr1 in the field row of the last column with **YearHired**. Save the query.

k. Use the Expression Builder or type to create an expression that measures how long each employee has worked. Assume that this year is 2008. The finished expression will look like this:

YearsWorked:2008 – [YearHire]

l. Run and save the query. Sort the output in descending order by the YearsWorked field. Close the database.

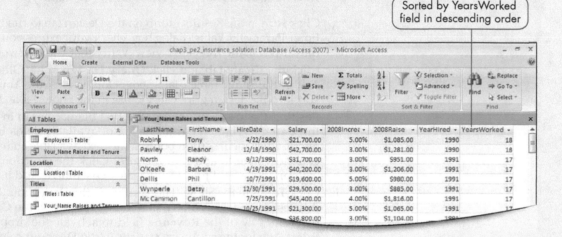

Figure 23 Raises and Tenure

3 Northwind Traders

Northwind Traders is a small, international, specialty food company. It sells products in eight different divisions: beverages, confections (candy), condiments, dairy products, grains and cereals, meat and poultry, produce, and seafood. The company offers discounts to some customers. Different customers receive differing discount amounts. The firm purchases merchandise from a variety of suppliers. All of the order and inventory information is stored in the company's database. This database is used by the marketing department to monitor and maintain sales records. You are the marketing manager. Your task is to determine the revenue from each order and to summarize the revenue figures by product category. This project follows the same set of skills as used in Hands-On Exercises 2 and 3 in this chapter. The instructions are less detailed to give you a chance to practice your skills. If you have problems, feel free to reread the detailed directions presented in the chapter. Compare your results to Figure 24.

...continued on Next Page

a. Copy the partially completed file *chap3_pe3_traders.accdb* to your production folder. Rename it **chap3_pe3_traders_solution.accdb**, open the file, and enable the content.

b. Click the **Database Tools tab** and then click **Relationships** in the Show/Hide group. Examine the table structure, relationships, and fields. After you are familiar with the database, close the Relationships window.

c. Click the **Create tab** and click **Query Wizard** in the Other group. Select **Simple Query Wizard** in the first screen of the dialog box. Click **OK**.

d. From the **Order Details table** select the **Quantity** and **Discount** fields to add the fields to the query. From the **Products table** select the **UnitPrice** and **ProductCost** fields. From the **Categories table** select the **CategoryName** Field. Click **Next**. This needs to be a detail query. Name the query **Your_Name Revenue**. Click **Finish**.

The UnitPrice field contains data on what customers pay to purchase the products. The ProductCost field contains data on what the company pays suppliers to purchase the products.

e. Right-click the query window tab and select **Design View** from the shortcut menu to switch to Design view.

f. Position the insertion point in the first blank column in the Field row. Create an expression that calculates revenue. Some customers receive discounts on their orders so you need to calculate the discounted price in the expression that calculates revenue.

Revenue:[UnitPrice] * (1 – [Discount]) * [Quantity]

g. Click **Run** in the Results group on the Design tab to run the query. (If you receive the Enter Parameter Value dialog box, check your expression carefully for typos.) Look at the output in the Datasheet view. Verify that your answers are correct.

h. Click the **Create tab** and click **Query Design** in the Other group. Click the **Queries Tab** in the Show Table dialog box. Double-click the **Your_Name Revenue** query to add it to the design grid. Click **Close** in the Show Table dialog box.

i. Position the insertion point in the first blank column in the Field row. Double-click the **CategoryName** field in the list of available fields in the Your_Name Revenue query. Click the insertion point in the next available column in the field row. Double-click **Revenue** to add it to the grid. Click the insertion point in the next available column in the field row. Double-click **Discount** to add it to the grid.

j. Click **Totals** in the Show/Hide group on the Design tab. The Total row will turn on in the design grid. This query should be grouped by the **CategoryName** field. Click in the Total row of the **Revenue** field to activate the drop down list and select **Sum**. Select **Avg** for the summary statistic in the **Discount** column.

k. Right-click the **Revenue** field name and select **Properties**. Click the box in the Property Sheet window to the right of **Format**. Select **Currency** from the drop down list to format the Revenue field as currency. With the Property Sheet Window still open, click the **Discount** field in the design grid. Click the box in the Property Sheet window to the right of **Format**. Select **Percent** from the drop-down list. Close the Property Sheet window by clicking the **X**.

l. Run the query. Verify the results. Name this query **Your_Name Revenue by Category**.

m. Close the database.

...continued on Next Page

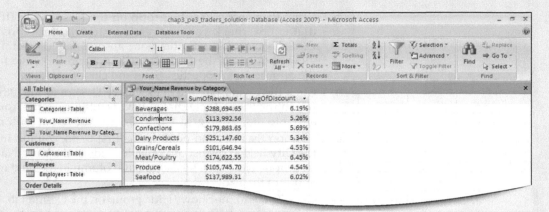

Figure 24 Revenue by Category

4 Member Rewards

The Prestige Hotel chain caters to upscale business travelers and provides state-of-the-art conference, meeting, and reception facilities. It prides itself on its international, four-star cuisines. Last year the chain began a member rewards club to help the marketing department track the purchasing patterns of its most loyal customers. All of the hotel transactions are stored in the database. Your task is to determine the revenue from each order and to summarize the revenue figures by location. This project follows the same set of skills as used in Hands-On Exercises 2 and 3 in this chapter. The instructions are less detailed to give you a chance to practice your skills. If you have problems, feel free to reread the detailed directions presented in the chapter. Compare your results to Figure 25.

a. Copy the partially completed file *chap3_pe4_memrewards.accdb* to your production folder. Rename it **chap3_pe4_memrewards_solution.accdb**, open the file, and enable the security content.

b. Click the **Database Tools tab** and then click **Relationships** in the Show/Hide group. Examine the table structure, relationships, and fields. After you are familiar with the database, close the Relationships window.

c. Create a new query using the Query Wizard. Click the **Create tab** and click **Query Wizard** in the Other group. Select **Simple Query Wizard** in the first screen of the dialog box. Click **OK**.

d. Add fields to the query. From the **Location table** select the **City**. From the **Orders table** select the **NoInParty** Field. From the **Service table** select the **PerPersonCharge** field. Click **Next**. This needs to be a detail query. Name the query **Your_Name Revenue**. Click **Finish**.

e. Right-click the query window tab and select **Design View** from the shortcut menu to Switch to Design view. Right-click **PerPersonCharge** and select **Properties** from the shortcut menu. Click the box to the right of **Format** in the Property Sheet. Select **Currency** from the drop-down. Click **X** to close the Property Sheet window.

f. Position the insertion point in the first blank column in the Field row. Create an expression that calculates revenue and format the field as **Currency**.

Revenue:[NoInParty] * [PerPersonCharge]

...continued on Next Page

g. Click **Run** in the Results group on the Design tab. (If you receive the parameter dialog box, check your expression carefully for typos.) Look at the output in the Datasheet view. Verify that your answers are correct. If they are, return to Design view and format the **PerPersonCharge** and **Revenue** fields as **Currency** by setting the appropriate properties. Save and close the query.

h. Click the **Create tab** and click **Query Design** in the Other group. Click the **Queries tab** in the Show Table dialog box. Double-click the **Your_Name Revenue** query to add it to the design grid. Click **Close** in the Show Table dialog box.

i. Position the insertion point in the first blank column in the Field row. Double-click the **City** field in the list of available fields in the Your_Name Revenue query. Click the insertion point in the next available column in the field row. Double-click **Revenue** to add it to the grid.

j. Click **Totals** in the Show/Hide group on the Design tab. The Total row will turn on in the design grid. This query should be grouped by the **City** field. Click in the Total row of the **Revenue** field to activate the drop-down list and select **Sum**.

k. Right-click **Revenue** and select **Properties** from the shortcut menu. Click the box to the right of **Format** in the Property Sheet. From the drop down menu select **Currency**. Click **X** to close the Property Sheet window. Run the query.

l. Click the **Home tab** in Datasheet view. Click **Totals** in the Records group to turn on the Totals row. Click the **SumOfRevenue** column in the Total row. Click the drop-down arrow and select **Sum**.

m. Save this query as **Your_Name Revenue by City**.

n. Run and save the query. Close the dialog box.

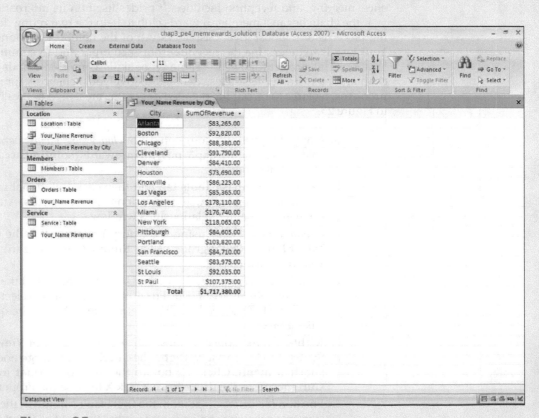

Figure 25 Revenue by City

Customize, Analyze, and Summarize Query Data

Northwind Traders is a small, international, specialty food company. It sells products in eight different divisions: beverages, confections (candy), condiments, dairy products, grains and cereals, meat and poultry, produce, and seafood. Although most of its customers are restaurants and gourmet food shops, it has a few retail customers, too. The company offers discounts to some customers. Different customers receive differing discount amounts. The firm purchases merchandise from a variety of suppliers. All of the order information is stored in the company's database. This database is used by the finance department to monitor and maintain sales records. You are the finance manager. Your task is to determine the revenue and profit from each order and to summarize the revenue, profit, and discount figures by salesperson. *Revenue* is the money the firm takes in. *Profit* is the difference between revenue and costs. The salespeople may offer discounts to customers to reward loyal purchasing or to appease an angry customer when a shipment is late. Occasionally the sales people discount so deeply that the company loses money on an order, that is, the costs exceed the revenue. It is important that your calculations are correct. If the firm's profitability figures do not accurately reflect the firm's financial health, the employee's paychecks (including yours) might be returned as insufficient funds. Compare your results to Figure 26.

a. Locate the file named *chap3_mid1_traders.accdb*, copy it to your working folder, and rename it **chap3_mid1_traders_solution.accdb**. Open the file and enable the content. Open the **Employee table**. Find and replace **Margaret Peacock**'s name with **your name**.

b. Create a detail query that you will use to calculate profits for each product ordered. You will need the **LastName** field from the **Employees table**. You will also need the fields for **Quantity**, **Discount**, **OrderDate**, **ShippedDate**, **UnitPrice**, and **ProductCost**. Save the query as **Your_Name Profit**.

c. In Design view, calculate **Revenue** and **Profit**. Because the discounts vary, some (not all) of the profit numbers will be negative. You must factor the discount into the price as you calculate revenue. If a product price is $100 and is sold with a 20% discount, the discounted price would be $80. Calculate **revenue** by multiplying the discounted price by the quantity sold. Calculate **total costs** by multiplying the product cost by quantity. Calculate **profit** by subtracting total cost from revenue. UnitPrice is the price for which the company sells merchandise. ProductCost is what the company pays to purchase the merchandise.

d. In the Datasheet view, add a Total row. Use it to calculate the **average discount** and the **sums** for **Revenue** and **Profit**.

e. Create a **Totals query** based on **Your_Name Profit**. Group by **LastName** and summarize the fields for **Discount (average)**, **Revenue**, and **Profit (sums)**.

f. Format the **Discount** field as a percentage and the **SumOfRevenue** and **SumOfProfit** fields as currency.

g. Add a Total row to the Datasheet view. Average the discount field and sum the **SumOfRevenue** and **SumOfProfit** fields.

h. Save the totals query as **Your_Name Profit by Employee**.

i. Capture a screenshot of the Your_Name Profit by Employee query. Have it open on your computer and press **PrintScrn**. Open Word and press **Ctrl+V** or click **Paste** in the Clipboard group. Save the Word document as **chap3_mid1_solution**. Print the Word document.

...continued on Next Page

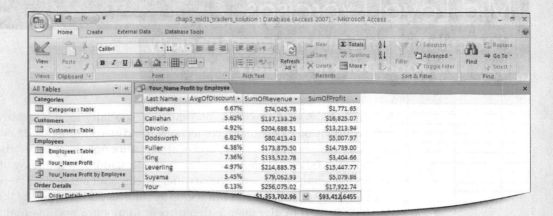

Figure 26 Profit by Employee

2 Calculating and Summarizing Bank Data in a Query

You are the manager of the loan department of the National Bank. Several customers have multiple loans with your institution. A single customer might have a mortgage loan, one or more car loans, and a home improvement loan. You need to monitor the total indebtedness of your customers to help them manage their debt load. Your task is to use the information stored in the database to calculate the loan payments for each loan and then to summarize the loans by customer. The PMT function requires five arguments. The first is the interest rate per period. The interest rates in the table are annual rates, so you will need to convert them to monthly rates in the function. The second argument is the number of periods (in years). Because the payments are monthly, you also need to convert the years for each loan to months in the function. The next argument is the PV, the present value of the loan—what the loan is worth today. It tells you how much each customer has borrowed. You generally supply zeros for the last two arguments, FV, and Type. FV shows the amount the borrower will owe after the last payment has been made—the future value of the monies borrowed. Generally this is zero. The type argument tells Access whether the payment is made at the beginning or the end of the period (month). Most loans accept payments and charge interest on the unpaid balance throughout the period. Use zero as the argument for this function. See Table 2 for more information about the arguments to the PMT function. Compare your results to Figure 27.

a. Locate the file named *chap3_mid2_nationalbank.accdb*, copy it to your working folder, and rename it **chap3_mid2_nationalbank_solution.accdb**. Open the file and enable the content. Open the **Customers table**. Find and replace **Michelle Zacco**'s name with your name.

b. Create a detail query that you will use to calculate the payments for each loan. You will need the following fields: **LastName**, **Amount**, **InterestRate**, **Term**, and **Type**. Save the query as **Your_Name Payment**.

...continued on Next Page

Customize, Analyze, and Summarize Query Data

c. In Design view, use the **Pmt** function to calculate the loan payment on each loan. Divide the annual interest rate by 12 and multiply the loan's term by 12 because every year has 12 months. Include a minus sign in front of the loan amount in the expression so the result returns a positive value. The last two arguments will be zero.

d. In the Datasheet view, add a Total row. Use it to calculate the **average** interest rate and the **sum** for the **payment**.

e. Create a Totals query based on Your_Name Loan Payment. **Group by LastName** and summarize the **sum** of the **Payment** field.

f. Format the **SumOfPayment** field as currency.

g. Add a total row to the Datasheet view that will sum the Payments. Save this query as **Your_Name Payment Summary**.

h. Capture a screenshot of the Payment Summary query. Have it open on your computer and press **PrintScrn**. Open Word and press **Ctrl+V** or click **Paste** in the Clipboard group. Save the Word document as **chap3_mid2_solution**. Print the Word document displaying the screenshot. Close the database.

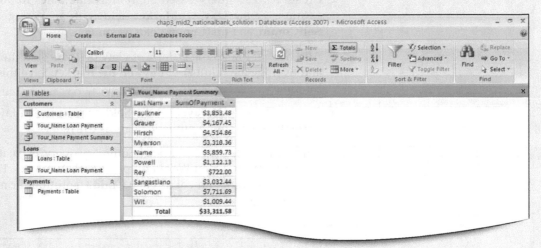

Figure 27 Payment Summary

3 Calculating and Summarizing Data in a Query, Working with Dates

You are the senior partner in a large, independent real estate firm that specializes in home sales. Although you still represent buyers and sellers in real estate transactions, you find that most of your time is spent supervising the agents who work for your firm. This fact distresses you because you like helping people buy and sell homes. Your firm has a database containing all of the information on the properties your firm has listed. You believe that by using the data in the database more effectively, you can spend less time supervising the other agents and spend more time doing the part of your job that you like doing the best. Your task is to determine the length of time each sold property was on the market prior to sale. Then calculate the commission from each property sale. Most real estate transactions involve two agents—one representing the seller (the listing agent) and the other the buyer (the selling agent). The two agents share the commission. Finally, you need to summarize the sales data by employee and calculate the average number of days each employee's sales were on the market prior to selling and the total commission earned by the employees. Compare your results to Figure 28.

a. Locate the file named *chap3_mid3_realestate.accdb*, copy it to your working folder, and rename it **chap3_mid3_realestate_solution.accdb**. Open the file and enable the content. Open the **Agents table**. Find and replace **Pa Lor**'s name with your name.

...continued on Next Page

b. Create a detail query that you will use to calculate the number of days each sold property has been on the market prior to sale. You will need the following fields: **LastName, DateListed, DateSold, SalePrice, SellingAgent, ListingAgent,** and **Subdivision.** Save the query as **Your_Name Sales Report.**

c. In Design view, build an expression, **DaysOnMarket,** to calculate the number of days each sold property has been on the market prior to sale. Subtract the **DateListed** field from the **DateSold** field. [Hint: The answers will *never* be negative numbers!]

d. Calculate the **Commission** for the selling and listing agents. Multiply the **SalePrice** by the Commission rate of **3.5%.** Name the newly created fields **SellComm** and **ListComm.** Both fields contain the same expression. They need to be named differently so that the proper agent—the listing agent or the selling agent—gets paid.

e. After you are sure that your calculations are correct, save the query. In Datasheet view, add a total row. Use it to calculate the average number of days on the market and the sums for the **SalePrice, SellComm,** and **ListComm** fields. Format the **SellComm, ListComm,** and **SalePrice** fields as **Currency.**

f. Create a Totals query based on **Your_Name Sales Report.** Group by **LastName** and summarize the **DaysOnMarket** field with an **average.** Summarize the **SalePrice, SellComm,** and **ListComm** fields as **sums.**

g. Add a Total row to the Datasheet view that will sum the price and commission fields and average the number of days on the market. Save this query as **Your_Name Sales Summary.**

h. Format the **AveOfDaysOnMkt** field so that it displays only two decimal places. Format the remaining numeric fields as Currency.

i. Capture a screenshot of the Sales Summary query. Have it open on your computer and press **PrintScrn.** Open Word and press **Ctrl+V** or click **Paste** in the Clipboard group. Save the Word document as **chap3_mid3_solution.** Print the Word document. Close the database.

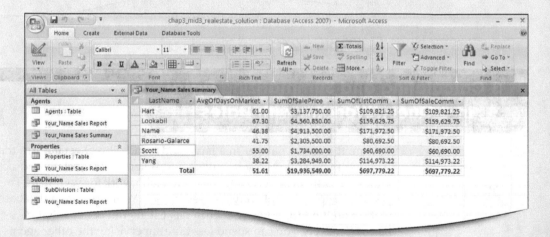

Figure 28 Sales Summary

Customize, Analyze, and Summarize Query Data

Capstone Exercise

Your boss expressed a concern about shipping delays. She believes that customers are not receiving the products they order in a timely fashion. Because your firm's reputation as a provider of high-quality customer service is at risk, she asks that you investigate the sales and shipping records for the last six months and report what you have discovered. In addition, the sales staff is permitted to discount the prices for some customers. Your boss is worried that the discounting erodes profits. She wants you to identify the sales staff who discount the most deeply.

Database File Setup

You need to copy an original database file, rename the copied file, and then open the copied database to complete this capstone exercise. After you open the copied database, you will replace an existing employee's name with your name.

a. Locate the file named *chap3_cap_traders.accdb* and copy it to your production folder.
b. Rename the copied file as **chap3_cap_traders_solution.accdb**.
c. Open the *chap3_cap_traders_solution.accdb* file and enable the content.
d. Open the **Employees table**.
e. Find and replace *Margaret Peacock's* name with your name.

Sales Report Query

You need to create a detail query to calculate the number of days between the date an order was placed and the date the order was shipped for each order. You also need the query to determine the amount of a discount, calculate the revenue, calculate the total cost, and calculate the profit. Furthermore, the query should calculate the employee's commission on the sale.

a. Set a criterion that limits the query to only the most recent six months' worth of shipped orders.
b. Sort the records in the datasheet view by order date to determine the most recent order, if you want.
c. Include the following fields: **LastName** (from the Employee Table), **OrderDate**, **ShippedDate**, **UnitPrice**, **ProductCost**, **Quantity**, and **Discount**.
d. Save the query as **Your_Name Sales Report**.
e. In Design view, build an expression, DaysToShip, to calculate the number of days taken to fill each order. Subtract the OrderDate field from the ShippedDate field. (Hint: The answers will never be negative numbers.)

f. Calculate the profit for each product ordered. Multiply the UnitPrice by the Discount to determine the amount of the discount. Then subtract the Discount amount from the UnitPrice and multiply the result by Quantity to calculate Revenue. Calculate TotalCost for each item ordered by multiplying ProductCost by Quantity. Subtract TotalCost from Revenue to calculate Profit.
g. Calculate the Commission for each profitable order. When the profit on the ordered item is positive, calculate Commission by multiplying profit by the commission rate of 3.5%. If the profit on the ordered item is negative (a loss), the salesperson receives no commission. Name the newly created field Commission.
h. Verify that the query calculations are correct and save the query.
i. In Datasheet view, add a total row to calculate the average number of DaysToShip and the sums for the Revenue, TotalCost, Profit, and Commission fields. Format the Revenue, TotalCost, Profit, and Commission fields as currency.

Totals Query

You need to create a totals query based on the Your_Name Sales Report query. You will group the totals query by last name to provide aggregate statistics that summarize each salesperson's performance and income. It also will provide the average number of days each salesperson's orders take to ship. Compare your results to Figure 28.

a. Create a **Totals** query based on Your_Name Sales Report. Group by **LastName** and summarize the **DaysToShip** field with an average. Summarize the **Revenue, TotalCost, Profit**, and **Commission** fields as sums. Format the Revenue, TotalCost, Profit, and Commission fields as currency.
b. Add a Total row to the Datasheet view that will sum the Revenue, TotalCost, Profit, and Commission fields and average the DaysToShip field.
c. Save this query as **Your_Name Shipping and Commission Summary**.
d. Capture a screenshot of the Sales Summary query. Open the query on your computer and press **PrintScrn**. Open Microsoft Word and press **Ctrl+V** or click **Paste**. Save the Word document as **chap3_cap_solution**. Print the Word document.

...continued on Next Page

Mini Cases

Vacation Time for Bank Employees

GENERAL CASE

The *chap3_mc1_safebank.accdb* file contains data from a small bank. Copy the *chap3_mc1_safebank.accdb* file to your working storage folder, name it **chap3_mc1_safebank_solution.accdb**, and open the copied file. Use the skills from this chapter to perform several tasks. The bank's employee policy states that an employee is eligible for three weeks of vacation after two years of employment. Before two full years, the employee may take two weeks of vacation. The Branch table stores the start date of each manager. You need to figure out how long each manager has worked for the bank. Once you have done that, you need to calculate the number of weeks of vacation the manager is eligible to enjoy. Set these calculations up so that when the query is opened in the future (for example, tomorrow, a month, or two years from now), the length of service and vacation values will update automatically. Summarize each customer's account balances. This summary should list the customer's name and a total of all account balances.

Performance Elements	Exceeds Expectations	Meets Expectations	Below Expectations
Create query	All necessary and no unneeded fields included.	All necessary fields included but also unnecessary fields.	Not all necessary fields were included in the query.
Compute length of service	Calculations and methods correct.	Calculations correct but method inefficient.	Calculations incorrect and methods inefficient.
Compute vacation entitlement	Calculations and methods correct, updates automatically.	Calculations and methods correct but fail to update.	Calculations incorrect, methods inefficient, no updates.
Summarize balances	Correct method, correct totals.	Correct totals but inefficient method.	Totals incorrect or missing.

Combining Name Fields

RESEARCH CASE

This chapter introduced you to the power of using Access Expressions, but you have much more to explore. Use Access help to search for Expressions. Open and read the articles titled *Create an expression* and *A guide to expression syntax*. Put your new knowledge to the test. Copy any of the database files that you used in this chapter and rename the copy with the prefix, **chap3_mc2**. For example, if you copy the safebank database, the filename should be **chap3_mc2_description_solution.accdb**. Open the file. Find a table that stores names in two fields: FirstName and LastName. Add your name to the table. Your challenge is to figure out a way of combining the last and first name fields into one field that prints the last name, a comma, a space, and then the first name. Once you successfully combine the fields somewhere, alphabetize the list. Print it. Write your instructor a memo explaining how you accomplished this. Use a memo template in Word, your most professional writing style, and clear directions that someone could follow in order to accomplish this task. Attach the printout of the name list to the memo. Save the Word document as **chap3_mc2_solution**.

Performance Elements	Exceeds Expectations	Meets Expectations	Below Expectations
Use online help	Appropriate articles located and memo indicates comprehension.	Appropriate articles located but memo did not demonstrate comprehension.	Articles not found.
Prepare list of names	Printed list attached to memo in requested format.	Printed list is attached but the formatting has minor flaws.	List missing or incomprehensible.
Summarize and communicate	Memo clearly written and could be used as directions.	Memo text indicates some understanding but also weaknesses.	Memo missing or incomprehensible.
Aesthetics	Memo template correctly employed.	Template employed but signed in the wrong place or improperly used.	Memo missing or incomprehensible.

...continued on Next Page

Coffee Revenue Queries

DISASTER RECOVERY

A co-worker called you into his office and explained that he was having difficulty with Access 2007 and asked you to look at his work. Copy the *chap3_mc3_coffee.accdb* file to your working storage folder, name it **chap3_mc3_coffee_solution.accdb**, and open the file. It contains two queries, Your_Name Revenue and Your_Name Revenue by City. The Revenue query is supposed to calculate product Price (based on a markup percentage on Cost) and Revenue (the product of Price and Quantity). Something is wrong with the Revenue query. Your challenge is to find and correct the error(s). Your co-worker also tried to use the Revenue query as input for a Totals query that should show revenue by city. Of course, since the Revenue query doesn't work correctly, nothing based upon it will work, either. After correcting the Revenue query, open, locate the errors in, and fix the Totals query. Run the queries. Display all of the Balance values as currency. Save the queries with your name and descriptive titles. Print the Datasheet view of the Totals query and turn the printout and file in to your instructor if instructed to do so.

Performance Elements	Exceeds Expectations	Meets Expectations	Below Expectations
Error identification	Correct identification and correction of all errors.	Correct identification of all errors and correction of some errors.	Errors neither located nor corrected.
Summary query	Correct grouping options and summarization selected.	Correct grouping but some summaries incorrectly selected.	Incorrect group by option selection.
Naming	Descriptive query name selected and employed.	Query name is only partially descriptive.	Query missing or default names used.

Access

Create, Edit, and Perform Calculations in Reports

Creating Professional and Useful Reports

bjectives

After you read this chapter you will be able to:

1. Plan a report.
2. Use different report views.
3. Create and edit a report.
4. Identify report elements, sections, and controls.
5. Add grouping levels in Layout view.
6. Add fields to a report.
7. Use the Report Wizard.

Hands-On Exercises

Exercises	Skills Covered
1. INTRODUCTION TO ACCESS REPORTS **Open:** chap4_ho1-3_coffee.accdb **Save as:** chap4_ho1-3_coffee_solution.accdb **Back up as:** chap4_ho1_coffee_solution.accdb	• Create a Report Using the Report Tool • Create and Apply a Filter in a Report • Remove Fields from a Report and Adjust Column Widths • Reposition Report Objects and Insert Graphic Elements in a Report • Use AutoFormat and Format Report Elements
2. CREATE, SORT, EDIT, NEST, AND REMOVE GROUPS FROM REPORTS **Open:** chap4_ho1-3_coffee_solution.accdb (from Exercise 1) **Save as:** chap4_ho1-3_coffee_solution.accdb (additional modifications) **Back up as:** chap4_ho2_coffee_solution.accdb	• Sort a Report • Create a Grouped Report and Sort It • Add Additional Grouping Levels and Calculate Summary Statistics • Remove Grouping Levels • Reorder Grouping Levels
3. REPORT WIZARD **Open:** chap4_ho1-3_coffee_solution.accdb (from Exercise 2) **Save as:** chap4_ho1-3_coffee_solution.accdb (additional modifications)	• Assemble the Report Data • Create a Query-Based Report and Add Grouping • Create Summary Statistics • Select Layout and AutoFormatting • Modify the Report

From *Exploring Office 2007 Volume I*, Robert T. Grauer, Michelle Hulett, Cynthia Krebs, Maurie Wigman Lockley, Keith Mulbery, and Judy Scheeren. Copyright © 2007 by Pearson Education. Published by Prentice Hall.

CASE STUDY
Northwind Traders

Northwind Traders is a small, international, specialty food company. It sells products in eight different divisions: beverages, confections (candy), condiments, dairy products, grains and cereals, meat and poultry, produce, and seafood. Although most of its customers are restaurants and gourmet food shops, it has a few retail customers, too. All of the order information is stored in the company's database. This database is used by the finance department to monitor and maintain sales records. You are the finance manager. Your task is to determine

Case Study

the revenue from each order and to summarize the first-quarter revenue for each month and by each category. You need only report on gross revenue—the total amount the firm receives. This report does not need to calculate any costs or expenses. It is important that you report accurately. Figure 1 presents a rough layout of the report. You must identify the source data; prepare a report; and group it to match the layout.

Your Assignment

- Copy the file named *chap4_case_traders.accdb*. Rename the copy **chap4_case_traders_solution.accdb**. Open the copied file and enable the content.
- Locate and rename the Your Name Revenue query with your first and last name. Use this query as the source for your report. It contains all the needed fields for the report plus several fields you do not need.
- Create a report based on the Your Name Revenue query. Use any report creation method you learned about in the chapter.
- Add appropriate grouping levels to produce the output shown in Figure 1. Name the report **Your Name First Quarter Sales by Month and Category**. You may select formatting as you want, but the grouping layout should match the design shown.
- Print the completed report.
- Compact and repair the file.
- Back up the database.

Appearances Matter

By now you know how to plan a database, create a table, establish relationships among table data, and extract, manipulate, and summarize data using queries. You generated output by printing table or query datasheets. If you look back at your earlier work, you will see that the information exists, but it is bland. You probably have worked in other application software sufficiently to wonder if Access can enhance the print files. Access provides a powerful tool, giving you the ability to organize and present selected data clearly. Most of the printed output generated by Access users comes from reports.

Enhanced data improves the functionality of database information. Just as in the other Microsoft Office applications, you can change the size, style, and placement of printed matter. You may highlight portions of output to call attention to them. You may also add graphs, pictures, or charts to help the report reader more easily convert the database data into useful information. Designing and producing clear, functional, and organized reports facilitates decision-making. Report production begins with planning the report's design.

In this section, you plan reports. First you create reports using the Report Tool, and then you edit the report by using the Layout view.

Planning a Report

A *report* is a printed document that displays information from a database.

A *report* is a printed document that displays information from a database in a manner that provides clear information to managers. You can design a report to create a catalog, a telephone directory, a financial statement, a graph showing sales by month, a shipping label, or a letter to customers reminding them about a past due payment. All documents you create using table data are Access reports. You should carefully consider what information you need and how you can optimally present it.

Access provides powerful tools to help you accomplish this goal. However, if you do not take the time to plan the report in advance, the power of the tools may impede the report process. You should think through what elements you need and how they should be arranged on the printed page prior to launching the software. The time invested planning the report's appearance at the start of the process leads to fewer surprises with the end result. The report plan helps you take charge of the computer instead of the computer controlling you.

(The report plan helps you take charge of the computer instead of the computer controlling you.)

Draw a Paper Design

The most important tool you use to create an Access report may be a pencil. If you sketch your desired output before touching the mouse, you will be happier with the results. As you sketch, you must ask a number of questions.

- What is the purpose of the report?
- Who uses this report?
- What elements, including labels and calculations, need to be included? What formulae will produce accurate results?
- Will the results be sensitive or confidential? If so, does there need to be a warning printed on the report?
- How will the report be distributed? Will users pull the information directly from Access or will they receive it through e-mail, a fax, the Internet, Word, or Excel?

Sketch the report layout on paper. Identify the field names, their locations, their placement on the page, and other design elements as you sketch. Figure 1 provides a sample report layout.

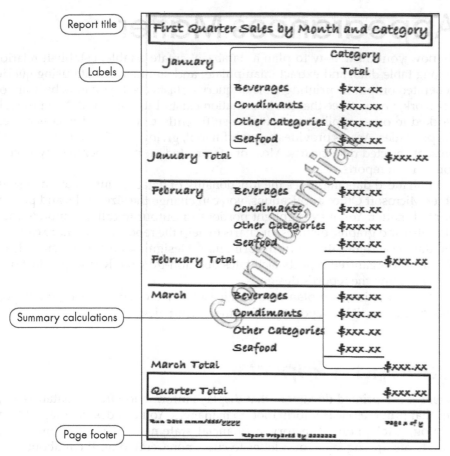

Figure 1 Report Plan

Identify Data Sources

In the next step of planning your report, you need to identify the data source(s) of each report element. You may use one or more tables, queries, or a combination of tables and queries as the report's source. Occasionally, a single table or query contains all of the records you need for the report. Typically, however, you need to specify several tables. When multiple tables are needed to create a report, you may assemble all necessary data in a single query and then base the report on that query. Reports frequently contain graphics as well as data. As you identify the sources of report input, you also need to specify the graphic source. Frequently, a company logo on an invoice or a watermark, indicating that the material is confidential or proprietary, is printed on the report.

Select a Reporting Tool

Access gives you several tools to facilitate report creation. Which one you select depends on the data source and complexity of the report design. Table 1 summarizes the available tools and their usage.

Create, Edit, and Perform Calculations In Reports

Table 1 Report Tools, Location, and Usage

Report Tool	Location	Data Source	Output Complexity
Report Tool	Create Tab, Reports Group, Reports command	Single table or query	Limited. This creates a report showing all of the fields in the data source.
Report Wizard	Create Tab, Reports Group, Report Wizard command	Single or multiple tables or queries or a mixture of tables and queries	More sophisticated. Include (or exclude) fields. Add grouping and sorting instructions. Choose between detailed or summary data presentation.
Label Wizard	Create Tab, Reports Group, Labels command	Single or multiple tables or queries or a mixture of tables and queries	Limited. This feature only produces mailing labels (or name badges) but does so formatted to fit a variety of commercially available mailing labels. The output displays in multiple columns only in Print Preview. Filterable to exclude records.
Blank Report	Create Tab, Reports Group, Blank Report command	Single or multiple tables or queries or a mixture of tables and queries	Limited and extremely complex. Use to quickly assemble a few fields from multiple tables without stepping through the wizard. Alternatively, use to customize the most sophisticated reports with complex grouping levels and sorts.

Using Different Report Views

You have worked with Datasheet and Design views of tables and queries to perform different tasks. For example, you cannot perform data entry in an Access table in Design view, nor can you establish query criteria in Datasheet view. Similarly, Access 2007 provides different views of your report. You view and edit the report using different views depending on what you need to accomplish. Because Access reports may be more sophisticated than queries or tables, you have more views available. Each view accommodates different actions.

Use Print Preview

The **Print Preview** displays the report as it will be printed.

The **Print Preview** displays the report exactly as it will appear on the printed output. You may look at or print your reports in this view, but you cannot edit the report data. You may specify which pages to print in the Print dialog box. The default value will print all pages in the report. Figure 2 shows an Access report in Print Preview.

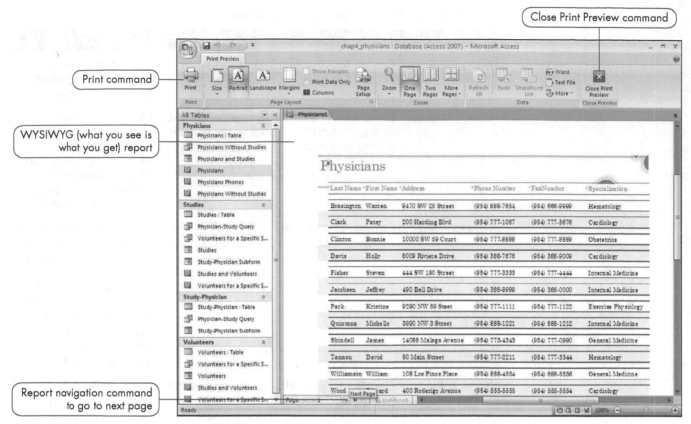

Figure 2 Print Preview of an Access Report

Close Print Preview command

Print command

WYSIWYG (what you see is what you get) report

Report navigation command to go to next page

TIP   Always Preview Access Reports Prior to Printing

Because databases contain a great deal of information, Access reports may become very long and may require many pages to print. Experienced Access users **always** preview their work and go to the last page of the report by using the navigation commands. Although some reports require hundreds of pages to print, many that have multiple pages may be reformatted to print on one or a few pages. The rule is preview before printing.

View and Interact with Data in Report View

Use the **Report view** to make temporary changes to data while viewing it as it will print.

The second way to view Access reports, the **Report view**, provides you the ability to see what the printed report will look like and to make temporary changes to how the data are viewed. You can identify portions of the output by applying a filter. For example, if you need a list of physicians practicing Internal Medicine, you can right-click the record value and select the appropriate filtering option, *equals Internal Medicine*, from the shortcut menu. All of the other types of physicians are hidden temporarily (see Figure 3). If you print the filtered report, the printout will not show the hidden records. When you close and open a filtered report again, the filter disappears, and all records appear in Report view. You may reapply the filter to reproduce the filtered results. The Report view permits you to copy selected formatted records to the Clipboard and paste them in other applications. Even when the security controls on the report have been tightly set by the database administrator, this view gives the report user a measure of customization and interactivity with the data.

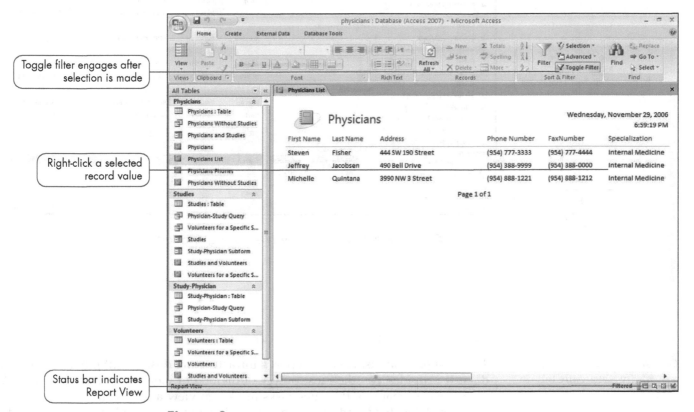

Figure 3 Filtered Report Output Shown In Report View

Modify Reports in Layout View

Use the **Layout view** to alter the report design while viewing the data.

The third (and perhaps the most useful) report view is the Layout view. Use the **Layout view** to alter the report design while viewing the data. You should use Layout view to add or delete fields to the report, modify field control properties, change the column widths or row height to ensure that the entire field displays without truncation, add grouping and sorting levels to a report, or to filter reported data to extract only specific records. Although the display appears as what you see is what you get (WYSIWYG), you will find sufficient variations between the Layout and Print Preview views that you will need to use Print Preview. You do most of the report's modification using Layout view. Figure 4 shows a report in Layout view.

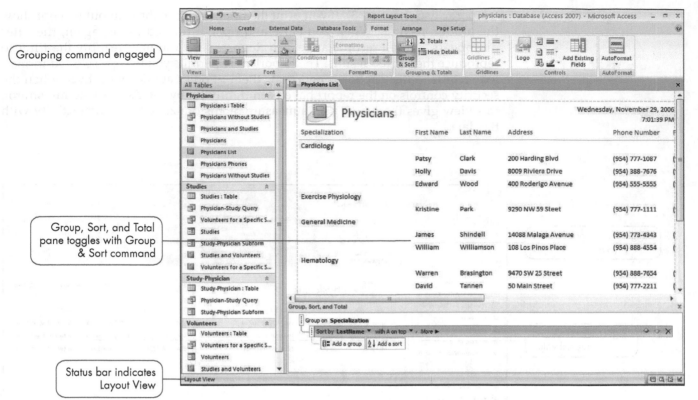

Grouping command engaged

Group, Sort, and Total pane toggles with Group & Sort command

Status bar indicates Layout View

Figure 4 Report in Layout View with Grouping and Sorting

Perfect a Report in Design View

The ***Design view*** displays the report's infrastructure but no data.

The ***Design view*** displays the report's infrastructure design, but it does not display data. It provides you the most powerful method of viewing an Access report. You may perform many of the same tasks in Design view as you can in Layout view—add and delete fields, add and remove sorting and grouping layers, rearrange data elements, adjust column widths, and customize report elements. You do not see any of the report's data while in this view. When the report is very lengthy, hiding the data as you alter the design may be an advantage because you save time by not scrolling. However, the Design view looks so different from the final output, it may be confusing. You need to experiment with using both the Layout and Design views and decide which view fits your style. Figure 5 displays the Physicians report in Design view. The next section provides explanations for all of the little boxes and stripes.

Create, Edit, and Perform Calculations in Reports

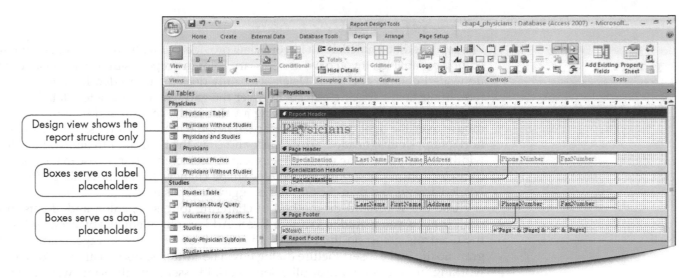

Design view shows the report structure only

Boxes serve as label placeholders

Boxes serve as data placeholders

Figure 5 Reports Shown In Design View Do Not Display Record Values

Create and Edit a Report

Access gives you several different methods to generate a report. You will first learn how to use the Report tool. Start by determining all of the fields needed for the report. To use the Report tool, you need to assemble all of the necessary data in one place. This tool is extremely easy to use and will adequately serve your needs much of the time. Occasionally, a table contains all of the fields for a report. More often, you will need to create or open a query containing the necessary fields. If an existing query has all of the fields needed for the report but also some unneeded fields, you will probably use the existing query. You can delete the extraneous fields.

Create a Report with the Report Tool

First you need to determine the record source for the report. Open the record source in Datasheet view. Click the Create tab and click Report in the Reports group. Access creates the report and displays it in Layout view (see Figure 6). If you like the look of the report, you may print, save, and close it from the Layout view. When you reopen the saved report file, Access automatically returns to the record source and loads the most recent data into the report.

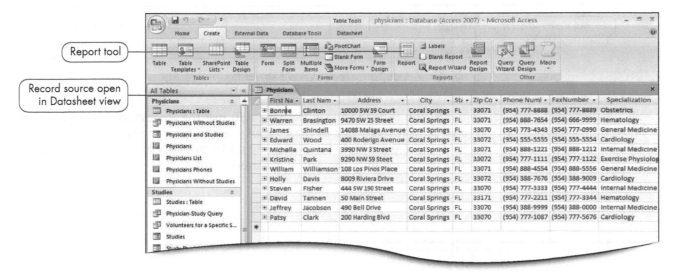

Report tool

Record source open in Datasheet view

Figure 6 Set Up for Using Report Tool

Create, Edit, and Perform Calculations in Reports

Edit a Report in Layout View

The report-editing functions in Layout view provide you with powerful and easy-to-use editing capabilities. If you have unnecessary fields in a report, simply click a value in the unneeded column and press Delete. Not only does the unneeded field go away; the remaining field's spacing adjusts to cover the gap where the deleted data had been. Change the column widths by clicking a value in the column and then moving your mouse over the right column boundary. When the mouse pointer shape changes to a horizontal, double-headed arrow, click and drag the boundary to adjust the column width. You may move an object by selecting it, positioning your mouse in the middle of the selection, waiting until the pointer shape changes to the move shape (the four-headed arrow), and then clicking and dragging to reposition.

Use the select-and-do method of changing font, size, color, and effects in the same way as you would in Word or Excel. Add graphic elements by clicking Logo in the Controls group on the Format tab. Then browse to the storage location of the graphic file in the Insert Picture dialog box. The editing skills you already know from working in other software applications work in essentially the same way when you edit an Access report in the Layout view. Access provides many predefined formats that you may apply to the report. Figure 7 shows a report in Layout view.

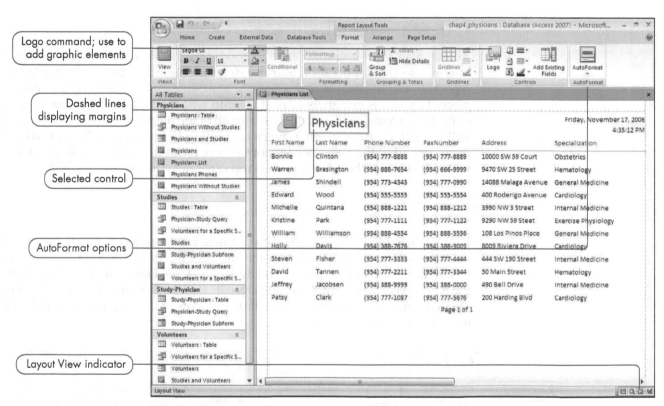

Figure 7 Report Layout View Elements

In the following exercise you will use the Report tool to generate an Access report. You will work in the Layout view to filter the report, remove unnecessary fields, resize and reposition columns, add graphics, apply AutoFormats to the report, and then customize the AutoFormatted results.

Hands-On Exercises

1 | Introduction to Access Reports

Skills covered: 1. Create a Report Using the Report Tool **2.** Create and Apply a Filter in a Report **3.** Remove Fields from a Report and Adjust Column Widths **4.** Reposition Report Objects and Insert Graphic Elements in a Report **5.** Use AutoFormat and Format Report Elements

Step 1	
Create a Report Using the Report Tool	Refer to Figure 8 as you complete Step 1.

a. Use Windows Explorer to locate the file named *chap4_ho1-3_coffee.accdb*. Copy the file and rename it as **chap4_ho1-3_coffee_solution.accdb**.

b. Open the *chap4_ho1-3_coffee_solution.accdb* file.

c. Click **Options** on the Security Warning toolbar, click **Enable this content** in the Microsoft Office Security Options dialog box, and then click **OK**.

d. Open the **Sales Reps table** and replace *Your Name* with your first and last names. Close the Sales Reps table.

e. Right-click the **Your Name Revenue** query in the *All Tables window* and select **Rename**. Replace *Your Name* with your first and last names.

f. Open the **Your Name Revenue query** in Datasheet view.

g. Click the **Create tab** and then click **Report** in the Reports group.

Access creates the report and opens it in the Layout view. The report opens with the Format tab active because you almost always need to modify the format of a newly generated report.

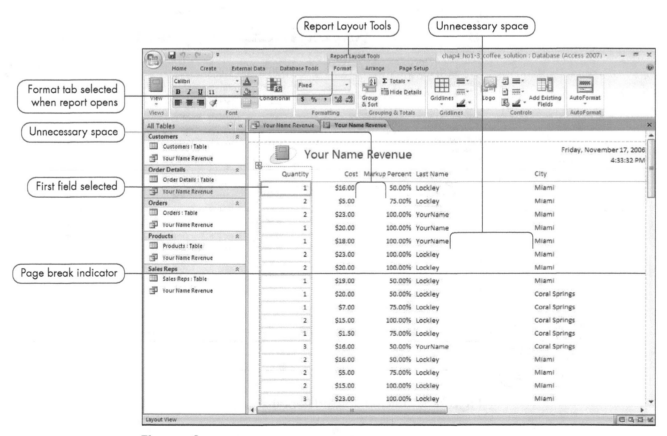

Figure 8 Newly Created Report Opens In Layout View

Refer to Figure 9 as you complete Step 2.

a. Right-click **Your Name** and select **Equals "Your Name"** from the shortcut menu.

You have created and applied a filter that displays only your orders. The status bar in the lower-right corner of the window tells you that the report has a filter applied. Only your records should display.

b. Right-click the word *Miami* and select **Does Not Equal "Miami"** from the short-cut menu.

Additional records are filtered out of the report, and a total for the Revenue field moves into view. Note that the total did not inherit the currency format from the source data. You may need to scroll right to see the total of the Revenue column.

c. Compare your selected fields to those shown in Figure 9 and then click **Save**.

The Save As dialog box opens with the default name (inherited from the source query) highlighted.

d. Type **Your Name Sales Outside of Miami**. Click **OK**.

e. Close the report and close the query.

You saved the report based on the query, so it no longer needs to be open. Although this is a small database, working with unnecessary objects open may slow your computer's response time. You should always close unnecessary objects.

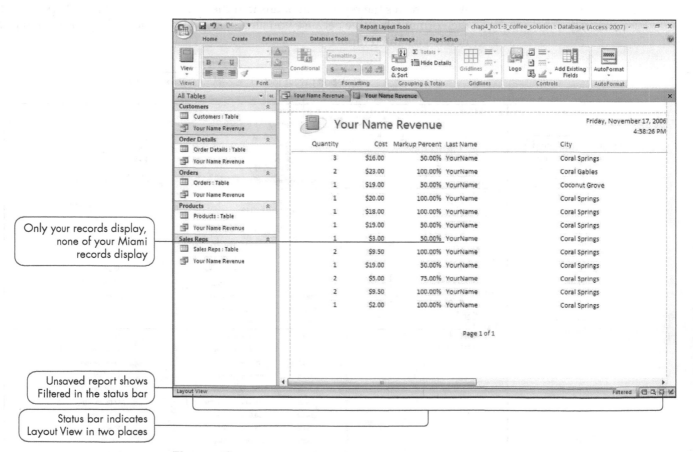

Figure 9 Filtered, Totaled Report

Refer to Figure 10 as you complete Step 3.

a. Open the **Your Name Sales Outside of Miami report**. Look at the right side of the status bar. It displays *Report View*. The status bar no longer indicates that the report is filtered.

When you reopen an existing report, it opens in Report view. This view lets you look at the report and permits limited filtering capabilities. Because this view provides limited editing interaction, you need to change to Layout view.

b. Right-click the **Your Name Sales Outside of Miami tab** and select **Layout View** from the shortcut menu.

c. Click the label **Quantity**.

A gold box surrounds the selected field name, and a dotted border surrounds the record values in the field.

TROUBLESHOOTING: The gold box should only be around the word Quantity. If it surrounds the entire label row, you are still in Report view. Switch to Layout view and then click Quantity again.

d. Press **Delete**.

The column disappears from the report. The remaining columns move left to fill the empty space.

e. Click on **your name** in any record. Move your mouse to the right boundary of the gold border and, when the pointer shape changes to a double-headed arrow, click and drag the boundary to the left to decrease the column width.

f. Click on a **city name** in any record. Move your mouse to the right boundary of the gold border and, when the pointer shape changes to a double-headed arrow, click and drag the boundary to the left to decrease the column width.

The report should fit on a single page now. You notice that the column heading for the Markup Percent column is much wider than the values in the column.

g. Click the **Markup Percent** column label to activate the gold border. Single-click **Markup Percent** again to edit the label.

You know you are in edit mode because the border color changes to black, and a flashing insertion point appears inside the border.

h. Position the insertion point to the left of the *P* in *Percent*. Press **Ctrl+Enter**. Click anywhere on the report to exit edit mode. Save the report.

The Ctrl+Enter command forces a line break. The word *Percent* moves below the word *Markup*.

TIP Forced Line Break

A similar command, Alt+Enter, may be used in Excel to force a line break, when the width of the column name greatly exceeds the width of the data displayed in the column. Although word wrapping may achieve the same effect, you can more precisely control which word prints on what line by forcing the break yourself.

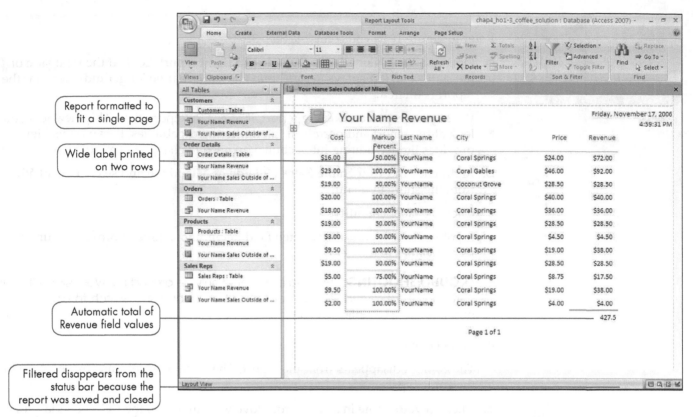

Report formatted to
fit a single page

Wide label printed
on two rows

Automatic total of
Revenue field values

Filtered disappears from the
status bar because the
report was saved and closed

Figure 10 Resized Report

Step 4

**Reposition Report
Objects and Insert
Graphic Elements
in a Report**

Refer to Figure 11 as you complete Step 4.

a. Click any record in the **City** column to select it. Move the mouse to the middle of the selected column. When the pointer shape changes to a *four-headed arrow*, click and drag to the left until the vertical gold line is on the left edge of the report. Release the mouse.

As you drag past other columns in the report, a gold line moves to tell you the column's current position. When you release the mouse, the City column moves to the first position.

TROUBLESHOOTING: When you begin to drag while located in a record, Access assumes that you want to change the height of the row until you move out of the column. While the mouse is inside the selected cell a black boundary forms across the entire row. Keep dragging left. As soon as the mouse moves outside the original boundaries, the gold line will appear.

b. Click any record in the **Last Name** column to select it. Move the mouse to the middle of the selected column. When the pointer shape changes to a *four-headed arrow*, click and drag right. Continue the drag until the vertical gold line is on the right edge of the report. Release the mouse.

The Last Name column is the last column in the report.

c. Click the report title, *Your Name Revenue*, to select it and then click it again to edit it. Type **Your Name Non–Miami Sales**.

d. Click the picture of the **report binder** to select it.

e. Click **Logo** in the Controls group on the Format tab.

The Insert Picture dialog box opens to the default folder, My Pictures, but the file you need is stored in the folder with the rest of the Access files.

f. Browse to your file storage folder; locate and open the file named *chap4_ho1-3_coffee.gif*. Click **OK**.

g. Move your mouse over the lower right corner of the picture until the pointer shape changes to a diagonal, double-headed arrow. Click and drag the lower-right picture corner until the picture's size roughly doubles.

The picture enlarges, but now it covers part of your name.

TIP Use the Properties Sheet to Exactly Size an Object

If you right-click the picture and select Properties from the shortcut menu, you may use measurements to exactly size the picture. You also may add special effects, like stretch or zoom.

---

h. Click the report's title, *Your Name Non–Miami Sales,* to select it. Position the mouse pointer in the middle of the box. When the pointer shape changes to the four-headed move arrow, click and drag the report title right and down (see Figure 11).

i. Click **Save** on the Quick Access Toolbar to save the design changes to the report.

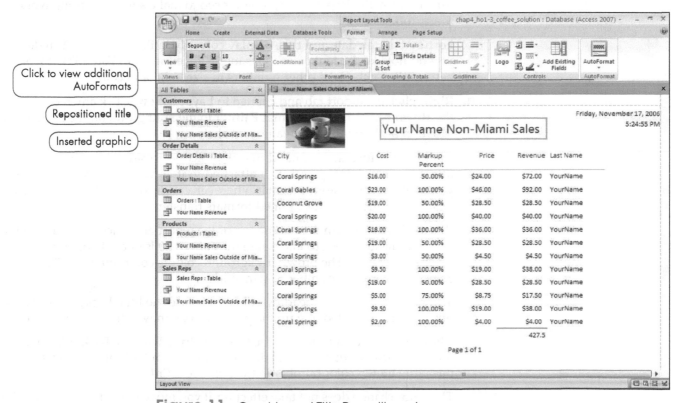

Figure 11 Graphic and Title Repositioned

Refer to Figure 12 as you complete Step 5.

a. Check to ensure the *Your Name Non–Miami Sales report* remains in Layout view. Right-click the **Revenue Total cell** (427.5) to select it and open the shortcut menu.

b. Select **Properties** from the shortcut menu.

The Property Sheet opens in the task pane.

c. Click the **Format tab** (if necessary) and then click the **drop-down arrow** in the *Format Property box* and select **Currency**.

You should see the value of the Revenue field total change to $427.50. Close the Property Sheet.

d. Click **AutoFormat** in the AutoFormat group on the Format tab (see Figure 12).

The AutoFormat list expands to display several formats. The last choice activates the AutoFormat Wizard.

e. Select the **Median AutoFormat** (2nd column, 3rd row) and click it.

The AutoFormat applies to the entire report. It does not matter what portion of the report you selected when you applied the AutoFormat. Every element of the report gets a format change. This effect may create problems.

f. Examine the results. Identify problems.

Although the Layout view gives you powerful editing capabilities, it does not perfectly duplicate the printed output. You need to use Print Preview to determine if the problem needs action.

g. Right-click the report tab and change to **Print Preview**. Examine the report's date and time. You should check the Report view, also. Right-click the report tab and change to **Report View**. Often, reports get copied and pasted or e-mailed directly from the Report view, so you need to make sure everything works there, too.

Fortunately, the date and time display correctly in Print Preview. You decide that you do not like the font color looks in the Revenue total. You think it would look better if it matched the other numbers in size, font, and color.

h. Right-click the report tab and change to **Layout View**. Click any record in the **Revenue** field. Click **Format Painter** in the Font group on the Format tab. Move to the **Revenue total** value and click it.

Clicking the format command instructs Access to save the source format. The mouse pointer has a paintbrush attached to it as you move to remind you that you will paint the stored format wherever you next click. When you reach the destination and click, the defined formats transfer.

i. Right-click the **brown area** at the top of the report and select **Properties** on the shortcut menu. Check to make sure the *Format tab* is open. Look in the *Back Color Property box*. The brown background color is color number **#775F55**. Select and **copy** the number or remember it.

You need to match the heading color to replace the blue background of the column headings. By looking up the property, you may make an exact color match.

j. Click the blue background for the **Cost heading**. Find the Back color property on the Format sheet. Click and drag to select its contents and press **Ctrl + V** to paste the brown color number in the box. Press **Enter**.

The color change does not take effect until you move to the next row. You like the new color but decide the type font will look better larger, centered, and bolded.

k. Click the **Font Size arrow** in the Font group and select **12**. Click **Bold**. Click the **Center text** command.

l. Scroll in the Property Sheet for the *Cost Heading* until you locate the Top Margin property. Type **0.1**.

m. Duplicate the format changes to the cost heading to the other headings by double-clicking **Format Painter** located in the Font group. Click the headings for *Markup Percent*, *Last Name*, *City*, *Price*, and *Revenue*. Press **Esc**.

Double-clicking the Format Painter permits painting a format to multiple areas without redefining the source after each painting. Pressing Esc or clicking the Format Painter again turns the Format Painter off.

n. Right-click the *Markup Percent* heading and change its Top Margin property in the Property Sheet to **0** (zero).

Because this heading is two lines, it needs to start higher up than the one line heading beside it.

o. Close the Property Sheet. Widen each column about a quarter inch so the entire page is filled (see Figure 12). Refer to Step 3e for instructions if necessary, except drag to widen rather than to narrow the column. Save your report.

TROUBLESHOOTING: Be sure to look at the report in Print Preview. Remember, the Layout view is not perfectly WYSIWYG. It is easy to make the right column a little too wide and push the report to an extra page. Check to make sure your report is still a single page. If it is not, make the columns a little narrower.

p. Click the **Office Button**, select **Manage**, and then select **Back Up Database**. Type **chap4_ho1_coffee_solution** (note *ho1* instead of *ho1-3*) and click **Save**.

You just created a backup of the database after completing the first hands-on exercise. The original database *chap4_ho1-3_coffee_solution* remains onscreen. If you ruin the original database as you complete the second hands-on exercise, you can use the backup file you just created.

q. Close the file and exit Access if you do not want to continue with the next exercise at this time.

TIP   Learning Software

Following step-by-step instructions is a way to begin learning application software. If you want to become proficient in software, you must explore on your own. The properties sheet contains dozens of features that you did not cover in this lesson. You have finished Hands-On Exercise 1 and saved your file. You should experiment a little. Make a copy of the report and experiment on the copy. Activate the Property Sheet for a field and change properties to see the results.

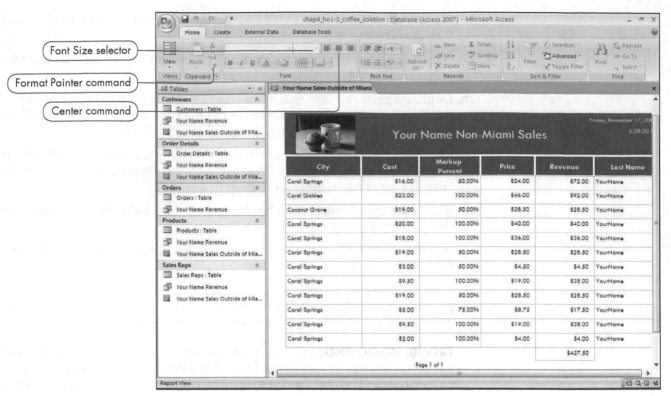

Figure 12 The Complete Single-Page Report

The Anatomy of a Report

You have produced reasonable, sophisticated output. Look at the report design depicted in Figure 13. It, too, contains summary statistics but on multiple levels. The desired layout contains indents to visually classify the differing elements. The finished report will likely require several pages. It would be much easier to read if the headings repeated at the start of each new page. Access can accomplish all of this, and more.

In this section you will learn more about a report's sections and controls. You will also learn how to group an Access report into nested sections.

Identifying Report Elements, Sections, and Controls

Access divides all reports into sections, although you only see the sectional boundaries when you display the report in Design view. You need to become familiar with the sectional areas so that you can control report output completely. For example, if you place an instruction to add field values together in the detail section, the resulting calculation will duplicate each record's value for that field. The field in the detail section contains a single value from a single record.

Understand Sectional Divisions

The *detail section* repeats once for each record in the underlying record source.

The *report header section* prints once at the beginning of each report.

The *report footer section* prints once at the conclusion of each report.

The *group header section(s)* appear once at the start of each new grouping level in the report.

The *group footer section(s)* appear at the end of each grouping level.

The *detail section* repeats once for each record in the underlying record source. If you copied the calculation and placed it in a report header or footer, the result would display the sum of all that field's values for the entire report. The *report header section* prints once at the beginning of each report. The *report footer section* prints once at the conclusion of each report. Should you find all the stripes and little boxes confusing, you still must learn something about them to accurately produce the output you desire. You will begin by learning about the stripes—the sectional boundaries.

In Figure 13, each blue stripe marks the upper boundary of a report area. The top stripe denotes the upper boundary of the report header. The bottom stripe displays the top boundary of the report's footer. The gray, grid-patterned area beneath the stripes shows the space allotted to that element. Notice that the report has no space allocated to the report footer. You may change the space between areas by moving your mouse over the stripe's bottom. When the pointer shape changes to a double-headed arrow, click and drag to move the boundary. Use this method if you decide to add a footer to the report. A gray, grid-patterned work space appears as your mouse drags down. If you expand or contract the space allotment for a middle sectional boundary, the lower boundaries all move also. The *group header section(s)* appear once at the start of each new grouping level in the report. The *group footer section(s)* appear at the end of each grouping level.

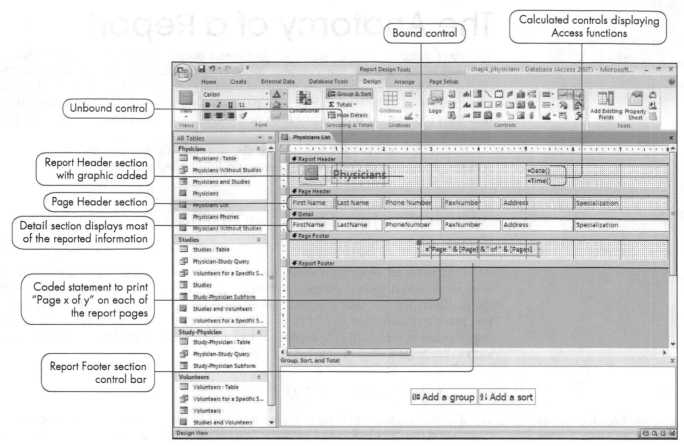

Figure 13 Reports Shown in Design View Do Not Display Record Values

If you decide that the allotted space for a particular section is not needed, you may reposition the top of the next sectional boundary so that the boundary stripes touch. The element will remain in the report's design but will consume no space on the printed output and will not show in any other report view. Use the page header section to repeat column headings on the top of each new page. You will place information like page numbers in the page footer. *Page headers* and *page footers* appear once for each page in the report at the top and bottom of the report's pages, respectively.

All reports contain several different sections; see the reference page for more information about their placement and usage.

Page headers and *page footers* appear once for each page in the report at the top and bottom of the pages.

Report Tools, Location, and Usage | Reference

Design Element	Location	Frequency	Usage	Required
Report Header	Top of the report	Once	Think of the report header as the title page. It includes information like the organization's name, the report's name, and the run date.	Yes
Page Header	Top of each page	One per page	Page headers generally contain the column headings. In a multi-page report, the labels repeat at the top of each page to provide clarity.	Yes
Group Header	At the start of each new group	One at the start of each new group (up to 10)	This element begins and identifies each new group. It generally contains the group name, i.e. in a report grouped by state, the state name would be the header. Any aggregating functions in a group header will summarize the group records, e.g., a SUM function will add all of the record values within the group.	No
Detail	Middle	Once per record reported	This element is repeated once for each selected record in the data source. If there were 500 records in the data source for the report, the report would have 500 detail lines. In a grouped report there may be multiple detail sections—one per group. Often, you omit the detail section entirely. You might show state total without population information showing the population per county. You might do this even when the state population was calculated by adding the county figures.	No
Group Footer	At the end of each group	Once at the end of each group (up to 10)	This element generally repeats the group name, e.g., in a report grouped by state, the state name would repeat in the footer along with a descriptor of aggregating information. An annual sales report might group by month, and one group's footer may display the Total Revenue in May. Any aggregating functions in a group's footer will summarize the group records, e.g., a SUM function will add all of the record values within the group.	No
Page Footer	Bottom of the page	Once per page in the report	Use this feature to print page numbers, page summary statistics, contact information, or report preparation/run date.	Yes, but it need not contain any data
Report Footer	End of the report	One per report	You would use this feature to print grand totals or other summary information for entire project. Often the date, authorship, or contact information displays here.	Yes

TIP Report Footer Placement

In Design view, the report footer section displays below the page footer section. However, all other views and the printed output position the report footer above the page footer. Although this effect can be disconcerting the first time you notice it, it makes good sense. It ensures that the page numbers and other page footer items print in the same position on the last page of the report as on other report pages.

Work with Controls

Use *controls* to position, display, format, and calculate the report data.

Bound controls allow you to pull information from the underlying table or query data.

Unbound controls do not have any record source for their contents.

A *calculated control* uses an expression as opposed to a record value as its data source.

The position and instructions about what to do with the data once retrieved from the table or query come through the use of controls (the little boxes in Design view). You use *controls* to position, display, format, and calculate the report data. Access reports use different types of controls for different purposes.

You use *bound controls* most frequently in preparing an Access report. These controls allow you to pull information from the underlying table or query data. Like the source data, the value of a bound control may be text, dates, numbers, pictures, graphs, or Yes/No values. The latter typically displays as a check box. The binding means that the control inherits most properties—size, formatting, and relationships—from the source table. For example, a text box may display a product's price in currency format. It is bound (tied) to the UnitPrice field in the Products table, which is also set to currency format. Most bound controls display with two small boxes in the report's Design view. The left box is the control's label, the right box or text box displays the record value. A bound control's label automatically comes from the field name or caption (if one exists).

Unbound controls do not have any record source for their contents. The values contained there exist only in the report and nowhere else in the database. You use them to display information (the report's title), cosmetic elements (borders or lines to visually separate report sections), boxes, and pictures.

A *calculated control* uses an expression as opposed to a record value as its data source. The expression usually is bound to the record values of the fields referenced. A report expression, like a query expression, combines field names, operators, constants, and functions to instruct Access on how to perform a calculation. For example, you might use an expression to calculate a discounted price in a sales report. For example:

$$=[UnitPrice] * (1-[Discount] * [Quantity])$$

This expression would likely retrieve the UnitPrice data from the Products table, and the Discount and Quantity values from the Order Details table if you are using a retail store database that contains records for products, including unit price, selling price, and quantity.

Adding Grouping Levels in Layout View

Access provides you with several methods of creating data summaries.

- Create a Totals query by specifying a group by field and the field or fields to summarize.

- Creat a grouped report using the Layout view's Sorting and Grouping tool.

- Create a grouped report using the Report Wizard and specifying the group layers within the Wizard.

Reports provide you with the same power as a Totals query and provide the added advantage of enhanced appearance. This section explores grouping and sorting in the Layout view method. The next section introduces you to the Report Wizard.

Engage the Group & Sort Tool

Open the report in Layout view. The report shown in Figure 14 contains over 2,000 records. Imagine that you must use this data to make decisions about your firm's operations. You would not easily identify trends and patterns by examining 50 or more printed pages. This data needs to be summarized. Begin summarizing by clicking Group & Sort in the Grouping & Totals group on the Format tab. The Group, Sort, and Total pane displays in the bottom of the report.

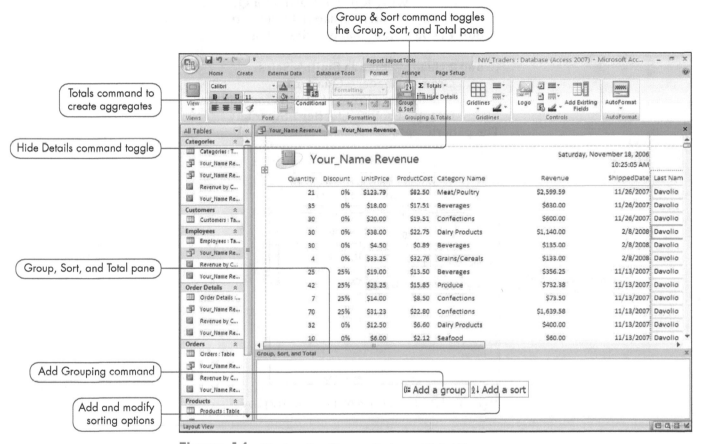

Figure 14 Display the Group, Sort, and Total Pane

Select the Primary Grouping Field

Nested groups provide a power-layering tool to organize information.

You may nest groups in different levels—up to 10. *Nested groups* provide a powerful layering tool to organize information. In this report, you need the sales figures summarized by the categories of products offered. Once created, each group contains introductory and summary information as well as the record values. Generally the group header provides identification information, for example the name of the category. You use the group footer to present summary information for the group. Figure 15 depicts the Add a Group command engaged with the categories field selected as the primary grouping level.

After you establish the primary group, you may add additional levels. This feature works much like an outline. Suppose you needed a sales report grouped by salesperson and then by quarter. Each successive grouping layer gets tucked between the header and footer of the previous layer.

Group 1 Header—Joe Adams' Sales
    Group 2 Header—Quarter 1
        Many Rows of Details for Quarter 1
    Group 2 Footer—Quarter 1 Summary

    Group 2 Header—Quarter 2
        Many Rows of Details for Quarter 2
    Group 2 Footer—Quarter 2 Summary

    Group 2 Header—Quarter 3
        Many Rows of Details for Quarter 3
    Group 2 Footer—Quarter 3 Summary

    Group 2 Header—Quarter 4
        Many Rows of Details for Quarter 4
    Group 2 Footer—Quarter 4 Summary
Group 1 Footer—Joe Adams' Sales Totals

Group 2 Header—Brenda Smith's Sales
    Group 2 Header—Quarter 1
        Many Rows of Details for Quarter 1
    Group 2 Footer—Quarter 1 Summary
The pattern repeats.

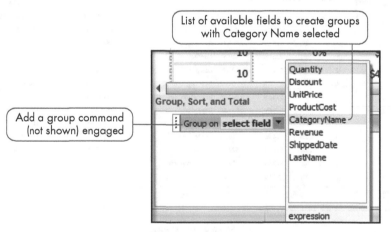

Figure 15 Select a Primary Grouping Level

Hide or Display Details

You must decide if the details—the values stored in each record that report used as a source—need to be displayed in the report. Many reports only display data summaries. How you decide to display details will depend on how the report will be used. Most Access report writers follow the general rule that the less detail and more summarizing information included, the more useful the report. Access makes it easy for you to add and remove detail levels. If you omit the detail and later discover that you need it, you can easily add it back. Engage the Hide Detail command to hide or display report details (see Figure 16).

> *. . . the less detail and more summarizing information included, the more useful the report.*

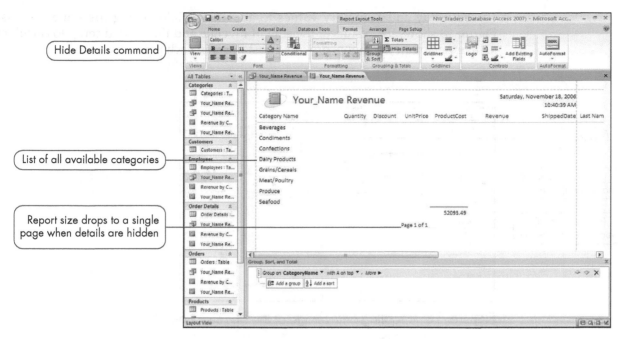

- Hide Details command
- List of all available categories
- Report size drops to a single page when details are hidden

Figure 16 Summary Report with Details Hidden

Calculate Summary Statistics

The report in Figure 17 displays a list of the names of the categories of merchandise sold by the firm. The Totals command in the Grouping & Totals group helps you summarize data. First select the control label for the data you want summarized. Then click Totals and select the necessary aggregating function from the drop-down list.

Decision-makers may wish to examine the same data using different aggregating functions to answer different questions. For example, a sum of all revenue generated by each product category will tell the manager important total sales information. Changing the report to display the maximum revenue will provide the decision-maker with information about which products generated the largest revenue. After you establish the grouping levels, Access makes it easy for you to examine the output in a variety of ways.

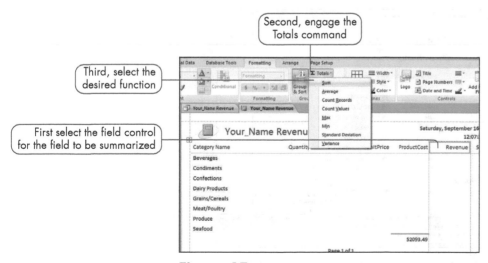

- Second, engage the Totals command
- Third, select the desired function
- First select the field control for the field to be summarized

Figure 17 Creating a Sum of the Revenue Field

You may add summary values to additional fields using the same process. Figure 18 shows the results of the sum of revenue and the needed setup to calculate an average of the discounts provided customers in each product category.

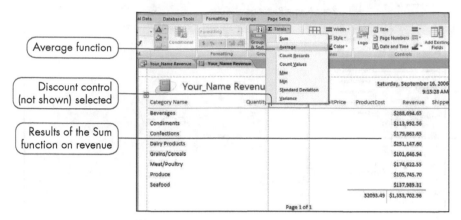

Figure 18 Creating an Average of the Discount Field

Add Additional Grouping Levels

You decide that having the report grouped by category is useful, but you also want to know who sells each category's products. You can add additional grouping levels to an existing report in Layout view by selecting the control that you need to group on and then clicking the Add a Group command in the Group, Sort, and Total pane. In the report displayed in Figure 19, you would first select the control for LastName field and then click the Add a group command. The figure displays the results of adding an additional grouping level to the report. The More command controlling the Category name group expands when selected, granting you access to additional features. The figure displays the settings necessary to display the totals (averages) for the categories below the salesperson totals.

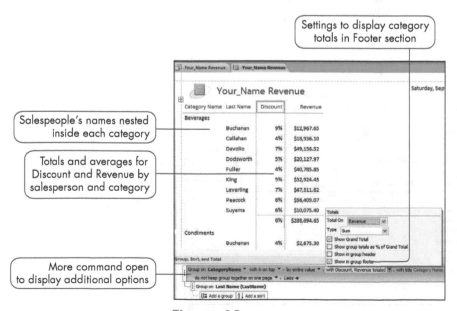

Figure 19 Nested Group Report with Totals Moved to Footer

Sort a Report

While working in the Layout view, you can interact with the sort order of the report's fields. Figure 20 shows a report with two sorting levels applied. The primary sort is the area of specialization. The secondary sort is by the physician's last name. This order groups the cardiologists together with Clark preceding Davis in the alphabetical listing.

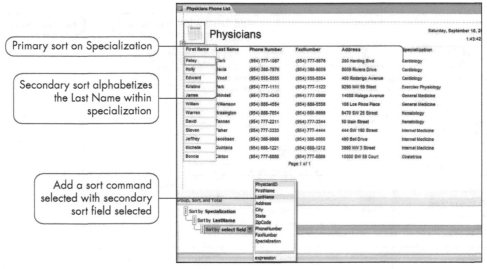

Figure 20 Sorted Report

Adding Fields to a Report

It is possible to omit a necessary field when designing a report. Even if a report has no errors, data needs change with time. You may need to add a new field to an existing report. Access provides an easy way to do that.

The *Field List pane* displays a list of all of the tables and fields in the database.

Open the report in Layout view. Activate the Format tab. Click Add Existing Fields in the Controls group. The Field List pane opens on the right side of the screen. The *Field List pane* displays a list of all of the tables and fields in the database. Once you locate the needed field in the Field List pane, drag and drop it on the report in the position that you want it to occupy. (Alternatively, you can double-click it.) Access creates the needed control to hold the new field, for example, a text box, and then binds the field to the newly created control (see Figure 21). Occasionally, you might want a different control type than the one Access creates for you. You may edit the newly created control's properties to get exactly the control you want. But, you cannot use Layout view to do so. You cannot change the control type property in Layout view. This change must be accomplished in Design view. Of course, you may only specify a control that is appropriate to that data type. For example, a Yes/No field might display as a check box, but you would rather have the words, Yes or No, display.

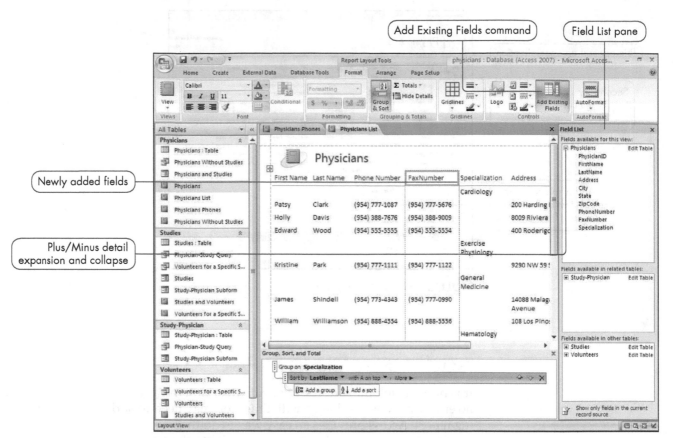

Figure 21 Sorted Report

In the next exercise, you will create a report, add sorting and grouping to refine the content, work with data aggregates, and add a new field to the report.

Hands-On Exercises

2 | Create, Sort, Edit, Nest, and Remove Groups from Reports

Skills covered: 1. Sort a Report **2.** Create a Grouped Report and Sort It. **3.** Add Additional Grouping Levels and Calculate Summary Statistics **4.** Remove Grouping Levels **5.** Reorder Grouping Levels

---

Step 1

Sort a Report

Refer to Figure 22 as you complete Step 1.

a. Open the *chap4_ho1-3_coffee_solution* file if necessary, click **Options** on the Security Warning toolbar, click the **Enable this content option** in the Microsoft Office Security Options dialog box, and click **OK**.

> **TROUBLESHOOTING:** If you create unrecoverable errors while completing this hands-on exercise, you can delete the *chap4_ho1-3_coffee_solution* file, copy the *chap4_ho1_coffee_solution* backup database you created at the end of the first hands-on exercise, and open the copy of the backup database to start the second hands-on exercise again.

b. Open the **Your Name Revenue query** in Datasheet view. Click the **Create tab** and click **Report**.

c. Click **Group & Sort** in the Grouping & Totals group to turn on the Group, Sort, and Total pane at the bottom of the screen.

> **TROUBLESHOOTING:** The Group & Sort command is a toggle. If you do not see the Group, Sort, and Total pane, click the Group & Sort command again. It may have been on, and you turned it off.

d. Click **Add a sort** in the Group, Sort, and Total pane.

A list box opens displaying the names of all the reports fields.

e. Click **LastName** from the list and select it.

Scroll through the list to see two names: Lockley and your name. If your name comes before Lockley alphabetically, your sales are reported first. If your name comes after Lockley alphabetically, Lockley's sales will be first. In the next step, you will sort the list so that your name is on the top—ascending or descending, depending on what letter your name begins with.

f. Find the **Sort with A on top drop-down arrow** in the Group, Sort, and Total pane. Click it to reveal two choices—with A on top and with Z on top. Click the choice that will position your name at the top of the list.

If your name is not on top, sort again, and select the other option.

g. Click the **Office Button**, choose **Save As**, and type **Sales by Employee and City**. Click **OK**.

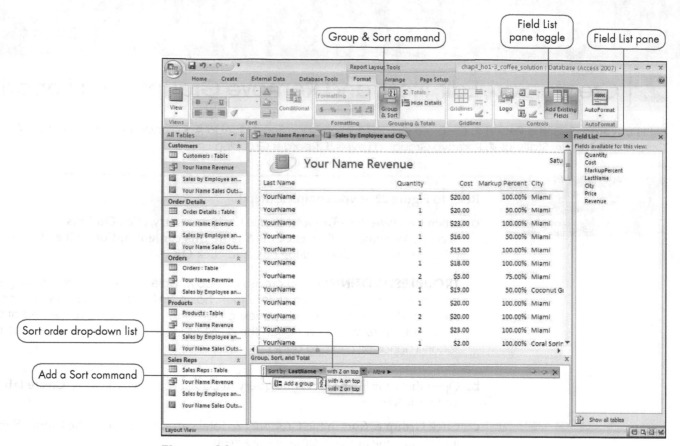

Figure 22 Correctly Sorted Report

Step 2	Refer to Figure 23 as you complete Step 2.
Create a Grouped Report and Sort It	**a.** Click **Add a group** in the Group, Sort, and Total pane.

a. Click **Add a group** in the Group, Sort, and Total pane.

A list box pops up asking you to select the field name that you want to group by.

b. Select the **LastName** field in the list box.

TROUBLESHOOTING: If your screen does not look like Figure 23, it may be because you selected a different group by value. Click close on the gold Group on LastName bar in the Group, Sort, and Total pane to remove the incorrect grouping. Then rework Steps 2a and 2b.

c. Scroll right until you can see the label control box for the **Revenue** field. (It is blue.) Click to select it.

d. Click the **Format tab** and click **Totals** in the Grouping & Totals group.

A drop-down list providing function options appears.

e. Click **Sum**.

f. Save the report.

A sum has been added to the Revenue field after each group. You probably cannot see it because it is scrolled off-screen. Use the scrollbar to see that your revenue is 1599.125.

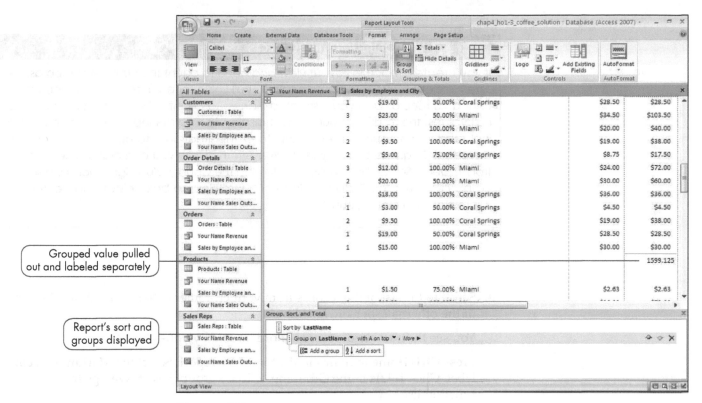

Grouped value pulled out and labeled separately

Report's sort and groups displayed

Figure 23 Correctly Sorted Report with Primary Group

Refer to Figure 24 as you complete Step 3.

a. Ensure that you are still in Layout view. Click **Add a group** in the Group, Sort, and Total pane.

b. Scroll left to locate and select the **City** field in the Field List box.

The Primary grouping level is still the salesperson's last name. Now the customer's city is grouped together nested inside the LastName field. During this period, you sold one order to a customer in Coconut Grove, once to a customer in Coral Gables, 10 orders to customers in Coral Springs, and the rest of your orders came from Miami-based customers. You decide to create summary statistics by city and salesperson to analyze the sales information.

c. Click the **Cost** label to select it. Click **Totals** in the Grouping & Totals group. Select **Average** from the function list.

Scroll down until you see the average cost for the orders to Coral Springs displayed. You will see the average cost of an order from a Coral Springs customer was only $12.10, while the average costs of orders to Coral Gables and Coconut Grove were much higher.

d. Scroll up and click the **City** label to select it. Click **Totals** in the Grouping & Totals group. Select **Count Records** from the function list.

The City field is defined as a text field. Access presents different functions depending on whether the field contains text or numbers.

TIP Counting Records

If you create a report in Layout view and need to count the number of records, be sure to select a field that contains a non-null value for each record. If a report contained 20 records and you instructed Access to count a field that contained two null values, the resulting count would display 18. The missing values would not be included in the count. An easy way to fix this situation is to count only fields that have their Required property set to Yes. Alternatively, you can edit the field's control property. Select the text box containing the Count value, right-click, and select Properties. Click the Data tab. In the Control Source box, select and delete the expression and type =count(*).

e. Scroll to the last of the records from your customers (that is just above the name of the other salesperson, Lockley).

You see the number of records of orders sold by you—39.

f. Press **Ctrl+Home** to return to the top of the report. Select the **Markup Percent** label. Click **Totals** in the Grouping & Totals group. Select **Average** from the function list.

g. Scroll to the right. Select the **Price** label. Click the **Totals** command in the Grouping & Totals group. Select **Average** from the function list. Format as currency.

Like the Cost field, the Price field records a per-unit cost, so it does not make sense to sum it.

h. Scroll to the right. Select the **Revenue** label. Click **Totals** in the Grouping & Totals group. Select **Sum** from the function list. Check to make sure the value is formatted as currency.

TROUBLESHOOTING: A group summary statistic should automatically inherit its formatting properties from the field's format. Occasionally the group total or average calculates correctly, but it is incorrectly formatted. To correct the format, right-click the incorrectly formatted value in the Layout view of the report and select Properties from the shortcut menu. Set the Format property to the correct value, e.g., currency, and close the Property Sheet. This action forces a format correction.

i. Narrow the first two columns so that the report fits on one page horizontally. Refer to Hands-On Exercise 1, Step 3e, if you do not remember how to do this step.

j. Save the report.

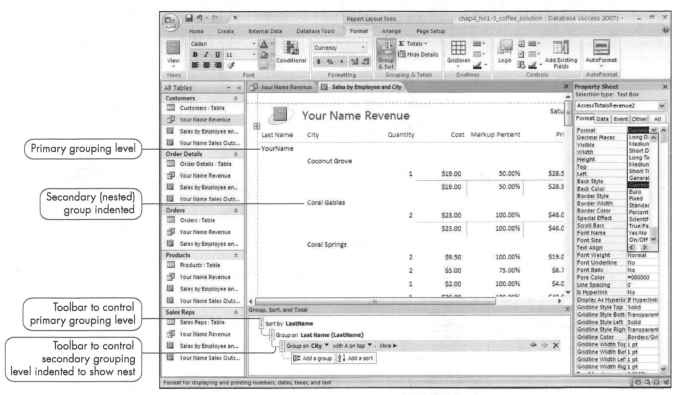

Figure 24 Report with Two Grouping Levels Added

Refer to Figure 25 as you complete Step 4.

a. Save and close the Sales by Employee and City report.

You need practice deleting grouping levels, but you need to preserve the work from Step 3. You will copy the report and delete the group levels in the copy.

b. Right-click the **Sales by Employee and City report** in the All Tables pane. Select **Copy** from the shortcut menu. Move your mouse to a white space in the All Tables pane, right-click, and select **Paste**.

c. Name the copy **Sales by Employee**. Click **OK**.

d. Move your mouse to a white space in the All Tables pane. (Do this a second time.) Right-click and select **Paste**.

e. Name the copy **Sales by City**.

TROUBLESHOOTING: If your monitor resolution is set low, you may have trouble finding white space in which to paste. This file was set to display tables and related objects in the All Tables pane. That view repeats multi-table query and report names. A view that uses less space is the Objects view. Click the All Tables pane title bar and select Object Type. That should free up some white space for you to paste the copied report. After your copied report is pasted and renamed, switch back to the Tables and related view.

f. Open the **Sales by Employee report** in Layout view.

g. Click **Group & Sort** in the Grouping & Totals group on the Format tab to display the Group, Sort, and Total pane (if necessary).

h. Click the **Group on City bar** to select it.

The entire bar turns gold when selected.

i. Click **Delete** on the far right of the bar (it looks like an X).

A warning box tells you that the group has a header or footer section and the controls there also will be deleted.

j. Click **Yes**.

The City grouping disappears, but the employee grouping remains.

k. Click **Save**. Close your report.

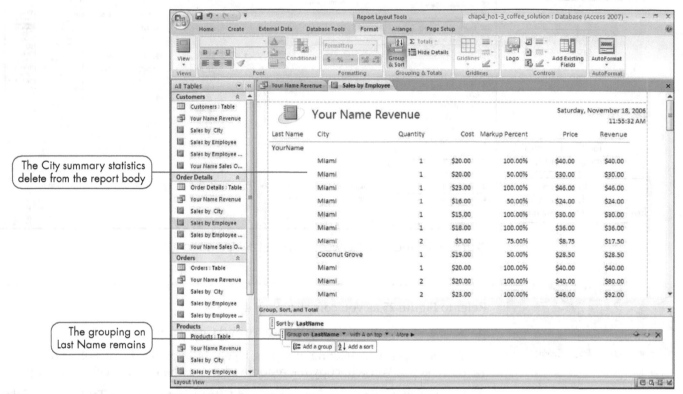

The City summary statistics delete from the report body

The grouping on Last Name remains

Figure 25 Sales by Employee

Refer to Figure 26 as you complete Step 5.

a. Open the **Sales by City report** in Layout view.

You are going to change the order of the grouping fields so that the primary group will be the City and the secondary group the employee.

b. Click **Group & Sort** in the Grouping & Totals group on the Format tab to display the grouping pane (if necessary).

c. Click the **Group on LastName bar** in the Group, Sort, and Total pane to select it.

d. Click the **down arrow** in the right side of the Group on Last Name bar one time.

You might have expected that the report would now be grouped by city and then by your sales and Lockley's sales grouped within each city. Your sales are together in the top of the report, Lockley's in the bottom of the report. Examine the grouping window more carefully. There is a sort in effect. It receives the top priority. So the employee sales will not group in each city.

e. Click the **Sort by LastName bar** to select it.

f. Click **Delete** (X) on the right of the Sort by Last Name bar.

When you delete the sort, the grouping prioritization changes; now, the employees are sorted within the cities as expected.

g. Check to make sure the formats of the group totals and grand totals are appropriately formatted. If not, apply the Currency format.

h. Click the text box containing the report title, *Your Name Revenue*. Click it again to edit it. Change the report name to **Your Name City Revenue**. Save the report.

i. Click **Group & Sort** in the Grouping & Totals group on the Format tab.

j. Click the **Office Button**, select **Manage**, and then select **Back Up Database**. Enter the filename **chap4_ho2_coffee_solution** (*note ho2 instead of ho1-3*) and click **Save**.

You just created a backup of the database after completing the second hands-on exercise. The original database *chap4_ho1-3_coffee_solution* remains onscreen. If you ruin the original database as you complete the third hands-on exercise, you can use the backup file you just created.

k. Close the file and exit Access if you do not want to continue with the next exercise at this time.

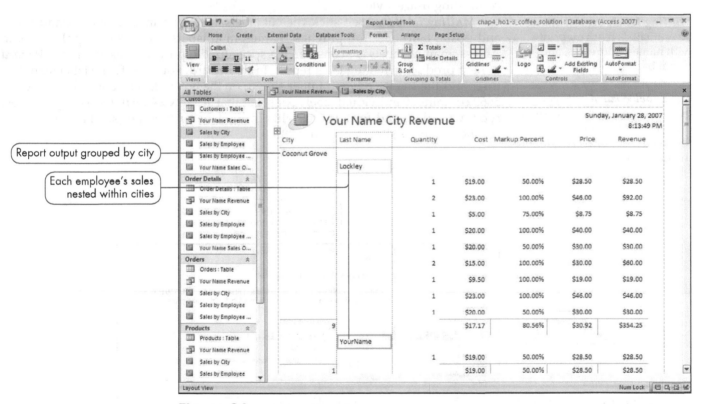

Figure 26 The City Report

The Report and Label Wizards

Earlier in this chapter you created a polished, professional report with grouping levels, sorts, and summary statistics by using the Report tool. You edited the report through a GUI interface and immediately saw the effect on the output. You may recall that Access provides four ways of creating a report (see Table 1). In this section you will create a report using the Report Wizard and edit it using both the Layout and Design views.

The ***Report Wizard*** asks you questions and then, depending on how you answer, generates the report. Many of the wizard's dialog boxes contain commands that lead you to further levels of options. As you read this section and work through the hands-on exercise, you should explore the additional options and think about how and when you might use them. Access provides so many methods of report generation because Access users require so many differing types of reports. As you gain experience you will learn which tool is most appropriate for your tasks.

If no query exists that assembles the necessary fields for a report, the Report Wizard is probably the best option. It enables you to pull fields from multiple sources relatively easily. Access reports generated by using the Report Wizard sometimes require extensive revision to make them intelligible. Occasionally the necessary revision time greatly exceeds the time needed to assemble the needed fields in a query in order to use the Report tool. You will need to experiment with the differing methods of report generation to discover which works most effectively with your data and computing usage style.

Mailing labels are self-stick, die-cut labels that you print with names, addresses, and postal barcodes. You purchase name-brand labels at an office supply store. In Access, mailing labels are considered a specialized report. You use the ***Label Wizard*** to help produce a mailing label report. In the wizard, you specify the label manufacturer and the label product number shown on the box of labels. For example, Avery 5660 contains 30 individual labels per sheet that are 1" x 2⅝". After selecting the label type, you place and format the fields in the label prototype (see Figure 27). The finished report is shown in Figure 28.

The ***Report Wizard*** asks you questions and then, depending on how you answer, generates the report.

Mailing labels are self-stick, die-cut labels that you print with names, addresses, and postal barcodes.

The ***Label Wizard*** asks you questions and then, depending on how you answer, generates the report formatted to print on mailing labels.

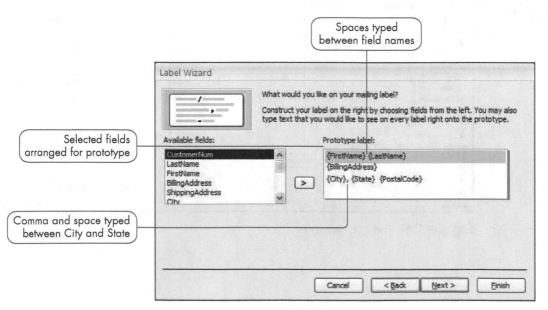

Figure 27 Label Prototype

Create, Edit, and Perform Calculations in Reports

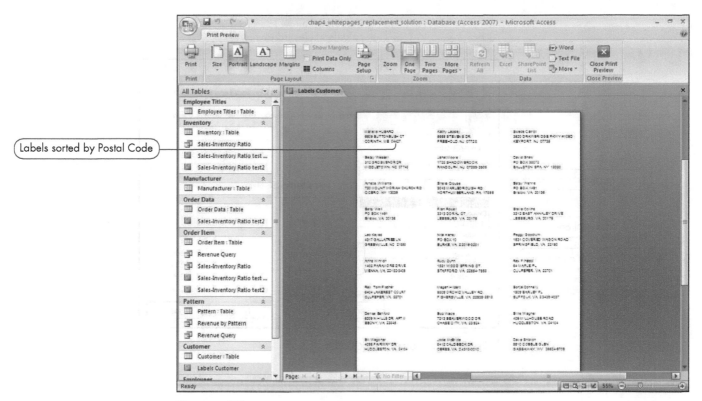

Figure 28 Completed Labels

Using the Report Wizard

Even when using a wizard to guide your report formation, you need to pre-plan the desired output. Suppose you needed a monthly sales report that grouped the products by category and provided summary statistics monitoring the average discounts offered to customers and the revenue generated from product sales. This report would require one grouping level and two summary calculations—one for total revenue and the other for average discount rate. Next you need to identify the report's record source. For this illustration you may assume that all necessary records exist in a query. In actual practice, you may need to first create the query assembling the needed records. Some Access users source reports directly from table data. After thinking through the design and record source, you launch the wizard.

> Even when using a wizard to guide your report formation, you need to pre-plan the desired output.

Start the Report Wizard

You do not need to have the report record source open to launch the Report Wizard like you do when using the Report tool. You may wish to close any open objects in your database before launching the wizard. Find the Report Wizard on the Create tab in the Reports group. The first dialog box asks you to specify the record source (see Figure 29).

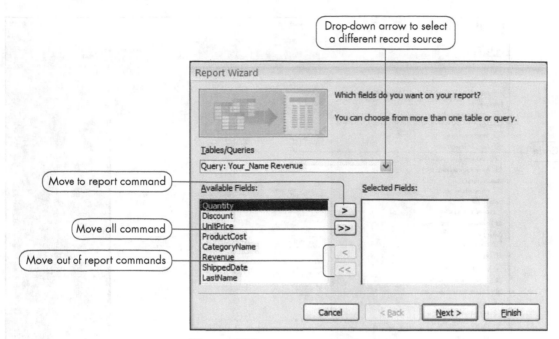

Figure 29 Select Records

Group Records

Grouping lets you organize and consolidate your data. You also can calculate aggregating information. In this report you need the data grouped by the Category Name field, so in the wizard's box under "Do you want to add any grouping levels?" you would identify and double-click the Category Name field. If you needed additional grouping levels, you would double-click those field names also. The order in which you select the groups dictates the order of nesting in the report (see Figure 30). The Priority commands let you change your mind and restructure the nest levels. If you select a date/time field to group by, click Grouping Options to find an interval specification box. Use it to designate the grouping interval, such as week, month, or quarter.

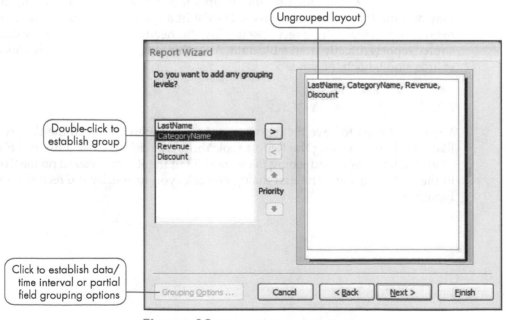

Figure 30 Specify Grouping Options

Create, Edit, and Perform Calculations in Reports

Figure 31 shows the grouping options set to group on Category Name. Once the group is established, the Grouping Options command activates. If the group field was a date/time field, you would establish the interval in the Grouping Intervals dialog box. Because this grouping field is a text field, the intervals displayed contain portions of the field name, i.e. the first two letters. You might use this feature if you were grouping an inventory list and the inventory IDs within a category started with the same letters. For example, FJW123, FJR123, FJB123 might be inventory numbers for the fine jewelry department for watches, rings, and bracelets. If you set the grouping interval option to the two initial letters, you would include the fine jewelry department's entire inventory.

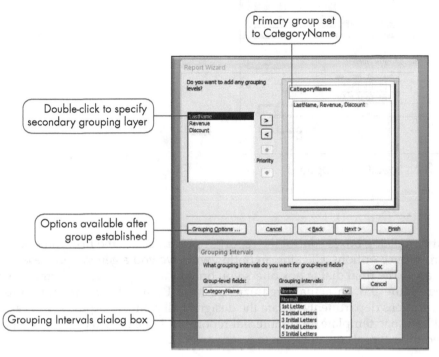

Figure 31 Grouping Options Set on Category

Add Sorts and Summary Instructions

The next dialog box asks "What sort order and summary information do you want for detail records?" Notice that the sorts apply only to a detail record. Some reports omit the detail, making the sort order moot. If this were a detail report, you might specify that the details be sorted first by category in ascending order and then by revenue in descending order. Because you have decided to create a summary report, you need to click the Summary Options command. This step takes you to a screen where you may choose summary statistics (sum, average, minimum, and maximum), and whether or not you want the details presented (see Figure 32). Clicking either OK or Cancel returns you to the wizard.

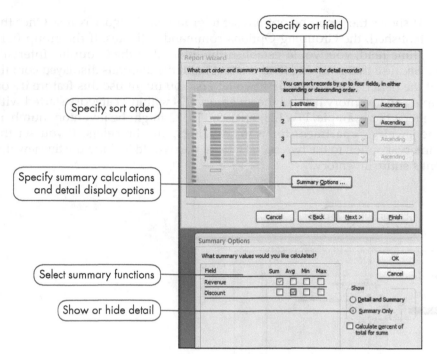

Specify sort field

Specify sort order

Specify summary calculations and detail display options

Select summary functions

Show or hide detail

Figure 32 Specify Sort Options

Design the Report

The next two dialog boxes control the report's appearance. In the first you select the layout from three options. Clicking an option will give you a general preview in the preview area. The final dialog box offers you options among the AutoFormats available (see Figure 33). In actual organizations, the Public Relations and Graphic Communications departments dictate the design of all printed output. The organization will have one template for all internal reports and one or two others for reports generated for external consumption (e.g., an invoice).

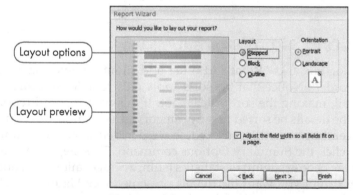

Layout options

Layout preview

Figure 33 Specify Layout Options

Create, Edit, and Perform Calculations in Reports

Ironically, the design selection variety makes life more difficult for students than for real-world practitioners. On the job, you typically employ fewer than five templates. You use them all day, every day. You become intimately acquainted with all of their quirks. You develop functional work-arounds. A *work-around* acknowledges that a problem exists and develops a sufficing solution. In a course, you use a variety of differing templates and never fully understand any of them. Figure 34 shows AutoFormat choices.

A *work-around* acknowledges that a problem exists, and develops a sufficing solution.

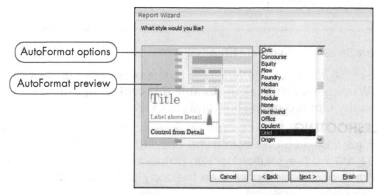

Figure 34 AutoFormat

Save and Name the Report

A well-designed database may contain only a few tables, but it may have many queries and reports. You should name all report objects descriptively to save you time and minimize frustration. Always name your report something that not only makes sense to you today, but also will communicate the report's contents to a co-worker or to you in six months (see Figure 35).

In this hands-on you exercise you will create a report using the Report Wizard and edit it using the Layout view.

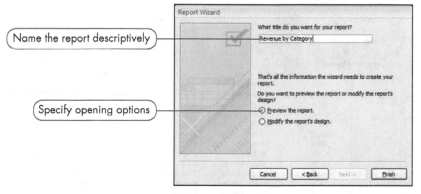

Figure 35 Use Descriptive Report Names

Hands-On Exercises

3 | Report Wizard

Skills covered: 1. Assemble the Report Data **2.** Create a Query-Based Report and Add Grouping **3.** Create Summary Statistics **4.** Select Layout and AutoFormatting **5.** Modify the Report

---

Step 1
Assemble the Report Data

Refer to Figure 36 as you complete Step 1.

a. Open the *chap4_ho1-3_coffee_solution* file if necessary, click **Options** on the Security Warning toolbar, click the **Enable this content option** in the Microsoft Office Security Options dialog box, and click **OK**.

> **TROUBLESHOOTING:** If you create unrecoverable errors while completing this hands-on exercise, you can delete the *chap4_ho1-3_coffee_solution* file, copy the *chap4_ho2_coffee_solution* backup database you created at the end of the second hands-on exercise, and open the copy of the backup database to start the third hands-on exercise again.

b. Open the **Your Name Revenue query** in Design view.

c. Add the **OrderDate** field located in the *Orders* table to the design grid by double-clicking it.

d. Add the **ProductName** field located in the *Products* table to the design grid by double-clicking it.

e. Click **Run** in the Results group on the Design tab to run the query. Scroll right to ensure that the newly added fields exist.

f. Save the changes. Close the query. Check to make sure the query name is selected in the Navigation pane.

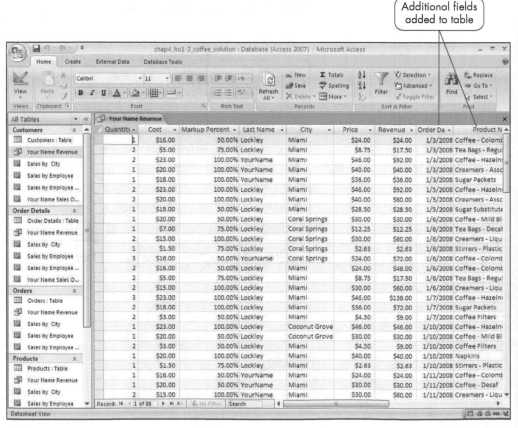

Additional fields added to table

Figure 36 Assemble the Record Source

Step 2

Create a Query-Based Report and Add Grouping

Refer to Figure 37 as you complete Step 2.

a. Click the **Create tab** and click **Report Wizard** in the Reports group.

The wizard launches, and the Your Name Revenue query selects as the record source because it was highlighted when you started the wizard.

b. Click the **Move All command (>>)** to move all of the query fields to the Selected Fields box. Click **Next**.

c. Double-click **OrderDate** in the grouping level box.

The right box displays the default date grouping, OrderDate by Month. In this case you want a monthly report so you do not need to change the grouping options command.

d. Double-click the **LastName** field in the left box to add it as a grouping level.

e. Compare your grouping levels to those shown in Figure 37. If they match, click **Next**.

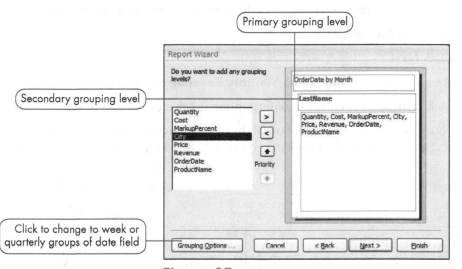

Figure 37 Create Groups

Step 3

Create Summary Statistics

Refer to Figure 38 as you complete Step 3.

a. Click the drop-down arrow beside the first sort box. Select **City** as the primary sort field.

b. Click **Summary Options**.

TROUBLESHOOTING: As long as the Report Wizard dialog box remains open, you can click Back and revisit your work.

c. Click the **Sum** check box for the **Revenue** field.

d. Click the **Calculate percent of total for sums** check box.

e. Compare your Summary Options to those shown in Figure 38. If they match, click **OK** and then click **Next**.

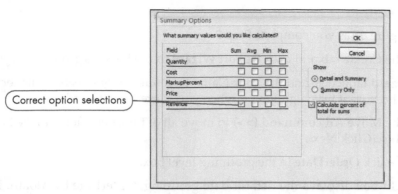

Correct option selections

Figure 38 Summary Calculation Specifications

Refer to Figures 39 as you complete Step 4.

a. Select a **Stepped** layout and a **Portrait** orientation.

b. Click **Next**.

Spend some time exploring in the Report AutoFormats of the wizard.

c. Select the **Module** style.

d. Click **Next**.

e. Name the report **Your Name Monthly Revenue by Salesperson.**

f. Make sure the **Preview the report** option is selected. Click **Finish**.

You successfully generated output, but it has flaws. Examine your work critically and then compare the problems you spot to those highlighted in Figure 39.

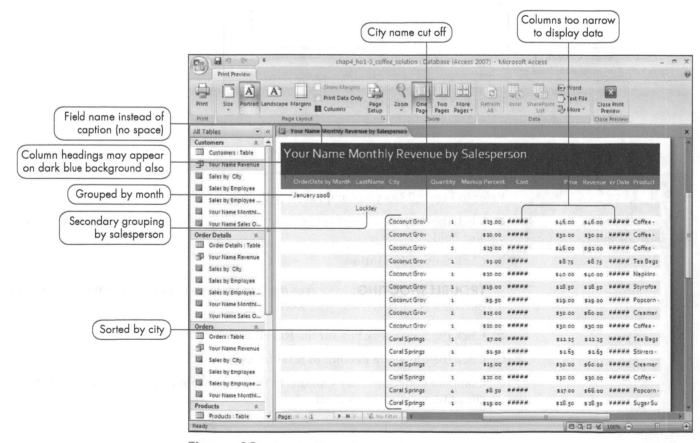

Figure 39 Create Groups

Create, Edit, and Perform Calculations in Reports

<table>
<tr>
<td valign="top">

Step 5

Modify the Report

</td>
<td valign="top">

Refer to Figure 40 as you complete Step 4.

a. Right-click the report tab and select **Layout View**.

b. Select the text box for the OrderDate by Month control. Click it again to edit the text to **Order Month**. Press **Enter**.

Ideally you should save and close the report, open the Orders table, switch to Design view and add a caption for the OrderDate field. Save the design change to the table and close it. Reopen the report. The caption will replace the field name in the text box in this and all other reports and forms that source on OrderDate. Because you also changed from OrderDate by Month to Order Month, it is excusable to make this a one-time change.

c. Ensure the **Order Month** control is still selected. Move your mouse over the right boundary and when the mouse pointer shape changes to the double-headed arrow, click and drag left about a quarter of an inch.

d. Select the text box for the **LastName** control. Click it again to edit the text. Type a **space** between Last and Name.

e. Select the **City** control text box and widen the column using the click and drag technique presented in Step 5c. Make sure the entire city name, Coconut Grove, displays.

You determine that the report is too crowded and that several fields do not need to be displayed. You decide to delete the Quantity, Markup Percent, Cost, and Price fields.

f. Click the **Quantity** field control text box and press **Delete**.

g. Delete the **Markup Percent**, **Cost**, and **Price** fields.

h. Widen the **Product Name** and **Order Date** fields.

i. Click the **Format tab**. Click **Hide Details** in the Grouping & Totals group.

The details of the report hide. This result makes it easier for you to find and edit the summary statistics.

j. Find the words, *Summary for 'LastName' = Lockley 47 detail records*. On the line below in blue, it says Sum. Look right. You should see a small text box with some numbers or pound signs in it. The control box is too small to display the value. Click the too-small control.

k. Mouse over the control's right boundary, get the double-headed resize arrows, and then click and drag to the **right** to widen the control.

When the box is large enough you will see that the value of Lockley's total revenue is 1836.5. It is not formatted as currency.

l. Enlarge the controls for **Sum Grand Total**. Check to see that the text boxes are large enough to display the percent values, too. Enlarge those text boxes if necessary.

m. Click the **Sum** value for Lockley, 1836.5. **Right-click** and select **Properties** from the shortcut menu. Set the **Format** property to **Currency**. With the Properties Sheet still open, click the grand total and format it as **Currency**.

All of the sums should display in Currency format. Because there are two grouping levels, the Report Wizard repeats the grand total twice. You want to keep the bottom one because it is in the report footer along with the words, *Grand Total*.

</td>
</tr>
</table>

n. Find the repeated Grand Total value (the one labeled Sum). Select it and press **Delete**. Select and delete the word *Sum*.

o. Click **Hide Details** in the Grouping & Totals group on the Format tab to return the details to the report.

You hid the details to format the totals. It moves them out of the way and makes it easier to format the total information.

p. Move the **Sum** and **Standard** control boxes left and position them under the Summary for 'LastName' = Your name. Align the total with the Revenue column. You also need to move the grand total controls.

q. Move the **percent** control boxes left under the Order Date column. Make the boxes wide enough to display the values. the control box containing **100%** and the **label**.

r. Locate the text box containing the **page number**. If necessary, move the right boundary left so that it no longer crosses the dotted line indicating the page break.

s. Right-click the report tab and select **Print Preview**.

t. Click **Two Pages** in the Zoom group. Use the navigation commands to preview the last page. Print the report. Save the report.

u. Click the **Office Button**, select **Manage**, and then select **Compact and Repair Database**.

v. Close the file and exit Access.

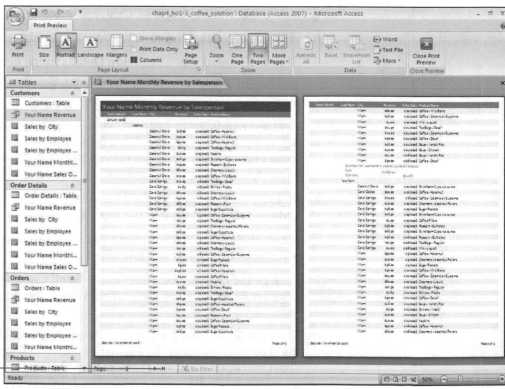

Figure 40 The Report in Print Preview

Summary

1. **Plan a report.** A report is a printed document that displays information from a database. Telephone directories, financial statements, shipping labels, and receipts are examples of reports. You should carefully consider what information you need and how you can optimally present it. A paper and pencil may be the best tools for planning. Develop a series of questions to ask to determine what the report should answer. Identify the data sources for the report. Select a reporting tool.

2. **Use different report views.** Access provides different views of your report depending on the operation you need to accomplish. Print Preview is an invaluable tool while designing reports. Use it liberally to preview your reports. Report view allows you to organize the data for the report by sorting and filtering it. Layout view enables you to alter the report design. This is the most powerful view and where you will spend most of your time. Design view displays the report's infrastructure design, but no data. This view has its advantages in large reports, but may be more difficult to use to make exact tweaks to the formatting.

3. **Create and edit a report.** To use the Report tool, you need to assemble all of the necessary data in one place. Occasionally, a table contains all of the necessary fields for a report. More often, you will need to create or open a query containing the necessary fields. If an existing query has all of the fields needed for the report but also some unneeded fields, you probably will use the existing query. You can delete the extraneous fields in Layout view. Access does a lot of the cosmetic work in your reports for you, by adjusting column widths as you add and remove columns. You can do the rest in Layout view.

4. **Identify report elements, sections, and controls.** Access divides all reports into sections, although you only see the sectional boundaries when you display the report in the Design view. Detail Section is the body of the report, containing each record. The Report Header (Footer) Section prints at the beginning (end) of each report. Group headers and footers appear at the tops and bottoms of each report group. Page headers and footers display at the top and bottom of each report page. You can edit these areas in the Design or Layout views. Controls display, position, format, and calculate the report data. You will use bound controls, those that are bound or tied to a source table or query, most frequently. Unbound controls have no record source in the underlying data. An example of an unbound control would be the report's title. A calculated control uses an expression as opposed to a record value as its data source. The expression usually is bound to record values of the fields referenced.

5. **Add grouping levels in Layout view.** Access provides several methods of grouping and summarizing data. You can create (1) a Totals query by specifying a group by field and the field or fields to summarize, (2) a grouped report using the Layout view's Sorting and Grouping tools, and (3) a grouped report using the Report Wizard and specifying the group layers within the wizard. Since most reports will have many thousands of records, you should sort them using the Group Sort tool. Nested groups make the report look similar to an outline. You also can hide and display details in reports and calculate summary statistics. You can add sub-groupings as needed.

6. **Add fields to a report.** Inevitably, after a report has been used, someone will say, "It would be nice to have this in the report, too." Use the Layout view to add additional fields to a report.

7. **Use the Report Wizard.** Access contains several wizards that will print common repeatedly used reports such as mailing labels. It is important that you organize your desired output for wizards just as you would if you designed the report from scratch. Unlike the Report tool, when using a Report Wizard, you should close any open objects in the data source. Like in the Report tool, you can customize the reports from the Report Wizard with groups, sorts, and summaries to tweak the overall design to best present your data. A well-designed database may only have a few tables, but dozens of queries and reports. Chances are good that they will be reused, so they should be saved and descriptively named.

Key Terms

Bound control	Label Wizard	Report footer section
Calculated control	Layout view	Report header section
Controls	Mailing labels	Report view
Design view	Nested groups	Report Wizard
Detail section	Page footer	Unbound controls
Field List pane	Page header	Work-around
Group footer section	Print Preview	
Group header section	Report	

Multiple Choice

1. Which statement most accurately describes the appropriate time to use a report in Access?

   (a) Entering data
   (b) Printing output for presentation
   (c) Querying data
   (d) Sorting records based on preset criteria

2. Which of the following is true?

   (I) You can edit the appearance of reports by changing fonts and styles.
   (II) You can add graphs, pictures, and charts to reports.

   (a) I but not II
   (b) II but not I
   (c) Neither I nor II
   (d) Both I and II

3. Which is an example of a report from a database?

   (a) a shipping label
   (b) a telephone directory
   (c) a sales receipt
   (d) all of the above

4. Which statement about saving a report is true?

   (a) Saved reports are static, and the data represented in a report will be the same every time you run a saved report.
   (b) Saving reports is generally not done in the real world because people rarely need the same information repeatedly.
   (c) You can edit a saved report to add additional fields at a later time.
   (d) Using a saved report can be costly and time-consuming.

5. The most important tool to create an Access report may be

   (a) the Report Grid tool
   (b) a calculator
   (c) a pencil
   (d) the Report Creator tool

6. It is always best to ask _____ questions about what the report should look like and do

   (a) the programmer
   (b) the end user
   (c) the customer
   (d) your manager

7. Which of the following are important things to know as you create an Access report?

   (a) Access cannot calculate data in a report.
   (b) Reports can be summarized, but the summaries have to be designed in the underlying query.
   (c) Reports cannot draw data from multiple tables.
   (d) What type of delivery mechanism will be used, fax, e-mail Word, Excel, PowerPoint, Internet, or printer, and what type and size of paper will be used for the report.

8. If you want to create mailing labels from your Customers table, the fastest and easiest tool would be Access':

   (a) Report Tool
   (b) Report Wizard
   (c) Label Wizard
   (d) Mailing Wizard

9. Which of the following is the most sophisticated and flexible tool for report generation?

   (a) Report Wizard
   (b) Report Tool
   (c) Free form report
   (d) WYSIWYG report

10. Use the _____ to see what the printed report will look like before printing. This step helps with the overall layout and makes the report easy to read and understand.

    (a) Report Tool
    (b) Report Wizard
    (c) Group Wizard
    (d) Print Preview

11. You should modify column widths and row heights for a report in:

    (a) Layout view
    (b) Print Preview
    (c) Group view
    (d) Report view

12. Which of the following is true?

    (I) Access can create a report from multiple tables.
    (II) You will usually have to create a new query to create a report.
    (a) I but not II
    (b) II but not I
    (c) Both I and II
    (d) Neither I nor II

... continued on Next Page

13. What happens if you click on a value in Layout view and press Delete?

   (a) The entire column is deleted from the report, and column widths are adjusted to use the empty space.

   (b) Nothing; you cannot change data in Layout view.

   (c) The record is deleted from the report but remains in the database.

   (d) An error message appears, saying that you should not attempt to manipulate records in a report.

14. Your pointer shape should be a _____ to widen or narrow a column in Layout view.

   (a) single arrow

   (b) hand

   (c) two-headed arrow

   (d) dashed-tail arrow

15. Which of these is not a sectional division used in Access?

   (a) Detail section

   (b) Report header and footer sections

   (c) Group header and footer sections

   (d) Summary section

16. Bound controls are so called because they are bound or attached to:

   (I) source data

   (II) the report's margins

   (a) I but not II

   (b) II but not I

   (c) Both I and II

   (d) Neither I nor II

17. Which of the following is true?

   (a) Unbound controls are used infrequently within reports.

   (b) Unbound controls are used to display cosmetic elements in a report.

   (c) Unbound controls must be saved separately because they are not part of a record.

   (d) Unbound controls cannot be used with bound controls in the same report.

18. To organize your data in a highly usable and readable report, you may use:

   (a) Nested tables

   (b) Nested groups

   (c) Nested queries

   (d) Calculated fields

Practice Exercises

1 Comfort Insurance Raises and Bonuses Report

The Comfort Insurance Agency is a midsized company with offices located across the country. The Human Resource office is located in the home office in Miami. Each year, each employee receives a performance review. The review determines employee eligibility for salary increases and the annual performance bonus. The employee data are stored in an Access database, which is used by the Human Resource department to monitor and maintain employee records. Your task is to prepare a report showing the salary increase for each employee and his or her performance bonuses (if any). You are the Human Resource department manager. If you correctly report the employee salaries and bonuses, you will receive a bonus. Work carefully and check the accuracy of the calculations. This project follows the same set of skills as used in Hands-On Exercises 1 and 2 in this chapter. If you have problems, reread the detailed directions presented in the chapter. Compare your results to Figure 41.

a. Copy the partially completed file *chap4_pe1_insurance* to your production folder. Rename it **chap4_pe1_insurance_solution**, open the file, and enable the security content.

b. Click the **Database Tools tab** and click **Relationships** in the Show/Hide group. Examine the table structure, relationships, and fields. After you are familiar with the database, close the Relationships window.

c. Rename the query with **your name**. Open the **Your Name Raises and Bonus query**.

d. Click the **Create tab** and click **Report** in the Reports group.

e. Click **Group & Sort** in the Grouping & Totals group, if necessary. Click **Add a sort** in the Group, Sort, and Total pane and select **LastName**.

f. Click the **LastName** label. Click it again to edit it and add a **space** between *Last* and *Name*. Click outside the text box to turn off editing. Move the mouse to the **right** control boundary, and when the pointer shape changes to the double-headed arrow click and drag the boundary about a half-inch to the left to make the column narrower.

g. Repeat Step f to add a space to the *FirstName* control and decrease its width. Also reduce the width for the *Performance* column. The report should only be one page wide. Add spaces to the *2008Increase* and *NewSalary* controls.

h. Click the **Report Graphic** (the picture in the upper left) to select it. Click **Logo** in the Controls group on the Format tab. Browse to and locate the file named *chap4_pe1_confident.jpg*. Click **OK** in the Insert Picture dialog box.

i. Click the report title *Your Name Raises and Bonuses* to select it. Point the mouse at the middle of the control box and when the pointer shape changes to the four-headed, move arrow, move the report title right.

j. Click the **Confidential graphic** and drag the **right** boundary right to enlarge the warning.

k. Right-click any number in the **New Salary** field and select **Properties** from the shortcut menu. Set the Format property in the Property Sheet to **Currency** and close the Property Sheet.

l. Right-click any number in the **Bonus** field and select **Properties**. Set the **Format property** to **Currency**. Close the Property Sheet.

m. Right-click the report tab and switch to **Print Preview**. If your report looks like the one in the figure, save the report as **Your Name Raises and Bonuses**.

...continued on Next Page

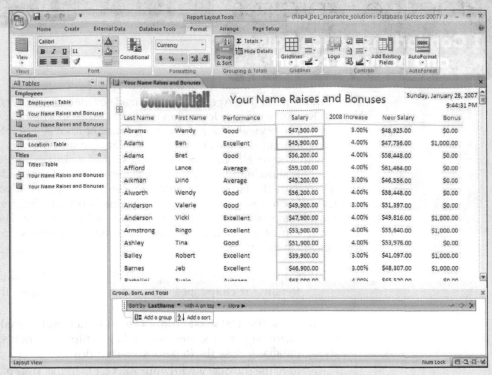

Figure 41 Raises and Bonuses Report

2 Comfort Insurance Raises by Location

The Comfort Insurance Agency is a midsized company with offices located across the country. The Human Resource office is located in the home office in Miami. Each year, each employee receives a performance review. The review determines employee eligibility for salary increases and the annual performance bonus. The employee data are stored in an Access database. This database is used by the Human Resource department to monitor and maintain employee records. Your task is to prepare a report showing employee raises and bonuses by city. You will need to total the payroll and bonus data for each city. You are the Human Resource department manager. If you correctly prepare the report, you will receive a bonus. This project follows the same set of skills as used in Hands-On Exercises 1 and 2 in this chapter. If you have problems, reread the detailed directions presented in the chapter. Compare your results to Figure 42.

a. Copy the partially completed file *chap4_pe2_insurance.accdb* to your production folder. Rename it **chap4_pe2_insurance_solution.accdb**, open the copied file, and enable the security content.

b. Click the **Database Tools tab** and click **Relationships** in the Show/Hide group. Examine the table structure, relationships, and fields. After you are familiar with the database, close the Relationships window.

c. Open the **Employees Query** in Datasheet view. Click the **Create tab** and click **Report** in the Reports group.

d. Click **Add Existing Fields** in the Controls group on the Format tab. The Field List pane opens on the right. In the bottom of the Field List pane is the *Fields available in related tables pane*. Click the **Show all tables** link. The Location table is listed with a plus sign next to it. Click the **plus sign** to reveal the hidden fields available in the Location table.

e. Double-click the **Location** field (not the LocationID field) to add it to the report. Because this field is in a table not in the original record source Access asks if it is OK to create a new query that contains the Location field. Click **Yes**. The city names add to the report. The new field is selected. Close the Field List pane.

f. Click the **Location** text box at the top of the field. Move the mouse to the middle of the selected Location field and when the mouse pointer assumes the four-headed move shape, click and drag the field to the **leftmost** position in the report.

...continued on Next Page

g. Click the **LastName** text box at the top of the field to select it. Click it a second time to edit it. Type a **space** between Last and Name. Add spaces to **FirstName, HireDate, 2008Increase, 2008Raise, YearHired,** and **YearsWorked**.

h. Select the **Last Name** field. Move the mouse pointer over the right boundary and when the pointer shape changes to a double-headed arrow, click and drag **left** to narrow the column. Repeat this step for the **First Name** field.

i. Right-click any record in the **2008 Raise** field and select **Properties** from the shortcut menu. In the Properties Sheet, set the Format property to **Currency**. Close the Property Sheet.

j. Select the **Year Hired** field and delete it. Adjust any field column widths as necessary to make sure all the columns fit on one page.

k. Click **Group & Sort** in the Grouping & Totals group to turn on the Group, Sort, and Total pane (if necessary). Click **Add a group** in the Group, Sort, and Total pane. Click **Location** in the Group on Select field box.

l. Click the **More Options** command on the Group on Location bar. Click the drop-down arrow beside "with LastName totaled." Click the drop-down arrow in the Total On box and select **2008Raise**. Click the **Show Grand Total** and **Show in group footer** check boxes. Click anywhere outside the Total by box.

m. Click the report title and change it to **Your Name**.

n. Click the **Office Button**. Select **Print** and then **Print Preview**. Print the report.

o. Save the report as **Your Name Raises by Location**. Close the database.

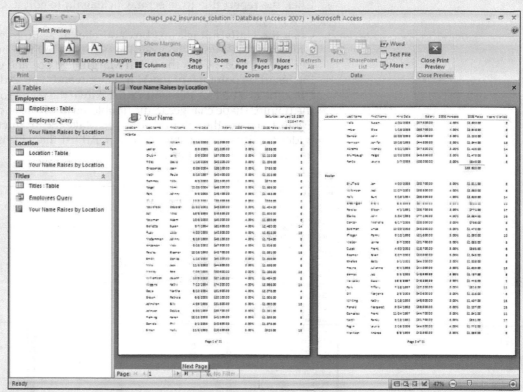

Figure 42 Raises by Location Shown in Print Preview

3 Northwind Traders

Northwind Traders is a small, international, specialty food company. It sells products in eight different divisions: beverages, confections (candy), condiments, dairy products, grains and cereals, meat and poultry, produce, and seafood. Although most of its customers are restaurants and gourmet food shops, it has a few retail customers, too. The firm purchases merchandise from a variety of suppliers. All of the order and inventory information is stored in the company's database. This database is used by the management to monitor and maintain records. You are the marketing manager. Your task is to prepare a report showing the profitability of the products in your inventory. You need to group the products by their categories. You also need to average the profit

...continued on Next Page

margin by category. (A profit margin is the profit divided by the price.) This project follows the same set of skills as used in Hands-On Exercises 1, 2, and 3. If you have problems, reread the detailed directions presented in the chapter. Compare your results to Figure 43.

a. Copy the partially completed file *chap4_pe3_traders.accdb* to your production folder. Rename it **chap4_pe3_traders_solution.accdb**, open the file, and enable the security content.

b. Click the **Database Tools tab** and click **Relationships** in the Show/Hide group. Examine the table structure, relationships, and fields. After you are familiar with the database, close the Relationships window.

c. Click the **Create tab** and click **Report Wizard** in the Reports group. Select the **Profit Margin query** in the first screen of the dialog box. Click the **Move all to Report command (>>)** to move all of the fields in the query to the report. Click **Next**.

d. Select **by Categories** to answer the "How do you want to view your data?" question. This step creates the necessary grouping level. Click **Next**. You already have established the grouping level so click **Next**, again two times.

e. Click **Summary Options** and indicate that you would like the **Avg** for the *PerUnitProfit* field. Click **OK** and then **Next.**

f. Ensure that **Stepped** layout and **Portrait** orientation are selected and click **Next**.

g. Select the **Aspect** style and click **Next**. Name the report **Your Name Profit Margin**. Set it to open to **Preview**. Click **Finish**.

h. Right-click the report tab and select Layout View.

i. Click the report title to select it. Click again to edit it. Change the title to **Your Name Category Profit Margins**.

j. Click the **UnitsInStock** text box and click it again to edit it. Insert a **space** between Units and In. Position the insertion point left of the **S** in Stock and type **Ctrl+Enter** to force a line break. Click the **Profit Margin** text box and click it again to edit it. Position the insertion point left of the **M** in Margin and type **Ctrl+Enter** to force a line break.

k. Click the text box for **Per Unit Profit**. Move the mouse over the **right boundary**. When the pointer shape changes to the double-headed arrow, click and drag the right boundary **left** to make the column narrower. Make the Product Name and Category columns wider to display the record contents. Adjust the widths of the remaining columns as necessary to fit all on one page.

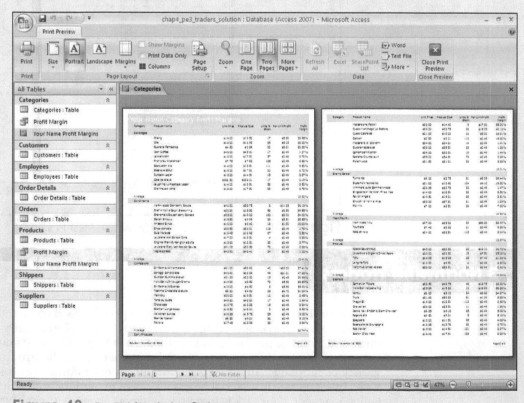

Figure 43 Profit Margin by Category

...continued on Next Page

Create, Edit, and Perform Calculations in Reports

l. Select the **Summary for Category Name . . .** and press **Delete**. Select **Ave** and replace it with **Average**.

m. Save the report. Print the report. Close the database.

4 Member Rewards

The Prestige Hotel chain caters to upscale business travelers and provides state-of-the-art conference, meeting, and reception facilities. It prides itself on its international, four-star cuisines. Last year, it began a member rewards club to help the marketing department track the purchasing patterns of its most loyal customers. All of the hotel transactions are stored in the database. Your task is to determine the revenue from each order and to summarize the revenue figures by location and service type. This project follows the same set of skills as used in Hands-On/Exercises 2, and 3. If you have problems, reread the detailed directions presented in the chapter. Compare your results to Figure 44.

a. Copy the partially completed file *chap4_pe4_memrewards.accdb* to your production folder. Rename it **chap4_pe4_memrewards_solution.accdb**, open the file, and enable the security content.

b. Click the **Database Tools tab** and click **Relationships** in the Show/Hide group. Examine the table structure, relationships, and fields. After you are familiar with the database, close the Relationships window. Rename the **Your Name Revenue** query with **your name**.

c. Open the **Your Name Revenue** query in Datasheet view.

d. Click the **Create tab** and click **Report** in the Reports group.

e. Click **Group & Sort** in the Grouping & Totals group to turn on the Group, Sort, and Total pane (if necessary). Click **Add a group** in the Group, Sort, and Total pane. Click **City** in the Group on list box. Click **Add a group** and select **ServiceName** in the Group on list box.

f. Click **Hide Details** in the Grouping & Totals group.

g. Click **Group on ServiceName** in the Group, Sort, and Total pane to activate the group bar. Click the **More** command. Click the **with City totaled drop-down arrow**. In the **Total On** box, select **NoInParty**. In the **Type** box select **Average**. Click the **Show in group header** check box.

h. Return to the Totals dialog box, click the drop-down arrow, and click **PerPersonCharge**. Set **Type** to **Average** and check **Show in group footer**.

i. Return to the **Totals** dialog box, click the drop-down arrow, and click **Revenue**. Set **Type** to **Sum** and check **Show in group header**.

j. Click **Group on City** to activate the group bar. Click **More**. Locate and click the **with City totaled drop-down arrow**. In the **Total On** box, select **NoInParty**. In the **Type** box select **Average**. Click the **Show in group footer check box**.

k. Return to the Totals dialog box, click the drop-down arrow, and click **PerPersonCharge**. Set **Type** to **Average** and check **Show in group footer**.

l. Return to the Totals dialog box, click the drop-down arrow, and click **Revenue**. Set **Type** to **Sum** and check **Show in group footer** and **Show Grand Total**.

m. Click the **ServiceName** text box and click it again to edit it. Insert a **space** between Service and Name. Click NoInParty to select and type **Number In Party**. Position the insertion point right of the **r** in Number and type **Ctrl+Enter** to force a line break. Click the **PerPerson Charge** text box and click it again to edit it. Add a space between Per and Person. Position the insertion point left of the **C** in Charge and type **Ctrl+Enter** to force a line break.

...continued on Next Page

n. Click the text box for **City**. Move the mouse over the **right boundary**. When the pointer shape changes to the double-headed arrow, click and drag the right boundary **left** to make the column narrower. Adjust the widths of the remaining columns as necessary to fit all on one page.

o. Right-click a value in the **Number in Party** field. Select **Properties** from the shortcut menu. Set the **Format** property to **Fixed**. Click the **Decimal Place** property and select **1**. Click a value in the Per Person Charge field. Set the **Format property** to **Currency**. Click a value in the Revenue field to set the **Format property** to **Currency**. Examine the formats of the city and grand totals and adjust their formats if necessary.

p. Right-click the report tab and select **Print Preview**. Save the report as **Your Name Revenue by City and Service**. Close the database.

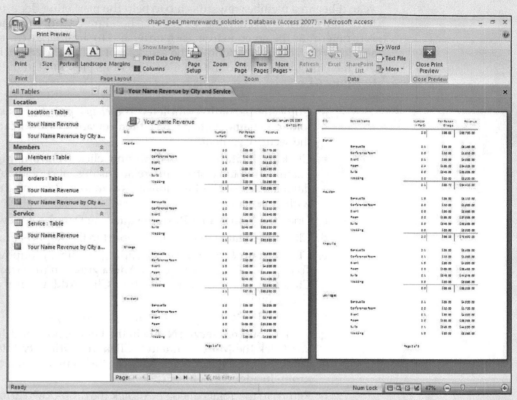

Figure 44   Revenue by City and Service

(Replacements, Ltd is a real company located in Greensboro, North Carolina. The data in the case file are actual data. The customer and employee information have been changed to ensure privacy. However, the inventory and sales records reflect actual transactions.)

Today is the first day in your new position as associate marketing manager at Replacements, Ltd., which has the world's largest selection of old and new dinnerware, including china, stoneware, crystal, glassware, silver, stainless, and collectibles. In preparation for your first day on the job, you have spent hours browsing the Replacements Web site, www.replacements.com. You classify the merchandise by category number where 1 is dinnerware, 2 is crystal/glassware, and 3 is flatware (knives and forks). You are responsible for managing several different patterns of merchandise. To accomplish this task, you need to closely monitor past sales in the various patterns to understand purchasing habits and product demand. You exchange information with the customer service representatives and monitor their performance. You need to create a report that summarizes sales by pattern for the merchandise in Product Category 1, dinnerware. Compare your work to Figure 45.

a. Locate the file named *chap4_mid1_replacement.accdb*, copy it to your working folder, and rename it **chap4_mid1_replacement_solution.accdb**. Open the file and enable the content.

b. Open the **Revenue query**. It contains information about all three product classifications. Today, you are interested only in dinnerware. Create a report and set a filter to select only product category 1.

c. Group the report on the **LongPatName** field. Click the **More Options** command on the group bar in the Group, Sort, and Total pane. Locate the Totals drop-down arrow and select Revenue. Eventually you will hide the details, so set the total to display in the group header.

d. Hide the details. Remove all of the fields except for the LongPatName and Revenue from the report. Replace the label, *LongPatName*, with **Pattern Name**.

e. Save the report as **Your Name Revenue by Dinnerware Pattern**. Title the report appropriately.

f. Insert the *chap4_mid1_replacement.jpg* picture in the logo area. This image depicts the Spode pattern. It is copyrighted by Replacements, Ltd., and is used with permission.

g. Select the **Wide** margin choice. **Enlarge** the picture and **move the controls** in the Report Header and Footer sections to make the report a single page and attractive.

h. Capture a screenshot of the report. Have it open on your computer and press **PrintScrn**. Open Word, type **Your Name and Section Number** and press **Enter**. Press **Ctrl+V**. Save the Word document as **chap4_mid1_replacement_solution**. Print the screen picture.

...continued on Next Page

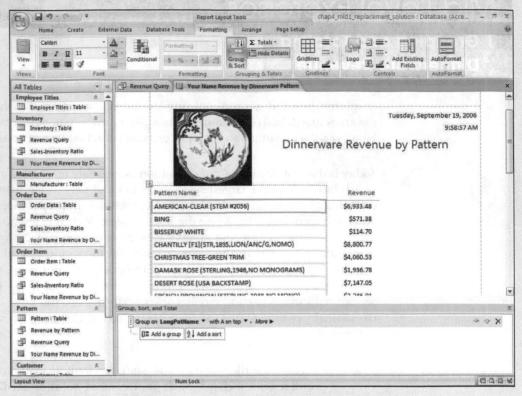

Figure 45 Dinnerware Revenue by Pattern

2 Calculating and Summarizing Bank Data in a Query

You are the manager of the loan department of the National Bank. Several customers have multiple loans with your institution. A single customer might have a mortgage loan, one or more car loans, and a home improvement loan. The loan department's database contains the records of all of the customer indebtedness. Your task is to use the information stored in the database to summarize the loan payments by month. Compare your results to Figure 46.

a. Locate the file named *chap4_mid2_nationalbank.accdb*, copy it to your working folder, and rename it **chap4_mid2_nationalbank_solution.accdb**. Open the file and enable the content. Open the **Customers table**. Find and replace **Michelle Zacco's** name with your name.

b. Open the **Payments Received** query. Use it to create a report.

c. In Report Layout view, use the Group, Sort, and Total pane to add a group. Group these data on the **Payment Date** field.

d. Click the **More** command on the Group on PaymentDate bar in the Group, Sort, and Total pane and set the grouping interval to **Month**.

e. Click the drop-down arrow beside with Amount Received totaled to launch the Totals box. Select **AmountReceived** as the value for Totals on. Show this total in the **group footer**. Also show a **grand total**.

f. Make the name fields narrower. Save the report as **Your Name Payments Received.**

...continued on Next Page

g. Add spaces as needed to the boxes controlling the report labels. Examine the report in Print Preview. Click and drag the Zoom slider to 75%.

h. Capture a screenshot of the Payment Summary query. Have it open on your computer and press **PrintScrn**. Open Word, then type **your name and section number**. Press **Enter** and then press **Ctrl+V** or click **Paste** in the Clipboard group. Save the Word document as **chap4_mid2_nationalbank_solution.docx**. Print the Word document displaying the screenshot. Close the database.

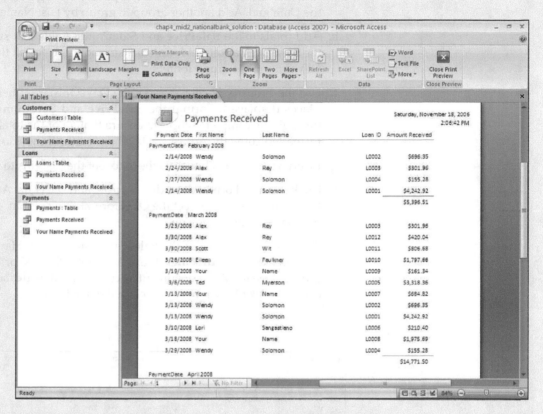

Figure 46 Payment Summary

3 Real Estate Report by Month and Salesperson

You are the senior partner in a large, independent real estate firm that specializes in home sales. Although you still represent buyers and sellers in real estate transactions, you find that most of your time is spent supervising the agents who work for your firm. This fact distresses you because you like helping people buy and sell homes. Your firm has a database containing all of the information on the properties your firm has for sale. You believe that by using the data in the database more effectively, you can spend less time supervising the other agents and spend more time doing the part of your job that you like doing the best. Your task is to prepare a sales report listing all recent transactions by month and salesperson. Finally, you need to summarize the sales and commission data by employee and calculate the average number of days each employee's sales were on the market prior to selling. Compare your results to Figure 47.

...continued on Next Page

a. Locate the file named *chap4_mid3_realestate.accdb*; copy and rename it **chap4_mid3_realestate_solution.accdb**. Open the file and enable the content. Open the **Agents** table. Find and replace **Pa Lor's** name with your name.

b. Rename the **Your Name Sales Report query** with **your name**. Open it. Create a report. Save the report as **Your Name Sales Report**. Open it in Layout view.

c. Add **spaces** as needed in the labels in the report header. Use **Ctrl + Enter** to force a line break between *On* and *Market* in *DaysOnMarket*. Make the **Subdivision** and **LastName** fields narrower so the report fits on a single page.

d. Activate the Group, Sort, and Total pane. Add a group to group the data monthly by the DateSold. Add another group to group by Last Name.

e. Add totals to the **SalePrice** and **SaleComm** fields that sum. Calculate the Average of the DaysOn Market field. Calculate grand totals for all three summary fields. Display all values in the group footers.

f. Use the Property Sheet to format the **DaysOnMarket** field as fixed with zero decimal places displayed. Format the **SalePrice** and **SaleComm** fields as Currency. Scroll through the complete report to ensure that all of the totals display fully and totals are formatted correctly. Adjust the text box widths if they do not.

g. Insert a picture of a house as the logo. Set the margins to wide.

h. Click the AutoFormat drop-down arrow and select the **AutoFormat Wizard** option. In the AutoFormat box select the Oriel format (3rd column, 4th row). View your report as two pages in Print Preview.

i. Capture a screenshot of the Sales Summary report. Have it open on your computer and press **PrintScrn**. Open Word and press **Ctrl+V** or click **Paste** in the Clipboard group. Save the Word document as **chap4_mid3_realestate_solution**. Print the screen. Close the Word document and close the database.

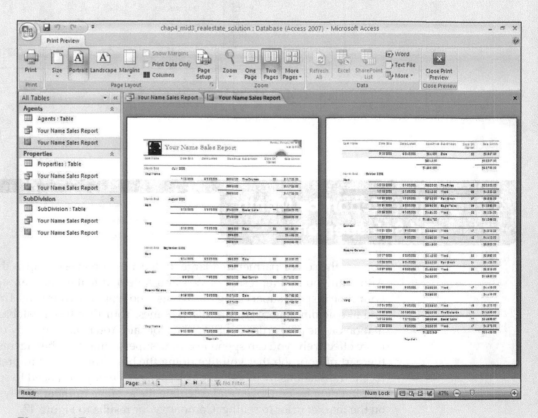

Figure 47 Sales Summary

Capstone Exercise

Your boss asked you to prepare a schedule for each speaker for the national conference being hosted next year on your campus. She wants to mail the schedules to the speakers so that they may provide feedback on the schedule prior to its publication. She believes that each speaker will find it easier to review his or her schedule if each speaker's schedule was printed in the same place. You assure her that you (and Access) can accomplish this task.

Database File Setup

You need to copy an original database file, rename the copied file, and then open the copied database to complete this capstone exercise. After you open the copied database, you will replace an existing employee's name with your name.

a. Locate the file named *chap4_cap_natconf.accdb* and copy it to a different folder.

b. Rename the copied file as **chap4_cap_natconf_solution.accdb**.

c. Open the *chap4_cap_natconf_solution.accdb* file and enable the content.

d. Open the **Speakers table**.

e. Find and replace **Your Name** with your name.

Report Wizard

You need to create a report based on the Speakers and Sessions with Rooms query. You decide to use the Report Wizard to accomplish this task.

a. Activate the **Report Wizard**.

b. Select **Query: Speakers and Sessions with Rooms** as the data source for the report.

c. Move all fields to the report.

d. You want to view your data by speakers. Select **by speakers** if necessary.

e. You want the **LastName** and **FirstName** fields established as the primary grouping level. If they are not already moved into a box at the top of the report, double-click LastName and then FirstName to group by them.

f. Click the drop-down arrow for the first box and select **Date** as the primary sort field. Click **Next**.

g. Select the **Stepped** and **Portrait** options.

h. Choose the **Flow** style.

i. Name the report **Your Name Speaker Schedule**.

Report Edits

The report opens in the Print Preview. You need to examine the report and look for problems. Once they are identified, you will need to switch to Layout view and correct them.

a. Switch to the two-page view.

b. Right-click the report tab and select **Layout View**.

c. Click the **Page Setup tab**. Click **Margins** in the Page Layout group. Select **Wide** from the drop-down menu.

d. Click the text box for **SessionTitle**. Insert a **space** between the words. Add a space to **RoomID**.

e. Move the **Date** field to the right of the Room ID column.

f. Resize the **FirstName** field by making it more narrow. Widen the **Session Title** field. Make the **RoomID** and **Date** fields more narrow.

g. Move the **Speakers** title right. Set the font size to **28 point**.

h. Click the **Logo command** in the Controls group. Insert a picture of a campus. Resize to about the same width as the Speakers title.

Additional Field

You realize the session times were not included in the query and you need them added to the report.

a. Click the **Add Existing Fields Command** in the Controls group.

b. Click **Show All Tables** in the bottom of the **Field List pane**. Find and **double-click** the **StartingTime** field in the Sessions table on the top of the Field List pane.

c. Click **Yes** in the warning box. Close the Field List pane. Add a **space** between Starting and Time. Adjust columns as needed to fit all columns on one page.

d. Scroll to the end of the page. Find and select the text box for the page number and move it left so the page number prints under the Starting Time field.

e. Change the view to Print Preview, two-page view.

f. Capture a screenshot of the Sales Summary query. Open the query on your computer and press **PrintScrn**. Open Microsoft Word and press **Ctrl+V** or click **Paste**. Save the Word document as **chap4_cap_natconf_solution**. Print the screenshot file. Close the Word document and close the database.

...continued on Next Page

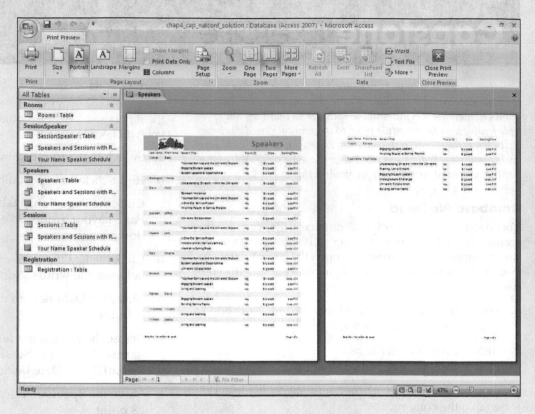

Figure 48 Speaker Schedule Report

Create, Edit, and Perform Calculations in Reports

Mini Cases

Use the rubric following the case as a guide to evaluate your work, but keep in mind that your instructor may impose additional grading criteria or use a different standard to judge your work.

Inventory Value

GENERAL CASE

The owner of a small bookstore called and asked for your help. Her insurance company requires that she provide the company with a report on the values of the inventory she stocks. Copy the *chap4_mc1_bookstore.accdb* file to your working storage folder, name it **chap4_mc1_bookstore_solution.accdb**, and open the copied file. Use the skills from this chapter to perform several tasks. Create a report that shows the publisher's name, the author's first and last names, the book title, the book price, the number in stock, and the value of the stock. The report needs to be grouped by publisher with appropriate summary statistics calculated. The books within each publisher's group should be listed in alphabetical order by the author's last name. The report needs to contain an appropriate graphic and a grand total. The file contains a query that you may use to create the report.

Performance Elements	Exceeds Expectations	Meets Expectations	Below Expectations
Create report	All necessary and no unneeded fields included.	All necessary fields included but also unnecessary fields.	Not all necessary fields were included.
Appropriate grouping and sorting	The grouping and sorting were correctly identified and executed.	Grouping correct but sorting incorrect or vice-versa.	Neither grouping nor sorting properly employed.
Summary statistics	Correct group aggregating information selected and appropriately displayed.	Correct group aggregating information selected, but the display had problems.	Group aggregating information not selected and/or inappropriately displayed.
Summarize balances	Correct method, correct totals.	Correct totals but inefficient method.	Totals incorrect or missing.

Producing Mailing Labels

RESEARCH CASE

This chapter introduced you to the power of using reports, but you have much more to explore. Use Access Help to search for mailing labels. Open and read the articles titled, *Use Access to Create and Print Labels* and *Learn Tips and Tricks for Creating Labels*. Put your new knowledge to the test. Copy the *chap4_mc2_arboretum.accdb* file and rename the copy as **chap4_mc2_arboretum_solution.accdb**. Open the file. It contains a query identifying volunteers who need to be invited to this year's gala. Your challenge is to figure out how to print the names and addresses as mailing labels. You have purchased Avery product number 5260 labels to print on. They are 1 ½" x 2 ⅝" with three columns of labels on each page. The mailing will be sent bulk rate, so the labels need to print sorted by postal code. After you successfully produce the report, print it on plain paper. Write your instructor a memo explaining how you accomplished this task. Use a memo template in Word, your most professional writing style, and clear directions that someone could follow in order to accomplish this task. Attach the printout of the labels to the memo. Save the Word document as **chap4_mc2_arboretum_solution**.

Each label should be set up in this fashion:
Mr. (Dr., Ms., Mrs.,) John Doe, Jr.
Street Address
City, State Postal Code

Performance Elements	Exceeds Expectations	Meets Expectations	Below Expectations
Use online help	Appropriate articles located and memo indicates comprehension.	Appropriate articles located, but memo did not demonstrate comprehension.	Articles not found.
Prepare labels	Printed list attached to memo in requested format.	Printed list is attached, but the formatting has minor flaws.	List missing or incomprehensible.
Summarize and communicate	Memo clearly written and could be used as directions.	Memo text indicates some understanding but also weaknesses.	Memo missing or incomprehensible.
Aesthetics	Memo template correctly employed.	Template employed but signed in the wrong place or improperly used.	Memo missing or incomprehensible.

Real Estate Development Report

DISASTER CASE

A co-worker called you into her office, explained that she was having difficulty with Access 2007 and asked you to look at her work. Copy the *chap4_mc3_realestate.accdb* file to your working storage folder, name it **chap4_mc3_realestate_solution.accdb**, and open the file. It contains a query, Your Name Sales Report. It also contains a report based on the query. The report is supposed to show each agent's total sales with each development listed under the agent's name. There should be totals for the sales and commissions columns for each salesperson and each development. Your challenge is to find and correct the error(s) and then to produce an attractive, easy-to-read report.

Performance Elements	Exceeds Expectations	Meets Expectations	Below Expectations
Error identification	Correct identification and correction of all errors.	Correct identification of all errors and correction of some errors.	Errors neither located nor corrected.
Grouping order	Correct grouping options and summarization selected.	Correct grouping, but some summaries incorrectly selected.	Incorrect group by option selection.
Aesthetics	Report design aids reader.	Inconsistent formatting, but all necessary data displays.	Controls improperly sized. Information obscured.

Create, Edit, and Perform Calculations in Reports

Glossary

All key terms appearing in this book (in bold italic) are listed alphabetically in this Glossary for easy reference. If you want to learn more about a feature or concept, use the Index to find the term's other significant occurrences.

Absolute cell reference A cell reference that stays the same no matter where you copy a formula.

Access function Predefined formula that performs an operation using input supplied as arguments and returns a value.

Access speed Measures the time it takes for the storage device to make the file content available for use.

Active cell The cell you are working in; the cell where information or data will be input.

Adjustment handle A control in the shape of a yellow diamond that allows you to modify a shape.

Aggregate A collection of many parts that come together from different sources and are considered a whole.

Align To arrange in a line so as to be parallel.

And operator Returns only records that meet all criteria.

Animation Movement applied to individual elements on a single slide.

Animation scheme A built-in, standard animation effect.

Annotation A note that can be written or drawn on a slide for additional commentary or explanation.

Append Process of adding new records to the end of the table.

Argument A necessary input component required to produce the output for a function.

Ascending order Arranges data in alphabetical or sequential order from lowest to highest.

Aspect ratio The ratio of width to height.

AutoFill An Excel operation that enables users to copy the content of a cell or a range of cells by dragging the fill handle over an adjacent cell or range of cells.

AutoFit The command used when formatting a spreadsheet to automatically adjust the height and width of cells.

AutoFormat A feature that evaluates an entire document, determines how each paragraph is used, then it applies an appropriate style to each paragraph.

Automatic replacement Makes a substitution automatically.

AutoNumber field A field that assigns a unique identifying number to each record.

AutoText A feature that substitutes a predefined item for specific text but only when the user initiates it.

AVERAGE function The function that determines the arithmetic mean, or average, for the values in a range of cells.

Back end Protects and stores data so that users cannot inadvertently destroy or corrupt the organization's vital data.

Background The area of a display screen found behind the desktop icons.

Background Styles gallery Provides both solid color and background styles for application to a theme.

Backup A copy of a file.

Bar chart A chart with a horizontal orientation that compares categories; useful when categorical labels are long.

Bar tab Does not position text or decimals, but inserts a vertical bar at the tab setting; useful as a separator for text printed on the same line.

Bibliography A list of works cited or consulted by an author and should be included with the document when published.

Bitmap image An image created by bits or pixels placed on a grid that form a picture.

Bookmark An electronic marker for a specific location in a document, enabling the user to go to that location quickly.

Border A line that surrounds a paragraph, a page, a table, or an image, similar to how a picture frame surrounds a photograph or piece of art.

Bound control A control that enables you to pull information from the underlying table or query data.

Breakpoint The lowest numeric value for a specific category or in a series of a lookup table to produce a corresponding result to return for a lookup function.

Brightness The ratio between lightness and darkness of an image.

Building Blocks Document components used frequently, such as disclaimers, company addresses, or a cover page.

Bulleted list Itemizes and separates paragraph text to increase readability.

Calculated control Uses an expression as opposed to a record value as its data source.

Calculated field A field that derives its value from a formula that references one or more existing fields.

Callout A shape that includes a line with a text box that you can use to add notes.

CamelCase notation Field-naming style that uses no spaces in multi-word field names, but uses uppercase letters to distinguish the first letter of each new word.

Caption A descriptive title for an image, a figure, or a table.

Caption property Specifies a label other than the field name that appears at the top of a column in Datasheet view, forms, and reports.

Cascade delete Searches the database and deletes all of the related records.

Cascade update Connects any primary key changes to the tables in which it is a foreign key.

Cascades Permit data changes to travel from one table to another.

Case-insensitive search Finds a word regardless of any capitalization used.

Case-sensitive search Matches not only the text but also the use of upper- and lowercase letters.

Category label Textual information, such as column and row headings (cities, months, years, product names, etc.), used for descriptive entries.

Cell The intersection of a column and row in a table or in an Excel spreadsheet.

Cell margin The amount of space between data and the cell border in a table.

Cell reference The intersection of a column and row designated by a column letter and a row number.

Center tab Sets the middle point of the text you type; whatever you type will be centered on that tab setting.

Change Case Feature that enables you to change capitalization of text to all capital letters, all lowercase letters, sentence case, or toggle case.

Character spacing The horizontal space between characters.

Character style Stores character formatting (font, size, and style) and affects only the selected text.

Chart A graphic or visual representation of data.

Chart area The entire chart and all of its elements.

Check box Enables you to select one or more items that are not mutually exclusive in a dialog box.

Citation A note recognizing a source of information or a quoted passage.

Clip Any media object that you can insert in a document.

Clip art A graphical image, illustration, drawing, or sketch.

Clipboard A memory location that holds up to 24 items for you to paste into the current document, another file, or another application.

Close button Removes a window from memory.

Clustered column chart A chart that groups similar data together in columns making visual comparison of the data easier to determine.

Codec Digital video compression scheme used to compress a video and decompress for playback.

Collapsed outline View that displays the title of slides only in the Outline view.

Colors gallery A gallery with a set of colors for every available theme.

Column Formats a section of a document into side-by-side vertical blocks in which the text flows down the first column and then continues at the top of the next column.

Column chart A chart that displays data vertically in a column formation and is used to compare values across different categories.

Column index number A number, indicated by col_index_num in the function, that refers to the number of the column in the lookup table that contains the return values.

Column width The horizontal space or width of a column in a table or in a spreadsheet.

Combine Feature that incorporates all changes from multiple documents into a new document.

Command An icon on the Quick Access Toolbar or in a group on the Ribbon that you click to perform a task. A command can also appear as text on a menu or within a dialog box.

Command button A dialog box item that you click to accept or cancel selections.

Comment A private note, annotation, or additional information to the author, another reader, or to yourself.

Compare Feature that evaluates the contents of two or more documents and displays markup balloons that show the differences between the documents.

Compatibility checker Looks for features that are not supported by previous versions of Word, Excel, PowerPoint, or Access.

Compress The process of reducing the file size of an object.

Connector A line that is attached to and moves with shapes.

Constant An unchanging value, like a birthdate.

Contextual tab A specialty tab that appears on the Ribbon only when certain types of objects are being edited.

Contrast The difference between the darkest and lightest areas of a image.

Control Panel Windows control center that enables you to change system settings, such as your background, screen saver, screen fonts, and accessibility options.

Controls Position, display, format, and calculate the report data.

Copy The process of making a duplicate copy of the text or object leaving the original intact.

Copyright The legal protection afforded to a written or artistic work.

COUNT function The function that counts the number of cells in a range that contain numerical data.

COUNTA function The function that counts the number of cells in a range that are not blank.

Criteria row Position in a query design grid where criteria may be entered.

PivotTable view Provides a convenient way to summarize and organize data about groups of records.

Placeholder A container that holds content and is used in the layout to determine the position of objects on the slide.

Plagiarism The act of using and documenting the ideas or writings of another as one's own.

Plain Text Format (.txt) A file type that retains only text when used to transfer documents between applications or platforms.

Plot area The area containing the graphical representation of the values in a data series.

PMT function Calculates a periodic loan payment given a constant interest rate, term, and original value.

PNPI Federal laws governing the safeguarding of personal, non-public information such as Social Security numbers (SSNs), credit card or bank account numbers, medical or educational records, or other sensitive data.

Pointing The use of the mouse or arrow keys to select a cell directly when creating a formula.

Portrait orientation Page orientation is longer than it is wide—like the portrait of a person.

Position Raises or lowers text from the baseline without creating superscript or subscript size.

Presentation graphics software A computer application, such as Microsoft PowerPoint, that is used primarily to create electronic slide shows.

Presenter view Delivers a presentation on two monitors simultaneously.

Primary key The field that makes each record in a table unique.

Print Layout view The default view that closely resembles the printed document.

Print Preview view Displays the report as it will be printed.

Program file Part of a software program, such as Microsoft Word.

Property A characteristic or attribute of an object that determines how the object looks and behaves.

Proportional typeface Allocates horizontal space to the character.

Public domain When the rights to a literary work or property are owned by the public at large.

Query A database object that enables you to ask questions about the data stored in a database and returns the answers in the order from the records that match your instructions.

Query design grid Displays when you select a query's Design view; it divides the window into two parts.

Query sort order Determines the order of items in the query datasheet view.

Query Wizard An Access tool that facilitates new query development.

Quick Access Toolbar A customizable row of buttons for frequently used commands, such as Save and Undo.

Quick Launch toolbar Contains program icons, making it possible to open programs with a single click.

Quick Style A combination of formatting options available that can be applied to a shape or graphic.

Radio button A mutually exclusive selection in a dialog box.

Range A rectangular group of cells. A range may be as small as a single cell or as large as the entire worksheet.

Record A complete set of all of the data (fields) about one person, place, event, or idea.

Recycle Bin Holds files and folders deleted from the hard drive.

Redo Command that reinstates or reserves an action performed by the Undo command.

Repeat Provides limited use because it repeats only the last action you performed. The Repeat icon is replaced with the Redo icon after you use the Undo command.

Referential Integrity The set of rules that ensure that data stored in related tables remain consistent as the data are updated.

Relational Database Management System Data are grouped into similar collections, called tables, and the relationships between tables are formed by using a common field.

Relational database software A computer application, such as Microsoft Access, that is used to store data and convert it into information.

Relative cell reference A cell reference that changes relative to the direction in which the formula is being copied.

Replace The process of finding and replacing a word or group of words with other text.

Report A printed document that displays information professionally from a database.

Report footer section Prints once at the conclusion of each report.

Report header section Prints once at the beginning of each report.

Report view Provides you the ability to see what the printed report will look like and to make temporary changes to how the data are viewed.

Report Wizard Asks you questions and then, depending on how you answer, generates the report.

Restore Down button Returns a window to the size it was before it was maximized.

Reviewing Pane A window that displays all comments and editorial changes made to the main document.

Revision mark Indicates where text is added, deleted, or formatted while the Track Changes feature is active.

Ribbon The Microsoft Office 2007 GUI command center that organizes commands into related tabs and groups.

Rich Text Format (.rtf) A file type that retains structure and most text formatting when used to transfer documents between applications or platforms.

Right tab Sets the start position on the right so as you type, text moves to the left of that tab setting and aligns on the right.

Row height The vertical space from the top to the bottom of a row in a table or in a spreadsheet.

Run a query Access processes the query instructions and displays records that meet the conditions.

Sans serif typeface A typeface that does not contain thin lines on characters.

Sarbanes Oxley Act (SOX) Protects the general public and companies' shareholders against fraudulent practices and accounting errors.

Scale or scaling Increases or decreases text or a graphic as a percentage of its size.

Scatter (xy) chart A chart that shows a relationship between two variables.

Screen saver A moving graphic or image that takes over the display screen when the user is idle.

ScreenTip A small window that describes a command.

Scroll bar Enables you to control which part of a window is in view at any time.

Search Companion Helps you locate files.

Section break A marker that divides a document into sections thereby allowing different formatting in each section.

Select All button The square at the intersection of the rows and column headings used to select all elements of the worksheet.

Select query Searches the underlying tables to retrieve the data that satisfy the query parameters.

Selection net Selects all objects in an area defined by dragging the mouse.

Selection Pane A pane designed to help select objects.

Selective replacement Lets you decide whether to replace text.

Serif typeface A typeface that contains a thin line or extension at the top and bottom of the primary strokes on characters.

Shading A background color that appears behind text in a paragraph, a page, a table, or a spreadsheet cell.

Shape A geometric or nongeometric object such as a rectangle or an arrow.

Sheet tabs The tabs located at the bottom left of the Excel window that tell the user what sheets of a workbook are available.

Shortcut A special type of file that points to another file or device.

Shortcut menu A list of commands that appears when you right-click an item or screen element.

Show Markup Enables you to view document revisions by reviewer; it also allows you to choose which type of revisions you want to view such as comments, insertions and deletions, or formatting changes.

Show/Hide feature Reveals where formatting marks such as spaces, tabs, and returns are used in the document.

Show row Area in a query design grid that controls whether the field will display in the query results.

Sizing handle The small circles and squares that appear around a selected object and enable you to adjust the height and width of a selected object.

Slide Show view Used to deliver the completed presentation full screen to an audience, one slide at a time, as an electronic presentation on the computer.

Slide Sorter view Displays thumbnails of slides.

SmartArt A diagram that presents information visually to effectively communicate a message.

Soft page break Inserted when text fills an entire page then continues on the next page.

Soft return Created by the word processor as it wraps text to a new line.

Sort Lists those records in a specific sequence, such as alphabetically by last name or rearranges data based on a certain criteria.

Sort Ascending Provides an alphabetical list of text data or a small-to-large list of numeric data.

Sort command The command that puts lists in ascending or descending order according to specified keys.

Sort Descending Arranges the records with the highest value listed first.

Sort row The area in the query design grid in which to indicate if you want the query results sorted in ascending or descending order for a specific field.

Sorting The action that arranges records in a table by the value of one or more fields within a table.

Spelling and Grammar Feature that attempts to catch mistakes in spelling, punctuation, writing style, and word usage by comparing strings of text within a document to a series of predefined rules.

Spin button A dialog box feature whereby you can click an up or down arrow to increase or decrease a selection.

Spreadsheet The computerized equivalent of a ledger that is a grid of rows and columns enabling users to organize data, recalculate formulas when any changes in data are made, and make decisions based on quantitative data.

Spreadsheet program A computer application, such as Microsoft Excel, that is used to build and manipulate electronic spreadsheets.

Stacked The vertical alignment of text.

Stacked column chart A chart that places (stacks) data in one column with each data series a different color for each category.

Stacking order The order of objects placed on top of each other.

Start button Provides access to programs and other system resources.

Start menu Displayed when you click the Start button.

Status bar The horizontal bar at the bottom of a Microsoft Office application that displays summary information about the selected window or object and contains View buttons and the Zoom slider. The Word status bar displays the page number and total words, while the Excel status bar displays the average, count, and sum of values in a selected range. The PowerPoint status bar displays the slide number and the Design Theme name.

Stock chart A chart that shows the high, low, and close prices for individual stocks over a period of time.

Storyboard A visual plan that displays the content of each slide in the slideshow.

Style A set of formatting options you apply to characters or paragraphs.

Subdocument A smaller document that is a part of a master document.

SUM function The function that adds or sums numeric entries within a range of cells and then displays the result in the cell containing the function.

Synchronous scrolling Enables you to scroll through documents at the same time in Side by Side view

Syntax The set of rules by which the words and symbols of an expression are correctly combined.

Tab Looks like a folder tab and divides the Ribbon into task-oriented categories.

Tab, Word Markers that specify the position for aligning text and add organization to a document.

Table A series of rows and columns that organize data effectively.

Table, Access A collection of records. Every record in a table contains the same fields in the same order.

Table, Excel An area in a worksheet that contains rows and columns of similar or related information. A table can be used as part of a database or organized collection of related information, where the worksheet rows represent the records and the worksheet columns represent the fields in a record. The first row of a table contains the column labels or field names.

Table alignment The position of a table between the left and right document margins.

Table of authorities Used in legal documents to reference cases, and other documents referred to in a legal brief.

Table of contents Lists headings in the order they appear in a document and the page numbers where the entries begin.

Table of figures A list of the captions in a document.

Table row The second row of the query design grid that specifies the tables from which the fields are selected to create a query.

Table style Contain borders, shading, font sizes, and other attributes that enhance readability of a table.

Task pane A bar that provides support for a currently selected item or window.

Taskbar The horizontal bar that allows you to move among open windows and provides access to system resources.

Template A file that incorporates a theme, a layout, and content that can be modified.

Text Any combination of entries from the keyboard and includes letters, numbers, symbols, and spaces.

Text box An object that enables you to place text anywhere on a slide or in a document or within a dialog box.

Text direction The degree of rotation in which text displays.

Text pane A special pane that opens up for text entry when a SmartArt diagram is selected.

Text wrapping style The way text wraps around an image.

Texture fill Inserts a texture such as marble into a shape.

Theme A set of design elements that gives the slide show a unified, professional appearance.

Three-dimensional pie chart A type of pie chart that contains a three-dimensional view.

Thumbnail A miniature display of an image, page, or slide.

Title bar The shaded bar at the top of every window; often displays the program name and filename.

TODAY function The function that is a date-related function that places the current date in a cell.

Toggle switch Causes the computer to alternate between two states. For example, you can toggle between the Insert mode and the Overtype mode.

Toolbar Usually found at the top or side of a window, contains buttons that are accessed more quickly than menu selections.

Total row Displays as the last row in the Datasheet view of a table or query and provides a variety of summary statistics.

Totals query Organizes query results into groups by including a grouping field and a numeric field for aggregate calculations.

Track Changes Monitors all additions, deletions, and formatting changes you make in a document.

Transition A movement special effect that takes place as one slide replaces another in Slide Show view.

Transparency Refers to how much you can see through a fill.

Type style The characteristic applied to a font, such as bold.

Typeface A complete set of characters—upper- and lower-case letters, numbers, punctuation marks, and special symbols.

Typography The arrangement and appearance of printed matter.

Unbound controls Do not have any record source for their contents.

Undo Command cancels your last one or more operations.

Ungrouping Breaking a combined object into individual objects.

User account A relationship between a user and a computer (requiring a username and password) defining individual desktop settings and file storage.

User interface The meeting point between computer software and the person using it.

Validation rule Checks the authenticity of the data entered in a field.

Value Number entered in a cell that represent a quantity, an amount, a date, or time.

Vector graphic An object-oriented graphic based on geometric formulas.

Vertex The point where a curve ends or the point where two line segments meet in a freeform shape.

View Side by Side Enables you to display two documents on the same screen.

Virus checker Software that scans files for a hidden program that can damage your computer.

VLOOKUP function The function that evaluates a value and looks up this value in a vertical table to return a value, text, or formula.

Web Layout view View to display how a document will look when posted on the Web.

Widow The last line of a paragraph appearing by itself at the top of a page.

Window An enclosed rectangular area representing a program or data.

Windows Desktop Search Helps you find anything on your computer by simply typing one or more keywords.

Windows Explorer Displays a tree structure of the devices and folders on your computer.

Windows Vista The newest version of the Windows operating system.

Windows XP The primary operating system (OS) for personal computers.

Windows XP Home Edition Focuses on entertainment and home use.

Windows XP Media Center Edition Coordinates multimedia elements.

Windows XP Professional Edition Designed to support business systems.

Wizard A set of guided instructions.

Word processing software A computer application, such as Microsoft Word, that is used primarily with text to create, edit, and format documents.

Word wrap The feature that automatically moves words to the next line if they do not fit on the current line.

WordArt Text that has a decorative effect applied.

Work-around Acknowledges that a problem exists, and develops a sufficing solution.

Workbook A collection of related worksheets contained within a single file.

Worksheet A single spreadsheet consisting of columns and rows that may contain formulas, functions, values, text, and graphics.

X or horizontal axis The axis that depicts categorical labels.

Y or vertical axis The axis that depicts numerical values.

Zoom slider Enables you to increase or decrease the magnification of the file onscreen.

Index